GROWTH OF HINDU RELIGION AND CULTURE

GROWTH OF HINDU RELIGION AND CULTURE

Brig. Jagdev Singh

GYAN PUBLISHING HOUSE
NEW DELHI-110002

Growth of Hindu Religion and Culture

Rs. 540

ISBN: 81-212-0893-9

Published in 2006 in India by
Gyan Publishing House
5, Ansari Road, Darya Ganj, New Delhi-110002
Phones : 23282060, 23261060 Fax : (011) 23285914
E-mail : books@gyanbooks.com
Website : www.gyanbooks.com

Laser Typesetting at : Master Computers, Delhi
Printed at : Salasar Imaging System, Delhi

Contents

Preface

Hindu religion claims to be one without beginning, i.e. it came into being with the beginning of time. Its roots are in timelessness, it came into being with the beginning of Creation and would dissolve into eternity once it has run its course. Then it is ready for another round of creation and go through another the cycle, and so the cycles would repeat ad infinitum. Hinduism claims to be Sanatan , ageless, with its routes embedded in eternity, and it takes birth with time, when Shrishti, creation, manifests itself. A lot of what exists as part of creation is the' Sanatanistic Hindu thought and content. It lasts as such till the next cycle is ready and gives the creation a new colour, and substance.

Another part of the Hindu concept is Maya. It is a complicated concept, but simplistically speaking it can be translated into illusion. According to Hinduism the whole creation is Maya, illusion, not a reality of substance, but just an illusion. At the time of dissolution all that happens is that the illusion vanishes and the reality manifests itself in all its glory. In their heyday Hindus were a vigorous, dynamic people who believed in free exchange of ideas and strived constantly to improve their living conditions and environments, their arts and culture, their scientific and engineering knowledge and skills, and believed that knowledge had to be disseminated down to the lowest level possible. They had faith in their beliefs, and not all of what they thought or practiced was based on the Veda, or some other philosophical cult. With time the philosophy tended to become more and more rigid and archaic, so that during the time of the Brahmanas the religion had come under the control of rigid rituals. The Brahmanas enunciated a philosophy but it was based on rigid basics, and this led to a kind of revolution in the philosophy, giving rise to different systems of philosophy which amply summarised the essence of the philosophical thought. These treatises do contain literature which has rich poetical content, and often contain ideas which are unique in meaning and substance. They form an important element in the dissemination of the essentials of the Hindu philosophical thinking.

The concept of Hindu Rashtra, or Hindu nation as such never took roots in the early history of the Hindus, and it was for that reason that the people of the subcontinent never were one great nation. It was a land riven between clans, and it took the people who decided to settle here took time to settle and then got organized into a viable social order. From loosely organized social organization they built, in time, a social order which did not reach heights, but tended to bring in the some kind of a national concept. In subsequent accounts there are accounts of Maharajas and kings who ruled and had armies and waged wars, and whose accounts, mostly garbled have been recorded and quoted in the literature. The two epics of Ramayana and Mahabharata, have been written in most ancient literature and are read with a lot of interest to this day. The epics talk of kings of faraway lands joining one side or the other. One of the kings joining the battle was Jarasandh; he has been described as powerful potentate who played an important part in the Kurukshetra War. Even the essence of the Krishna legend is based in this war.

That kingship was firmly established during this early period and the states have been shown fighting, and organizing their states have been brought out in the accounts of the battles fought, and the treaties finalized and the alliances made as part of state raft. The kings and the potentates of the time showed the war ambitious and showed their prowess both in the field of battle and in state craft. We have accounts of kings who roamed their states in disguise to get a true picture of the way their officials worked. They almost always had an effective intelligence system under their direct control to keep abreast of the developments. The rulers kept a keen eye on the functioning of their subordinates. On the basis of the experience gained and the information gathered about the functioning of the rival states they generally evolved workable systems of check and punishments. One of the masters of the statecraft of his time was Chanakya, who devised a system wherein there was no scope for emotions while handling the affairs of the state. His teachings imparted firm roots to state craft, though it offended the sensitivities of the common man and he revolted against it when he got the opportunity.

Revenue collection was an important business of the state. Without adequate revenue no state had a chance to survive for long. But a deficit in revenue collection invariably caused the demise of the state. So the rulers always appointed clever and experienced persons to take care of this branch of State administration.

This book covers the art of governance as adopted by the rulers of yore which no doubt was based on the collective experience of the ruling community, and in gradual stages covers the techniques adopted by them, and if they failed in the process, the reasons for that. The systems adopted by different rulers were different, in keeping with the trends to suit their subjects and their threat perceptions. Many a ruler fell because their subjects defaulted in payment of taxes; even great kings like Ashoka often felt threatened when there were shortfalls in tax collections, and often many old established kingdoms had to face sad situations. Rulers had to have a strong well established system to run their states well. Any failure brought them a lot of grief.

Brig. Jagdev Singh

1

The People

The Hindus are a multi-cultural, multi-ethnic and a multilingual people. Their religion is not based on the directions or utterings of any single person. It has evolved from the collective wisdom of the people. The word Hindu is derived from Sindhu, the old name of river Indus. The Iranians used it for the people of the Indus basin. From Sindhu it became Hindu, and Hind for their country, Hindi the people of Hind, Hindia their country, India.

For some unknown reason few skeletal remains of the early inhabitants of this subcontinent have been found and, therefore, their movements have not been reconstructed with any degree of accuracy. However, the generally held view is that people of the subcontinent are basically migrants, and they got characterised only while being here, that, in time, some out of them have moved out of here and settled in other lands. The basic migratory groups have been discussed in the succeeding paras.

Negritos

Of Brachycephalic head construction, probably from Africa, they have all but vanished from the mainland except for small groups surviving in the Andamans, Cochin and Travancore Hills, Assam (Angami Nagas) and Eastern Bihar. Of black complexion and height around five feet (females are smaller) they have been a restless people, and moved extensively. They got absorbed by the People following them, like the Proto Australoids, the Mongoloid groups or the Dravidians of the Palaeo-Mediterranean class. From the evidence of frescoes it seems they survived on the mainland upto the Gupta period. They were essentially food gatherers rather than food producers, and had developed skills for seafaring which got them to the Andaman Islands. They travelled to other lands as well, by land and sea, and still survive in Malaya, Indonesia, Philippines and New Guinea. Their original speech has survived in the Andamans, but as far as the present day Indian dialects are concerned, they have made no contribution except for a few words connected with flora and fauna.

They worshipped trees for fertility, and believed that human being possessed a soul. They narrated accounts of the travel of the soul after death to paradise guarded by an avenging demon who inflicted punishment on the basis of the "sins" committed during the life time as a human being, before permitting entry. Such ideas were widespread in Europe, Africa and India of these days.

Proto-Australoids

Dolichocephalic, they were probably an offshoot of an earlier Mediterranean race, possibly from Palestine. Near black complexion, had an average height of five feet six inches. There is also the view that they evolved from a subhuman species over the Indian subcontinent itself and then moved outwards in all directions. The aborigionals of India are almost entirely of this stock, though their characteristics have been vastly diluted through intermingling with other stocks. Part of this group moved over to Australia in very early times, and formed the base for the Malenesians and the Polynesians, spreading to the Pacific islands and, possibly to the South and Central America, inter-breeding with other racial groups during their long march eastwards. They are an important group in India, and arrived from the west over a number of routes, and intermingled with other groups like the Negritos and the Mongoloids. Of those who emigrated to the east, some came back in later times as Melanesians and Polynesians and made their contributions to the culture and economy of this country; they have since been completely absorbed by other groups. The conspicuous contributions of these people have been the outrigger canoe, head hunting, disposal of the dead by exposure, communal housing and the coconut.

The spread of the Proto-Australoids over the subcontinent has been wide, although in their near original form they can be identified only amongst a few aboriginal tribes, like the Mundas and Kols of Chhota Nagpur. But they have mixed extensively with other groups and imparted to them their traits and characteristics. A majority of people in rural India today carry, to a large or small extent the Proto-Australoid strain in their blood. The languages they speak are grouped under the head "Austric" and these have made a substantial contribution in the development of Hindustani language.

As for other views about their cradle land, William Hevesy places it in Hungary-Western Siberia area, and suggests that there was a major offensive/immigration into India by the Finno-Ugrians or Ugrian tribes during the prehistoric times, that Kol and Mundas are the result of inter-breeding between these tribes and the local inhabitants like the Negritos. The generally held view as put forth by Jean Pryzluski and others, however, is that Proto-Australoids are a very old offshoot of the Mediterranean race, that during their movement to India, over a period of time, a number of them dropped off en route, in Mesopotamia, Iran and other places, and in course of time formed the base of notable civilisations. Pater W. Schmidt has given the view that Austric family of languages have two main streams: one, which is spoken by Melanesians and Polynesians and the people of the islands of the Pacific, and the other as spoken in South and South-East Asia. This view is generally accepted.

The transition of the subcontinent from the Palaeolithic culture to the Neolithic was the achievement of the Proto-Australoids. They developed pottery and used boomerang, and cultivated, including cultivation of rice in terraces; this was taken on in many parts of South-East Asia. For cultivation they used the hoe and the digging stick.

They developed a good knowledge of the animal and human anatomy and the characteristics of the organs of the body, and a system of cure by using local flora; they cured ailments with medicines made from the extracts of herbs; this later developed into the Siddha System. They developed trade and commerce and devised a system of count upto twenty (kodi); this system was in vogue in most parts of India till the onset of Independence, and even subsequently in some backward areas. Their main occupation during the Neolithic period was agriculture. Apart from the staple crops of rice and wheat they cultivated cotton, sugarcane, vegetables, areca nut and betel vines, and extracted sugar from cane, and weaved cotton cloth and lived in thatched dwelling units.

Red colour they recognised as colour of life (being the colour of life sustaining blood) and considered it sacred, and applied it (or its variants vermillion or turmeric) on stones or whatever else they worshipped. In keeping with this thought the dominant colour in a marriage ceremony including that of the bridal attire, was red. For the same reason a married Hindu woman applied vermillion in the parting of the hair on her head.

Hindu religion and culture have interwoven strands of ideas and beliefs of different people who settled on this subcontinent, although the customs and ideas which eventually prevailed are an amalgam of what was practised by the Proto-Australoids, the Dravidians and the Aryans. The Proto-Australoid ideas of cosmic and creational myths have come to be known widely through the modified Puranic writings—the mythical account of "Amrita Manthan" wherein the good and the evil gods strive to scare the ambrosia for eternal life, is Austric based, and so arc the enumeration of the days by the phases of the moon, "Tithis", and some other ideas on astronomy. Corresponding ideas can be traced amongst the Melanesians and Polynesians. Myths about the creation of the world out of an egg, or the tribal totems being worshipped as zoomorphic deities—Nagas, the snake deities, the tortoise, "makra" or the crocodile, the monkey god Hanuman, or Ganesha of the elephant head—or magico-religious rituals, like removal of evil eye by performing "neochhawar" or observing some taboos, or a lot of material of the black Yajur Veda relating to magic spells, are all based on Austric tradition. Linga worship following from using the digging stick as plough-share, or the sex act, the act of copulation which triggers creation, is also Austric.

Austric Proto-Australoids left pockets of population all among their route to India. Those of them who settled in Afghanistan and the Indian northern plains became Aryan speaking during the second and the first millennium BC and from the study of civilisation and culture that they produced prior to the arrival of the Aryans proper, has misled many a modern historians into believing that this itself was the cradle land of the Aryans.

As for the characteristic traits of the Austric people it can be said that were gregarious, happy-go-lucky, superstitious and somewhat timid, in that they were for the beaten track and reluctant to strike out on their own and take risks. But they were not cowards when it came to defending their base values. They were simple folks, generally content with their lot, not in favour of creating dissensions or raising a voice of disagreement, revolt, against the established tradition, typical traits of people who might have evolved as food gatherers. They were, for this reason, easily overpowered by people who followed them and were more aggressive; they have generally served as the underdog. The Aryans ridiculed their ugliness, their snub noses and dark colour, and called them "Nishads", the dark skinned Austric dwellers of the forests. Their contribution to the development civilisation has been noteworthy. It has not been in their nature to aggressively take on the challenges of time to surmount the problems; they believed in getting over them by adopting passive means. They did not have to fight the rigours of the Ice Ages, and when challenged by those who had to, they simply were inadequate in holding out against them. But their persistent passivity and dogged steadfastness when their base values were threatened, often succeeded in converting their opponents to their own cause. They often managed to convince them that aggression solved nothing. They have the capability to do well, but have generally been condemned to poverty and destitution because of the deprivation inflicted upon them by more aggressive classes. They have been an important strand in the social, cultural and religious fabric of this subcontinent.

The Dravidians

They are dolichocephalic with the colour of the skin varying between the whitish and the dark. They came from the west, from the Mediterranean region, over a long period of time via any number of routes into the subcontinent: north-western border, the Indus delta or the coast to its south. There have been African infiltrations too along the coast but those people have since merged with the Dravidian stock, and by and large, are no longer recognisable. Incoming Dravidians can be classified into three main streams, viz, Palaeo-Mediterraneans (very black, bordering on almost black), the Mediterraneans, and the Orientals; the last category has people of lighter complexion from areas east of the Mediterranean. The last two categories were highly civilised people and came from developed areas who were leaders in economics, culture and statecraft. The Mediterranean proper, taller and fairer than the palaeo variety, inhabit the Punjab and the upper Gangetic plane, and were an important constituent of the Indus Valley Civilisation, and were later Aryanised, in so far as the language was concerned. They were important players in the development of Hinduism in northern India. As for the Orientals, they can be recognised by their pronounced longish noses and fair skin and inhabit the Punjab, Sind, Rajasthan and western Uttar Pradesh; infact, a fair scattering of theirs can be found almost all over India.

Palaeo Mediterraneans were almost the first to arrive, spreading extensively and intermixing with the inhabitants, Negritos and the Austric Australoids. Down south along with some Mediterraneans and Orientals they settled in what are now called the states of Tamil Nadu, Kerala, Karnataka and Andhra Pradesh. The languages and dialects in these areas are distinctly similar. In the north, however, the Dravid group of languages are not in use; here the languages, and speech are thoroughly Sanskrit based. In an area in Afghanistan, "Brahui" a Dravidian language, is spoken. Actually, the Dravidians, at one stage inhabited a large area which in the north-west extended as far as Iran and Afghanistan. The mix of their language with Austric languages and Sanskrit produced the regional languages of the non-Dravidian areas in India.

The words "Dasa" and "Dasyu" were used by the Aryans for the Dravidians. The words were in use when the two races lived side by side in Iran, and possibly meant "country" and were not derogatory references which they came to suggest in later times; the meaning possibly changed after the two racial groups had turned mutually hostile, which possibly had happened during their stay in Iran itself. According to A.C. Bouquet, in his book *Hinduism*, the ancient and longstanding elements in institutional Hinduism existed in the Mediterranean and Asia Minor of that time, and the megalithic culture of early India is closely allied to what prevailed in Bronze Age Europe, including Britain. Likewise the snake cult of the Indians is similar to that of Crete, and the Indian bull-worshipping and bull-fighting practices resemble those of early Mediterranean. It is almost certain that the fire-walking ceremonies of South India were associated with the cult of Artmis in Cappadocia. Also noteworthy are the slender waists of the males in Cretan paintings which are like those of males in some parts of South India. In religion the Dravidian thoughts and practices have made a significant contribution. The Aryans worshipped a vague set of deities when they came here, like Dyaush Pita (Zeus in Greece) the sky father and the Prithvi Mata the mother earth. Similarly Austrics had Sun god (Sin Bonga) and the Moon goddess (Ninda Chando). Only the Dravidians had a concept relating to the cosmic energy creating the universe and within that the rise of the force of life. God was equated to the father, the Creator, and Mother Goddess, the life sustaining force. They already believed in these concepts when they arrived from their homeland in the islands of the Aegean Sea and the bordering countries like Greece and Asia Minor.

The Aryan worship ceremonies included animal sacrifice *(homa)*, while the Dravidian worship was with the offerings of grains and flowers *(pooja)*, a practice followed almost all over India today in most variations of Hinduism. Siva is a Dravidian god and Durga their goddess, while Vishnu and Krishna are only partly Aryan; there is a tinge of Dravidian thought here. The phallic symbol was Austric; only in later times was it tied to the concept of Siva. Aryans did not believe in idol worship; they worshipped only fire. Most zoomorphic deities were Austric. It can be said that the religion and culture of the Hindus today are based on the contribution of the people of non-Aryan origin.

A word about the people of the southern part of the peninsula: the Tamilians of those times lived in small city states. The concept of kingship was well developed. There were palaces and courtiers and other frills and fanfare to bolster the image of the king and the ruling hierarchy. They had a language and script, and wrote on palmyra leaves and compiled books and ardently believed in God, and made temples in His honour. They made laws covering various aspects of living (though they had no lawyers) and followed the prescribed customs, and had the institution of marriage. They possessed good knowledge of common metals and astronomy and agriculture, and lived in well organised dwelling units in properly planned towns, and knew weaving, spinning, dyeing and pottery, and were well versed in martial arts and the use of bows, arrows, spears and swords.

The Mongoloid Group

Of this group, the tribes living in Assam and along the Indo-Myanmar border, constitute one part (they have dolichocephalic heads), while those with round heads found amongst the less primitive tribes in Myanmar and Chittagong Hills, form the other. There is also the more modern group of the Tibeto-Mongoloids of Sikkim and Bhutan, evolved as a result of intermingling of the Proto-Australoids and the Mongoloid stocks; the Mongoloid stock is from Tibet come down in comparatively recent times. However, these groups live only at the fringes of the subcontinent and have made little contribution to the development of Hindu religion and culture. Till recently, isolated in the jungles and mountains of the north and the east, they lived like the people of the Neolithic age. Christian missionaries took advantage of their isolation, particularly along the eastern border and converted a number of them to Christianity, establishing churches in their villages and educating them to some degree along Christian lines, securing for them jobs from their co-religionists, the Empire builder British bureaucrats of the Government of India at New Delhi as well as London. In this activity not only the British but the entire Christian Church participated with resources, like money, medicines, rations, shelters for the dispossessed and other philanthropic activity, and virtually won over the entire region to their side. But inspite of the efforts, north-east continued to be inhabited by tribes who were marked for their being primitive as compared to the most of India. These people generally inhabit the Himalayan foothills, though in recent times they have moved southwards and intermingled with the Indians of the plains and are getting assimilated in the Indian cultural, economic and social main stream.

Western Brachycephals

This group which spread all over India comprises the Alpinoids, the Dinarics and the Armenoids. Of these, the Alpinoids are a subdivision of a Caucasian race who lived mostly around the Alps. In India a majority of them live in Gujarat; their broad headed variation live around the west coast. They arrived before the Aryans but spoke the Aryan dialect. The Dinarics are from the Yugoslavian mountainous region and have settled in Orissa, Kathiawar, Kannada and Bengal, and to some extent in Tamil lands. In their near original form they can be identified in Coorg. As for the Armenoids, originating in Armenia, they possibly arrived with the civilised Mediterraneans, that is, the Dravidians, and spoke their language. The Parsis of Mumbai are a typical example of them; they are different from the long-headed Iranian Zoroastrians still living in Iran.

Nordic Aryans

The last of the major groups to arrive in the subcontinent is of the Nordic Aryans. They originated by most accounts, in the Eurasian steps and arrived on the subcontinent around the middle of the second millennium BC, and settled down in the north-western plains and highlands, including parts of Rajasthan, Punjab (on both sides of the Indo-Pak boundary), and hills and plains of western Uttar Pradesh. East of Uttar Pradesh they have intermingled with other racial groups. They were a fair skinned people, tall, mostly with blond hair and blue eyes, but under the pressure of natural selection and intermingling with other racial groups over long period of time, they are now light brown in complexion and the colour of their eyes and hair is no longer blue and blond. They can be identified over many parts of the subcontinent. They were dynamic people, and through their efforts to synthesize the different cultures and spread the one language, Sanskrit, they welded the sub-continent into one country. They were great organisers, and gave detailed attention to philosophy, arts, crafts, sciences, and every vocation that the society of their times took part in. To an appreciable extent the Hindu society of today is still governed by the rules and traditions that they set out during the second and first millennium BC.

Other Groups

In addition to the people described in the previous subparas, there were others too, like the Sythians, Huns, Greeks, Mongols, Tartars, who arrived from time to time and stayed on. Their number was small and, hence, their contribution to the development of Hindu civilisation was limited. Nonetheless their ideas and cultures did impact Hinduism. Hinduism did not accept conversions, but it has been fiercely competitive and modified itself where ever it felt threatened, although it stayed firm on the basic tenets; it would not accept changes in them, for it claimed to be "sanatana" eternal, having its origin with the birth of time. There is no point of its start; it just evolved with the growth of human awareness of the world and the universe, and it will cease at the time of the folding up of the universe.

North-western India has a larger concentration of the Nordics compared to the rest of the subcontinent; the area also has a marked presence of the Mediterraneans and the Orientals. The peninsular people are predominantly of the Palaeo-Mediterranean stock, while to the east and west are Alpo-Dinarics and the Armenoids, some in fairly original state while others as intermixture with other groups. Dark Australoids are visible everywhere, mostly as intermixture, primarily with Palaeo-Mediterraneans; they are of the poorer sections. Mongoloid people inhabit the cast and the mountainous north although their strain can be recognised in far off Bengal and Orissa. The racial groups are classified on the basis of speech families, like the Austric (Kol or Munda), Sino-Tibetan, the Dravidian, or the Indo-European (Aryan). But inspite of the differences, the common type of economic life based on agriculture has evolved a common Indian culture and the Indian archetype.

Except the Aryans no group on the subcontinent had to face the rigours of the Ice Age. The groups which had survived the Ice Age, were more intelligent and stronger, for they had to hunt extensively, and this required ingenuity and toughness. As meat eaters they consumed more proteins which contributed to their physical and intellectual well being and made them stronger and better equipped to over power the mere food gatherer. Paranthropus, a human-like vegetarian primate, was possibly eliminated by the hunter, meat eating Australopithecus, another type of primate who made tools and was, therefore, cleverer and more intelligent. Likewise this primate went extinct with the arrival of more advanced primates with better gains and capability to produce better tools,

During the existence threatening environments of the Ice Age the communities of the north had to expend considerable effort to survive against the fury of the elements while those living in the softer climes in the south could devote all the attention to the development of their civilisations. But with the mellowing of the Ice Age the northerners emerged as more competent and tougher competitors, for the hunter living style had given them superiority in survival capability, ingenuity, brain power. They operated in well-organised teams; effective team work was essential to the hunter.

2

The Indus Valley Civilisation

Many centuries before 3500 BC, people from the Mediterranean region and the areas cast of it were emigrating to western India. These emigrations were from lower Mesopotamia (Sumer) in the west and included Elam, southern Iran and Baluchistan. This tract is arid with scanty rainfall and any settlement depended on the rivers for their water. This happened during the Bronze Age and in the absence of steel good cutting tools were not yet developed. Some river valleys were level and not extensively wooded, and were fertile and could produce grains and vegetables and green fodder to support sizeable populations; infect some areas produced surplus for export and trade and commerce. Once the settlements had stabilised it was the development of industry and trade and commerce. This brought wealth and leasure. They developed their language, script, and rules and laws of business and governance. They were one of the oldest civilisations.

Before the Mohenjodaro and Harappa, settlements possessing remarkable organisational skills existed in south-east Afghanistan, Baluchistan and Sindh; they were almost at their prime around 3500 BC. Some of the better known amongst them are Mundigak in south-east Afghanistan (Quetta), Rana Ghundai in north Baluchistan and Nal, Nundara and Kulli in south Baluchistan. There were a number of them located in the present day Sindh province of Pakistan, starting from Bahawalpur; and then along the Indus river, going as far south as the Somnath in Kathiawar and Mehgam, Telod and Bhagatrav in the Deltas of the Narmada and the Tapti rivers. In the north these extended as far as Harappa and Ropar in the Punjab.

All pre-Harappan settlements were located in the close vicinity of established water sources, the region then received more rainfall than what it does now. The hill slopes had more trees and vegetation, rivers Ghaggar, Sarasvati (of the Vedic times) and Drisadvati carried substantial perennial water. At the time of Alexander's invasion, however, as stated in Greek accounts, climatically this area was as it is today. Alexander came almost 2500 years or more after the peak of the Indus Civilisation. The migrating Mediterraneans comprised labourers, agriculturists, artisans and men of trade and commerce. The laid out their settlements with care, utilising experience and skills developed in their mother country. They believed in orderliness and possessed organisational skills. Their houses were laid out in blocks of buildings constructed out of mud bricks or stones and were provided wooden doors. In some cases the houses had stone foundations, or flat roofs with staris leading to them. The passage way between houses could be six to eight feet in width, though in congested areas the width of the alley could be barely two to three feet.

Cemetries have revealed interesting information. In pre-Harappan days the burials were mostly fractional, that is burial after the bodies had been exposed to birds like vultures and animals and only parts of the skeletons remained. Some graves had more than on skeletons. Grave goods comprised pottery items, bones of animals killed possibly to support the soul in the after-life—their number and type depended upon the status of the dead person(s). Some graves had implements like axes. Most had red pigment while women graves had bangles of pottery and shell; this was mostly in graves in Sindh. Pottery of the pre-Harappans was of high quality. Nal and Amri are of fine soft buff or pinkish colour and in other settlements some are grey, brown or even black. The very thin walls of the vessels show the excellence of workmanship. Pottery is wheel turned and has painted upon it several types of geometrical designs or figures of animals including lions, fishes and birds, occasionally ox, sometimes leaves of peepal, the sacred fig. The tools and implements forming parts of the grave goods are of copper which contains small percentages of lead, nickel and arsenic. Stamp seals, even though these were prevalent during the Bronze Age culture of Iran and Mesopotamia are conspicuous by their absence, except for a lone steatite seal recovered from Nal cemetry. This seal is of irregular shape and has the like of kite etched upon it. The kite has a snake held in its claws—could possibly be the later day Garuda, the vehicle of the important Hindu god Vishnu.

The Kulli settlement was located on the western bank of river Hingol in southern Baluchistan, and proceeded Harappa by a couple of centuries. It evolved very like the Harappan culture, which was very similar to the culture of north-west India till the early years of the last century. They produced clay figurines of women, possibly for the worship of mother goddess, and of cattle, particularly of the humped bull; the bull was regarded as a sacred animal. Of the numerous figurines of cattle some, no doubt, served as toys, but were meant for religious purposes. Most female figurines at Kulli terminate at the waist on pedestals of flat base. Little attention has been paid to the facial details, but the necks have been adorned with strings of beads and necklaces. Some figurines have ornaments as are worn by Indian ladies of wealth even to this day, particularly in Gujarati Kathiawar, Sind and north-western area Rajasthan. Likewise in hairstyle, the high curls piled up in front and supported by a fillet above the forehead, and the hair at the back resting on the nape in a heavy tress, or hair arranged in two braids resting on the shoulders, or the fore-arm carrying a number of bangles, sometimes going above the elbow, are recognizable amongst the women of western part of India even today.

Soft stoneware of the Kullis, and the copper and bronze objects made by them and other village settlements along the river—of particular interest is the five inches diameter bronze mirror from Mehi—prove the existence of the settlements with Mesopotamia and Syria. In fact, there is a remarkable similarity in the cultural pattern followed by these settlements and the smaller communities of Mesopotamia, Elam and Iran. Originally even the trade was amongst them only and extended to the Harappans four or five centuries later.

Apart from the figurines of women, possibly representing Mother Goddess as the guardian of the dead and the patron deity of fertility, no other evidence of fertility cult has been found in southern Baluchistan. In Northern Baluchistan, however, a carved stone phallus was recovered from Moghul Ghundai and in a nearby site a female figurine with exaggerated vulva and thighs was found; Ghundai precedes Kulli by six or seven centuries. Next where similar evidence of fertility has been found is Harappa.

By early fourth millennium BC, village life in most parts of habitable India, including Baluchistan and Afghanistan, had fairly developed. People cultivated type land and weaved and made pottery and polished stones into microliths for use in implements like arrows, knives and swords. In the latter half of the fourth millennium BC more Sumer tribes arrived. They cultivated barley and strains of wheat which have been cultivated in most parts of India till recently, and bred cattle, used bronze implements, engraved or painted their wheel turned pottery, and worshipped a nude fertility goddess. They were the people of the pre-Harappan village cultures like Kulli or Rana Ghundai.

The Rise of the Cities

The cultures of the settlements in Baluchistan and south Afghanistan, though broadly similar, varied from one another in finer detail. For example, they did not have a common system of weights and measures, nor was there any uniformity in the design of their buildings or housing blocks, or in the detail on their pottery, or, possibly in their religious concepts. Actually these settlements were quite apart from one another in time and space; for example, Rana Ghundai preceded Kulli by nearly seven centuries, and then Kulli being closer to the sea and located on a fairly level area, had better communications and transportation system compared to uplands of Rana Ghundai. But still to the east were easier areas which received good rain and where the streams carried abundant water, and the soil was fertile and level and inter-settlement communications were easier. This kind of an environment gave rise to the development of central authority and the getting together of settlements into cities.

By about the middle of the first half of the third millennium BC a city civilisation was established in the Indus Valley; it was almost at its prime then, and had been organised by people who drew their inspiration from Sumer. There is a good reason to believe that the people who spear headed the organisation of the cities were either from Sumer or drew their inspiration from there. A few contiguously located settlements combined together to form centrally administered conglomerates which operated like cities. Such activity extended over an area which stretched from the Makran coast in the west to Sindh and Kathiawar and in the north included Harappa and Ropar in the Punjab, going right up to the Himalayan foothills, and in the east covering the Ganges-Yamuna Doab, a vast area enclosed by a rough triangle measuring around 1.3 million square kilometres; total area of the present day India is 3.3 million square kilometres. The two prominent city states which came up in this area are Harappa and Mohenjodaro. The cities appear to be under well organised central authorities who had standardised most aspects of the living activities of their citizens, including weights and measures, the arts and crafts, the designs on the pottery they made, the houses they lived in, the blocks formed by clusters of houses, the width of the streets, the design of the sewage disposal system, and so on. The two cities of Harappa and Mohenjodaro stood at a distance of around 550 mile from each other, they could be two trading capitals in the area of the Indus Valley set up. Each of the two cities covered an area of almost a square mile and were designed and constructed identically. They used baked bricks of standard dimensions.

The near uniformity of the Harappan goods suggests the existence of a strong central authority. They apparently regulated all sale and purchase, discouraging innovations and maybe even initiative or experimentation. But that perhaps, was the need of the time in order to ensure smooth progress in trade and commerce.

At Mohenjodaro nine different levels of foundations have been dug, and the lower most level has still not been reached, for beyond this it is the subsoil water, while at Harappa six successive settlements can be traced, one on top of the other. As Indus carried far more water, its floods inflicted more punishment on Mohenjodaro, located on its west bank, than did its tributary, Ravi, on Harappa, located on its eastern bank. Therefore, more information about the Civilisation has come from Harappa, although the layout of the cities has been obtained almost entirely from Mohenjodaro (the city of the dead). Located near Larkana in central Sindh this city was laid out in roads and streets running almost parallel in east-west and north-south directions creating blocks of buildings which were again subdivided by smaller and not so regular streets meant to provide access to individual houses. The size of a block was around 800 feet in the east-west direction and 1200 feet in the north-south direction and the width of the unpaved main streets could be as much as 30 feet. At the river end of either city there was citadel. What exactly the function of these citadels was, is not clear. Could be, in the style of Sumer, the high platforms within the citadels had temples, but there is no evidence of it. Nor is there indication of fortifications. At Mohenjodaro the layout within the citadel appears to have been dictated by the Great Bath, the Collegiate building, the Pillard Hall, and, may be, by the temple which some believe lies underneath the Stupa—this Stupa must have been constructed at a later date. The temple is deduced from the Great Bath which kind of structure accompanies most Hindu temples of any reckoning. Pillard Hall could also be for a religious purpose, like community prayer, or meditation. At Harappa the Citadel had ceremonial terraces approached by a processional pathway. Terraces have been provided guard rooms along the periphery. It appears the terraces had a ceremonial function which required a processional approach, but such a function could be religious or secular or both.

Most buildings were erected with baked bricks; sun-dried bricks were used for inner-walls and for filling of platforms or other structures where a lot of construction was required, like protective works or the ramparts. The standard of workmanship was high, including for the construction jobs, for houses and sewerage system. The latter ran under the streets and served the houses on either side. The drains could be cleaned by lifting the brick-made manhole covers. All sewers emptied into soakage pits and not in the river, a remarkable measure to prevent pollution of water. There is no indication about the provision of lavatories; they could have been located at the roof level of the building. Before the advent of the modern water-borne sanitation system, in most Indian towns and cities the lavatories were at the roof, from where excreta was removed manually.

A house was built around a courtyard; it had rooms of varying sizes around it or on its three sides. The bathrooms were located in the corner closest to the street drain while in the other comer close to the street was the kitchen; this kind of an arrangement was followed by type Babylonians. A house generally had two or more storeys and was provided with vertical drain pipes to drain the bathrooms and the kitchen at the higher floors. Some houses had doorless chambers at the bottom-most level which could be for the servants, or, maybe, even for cess-pits for the latrines or storage vaults, or were meant to strengthen the foundations against floods. Almost all houses had their own wells. In addition every two houses or so had a common well. Numerous sherds found around some public wells show that people preferred to discard the clay cup after drinking from it; drinking twice from the mine cup was taboo as it was till the recent times. Rubbish-shoots emptied into rectangular bins outside the house from where the refuse was possibly removed under municipal arrangements. Wooden beams and rafters and columns were used for roofs which were flat and had rash and bamboo matting covered with earth for protection from the elements. Sizes of the houses varied possibly in keeping with the status of the owner. Workers had small houses.

Granaries were near the river front and had loading ramps, quays, and labour quarters. The Industry was well organised, and a powerful bureaucracy decided what was to be produced and how much and its distribution, including export. In the opinion of Stuart Piggot (author of Prehistoric India), Harappa must have possessed the first really organised industry in Western Asia.

The Indus Civilisation comprised numerous small and large towns and villages, and at quite a few sites burnt bricks were not used, though where ever they were, they were of a standard size of

11 inches by 5.5 inches by 2.5 inches. In some places, however, some variations in the sizes have been noted. In some places stone has been used for foundations, or stone walls have been constructed upto a height of five feet or so from the foundations, whereafter the construction is in mud bricks. There has been no indication of construction of fortifications, except at Ali Murad where a three to five feet thick wall surrounds the housing complex, or at Surkagen-Dor in the Makran where more massive fortifications, duly provided with batter to the outer face, protect the living area; this probably was a strongly defended outpost the like of which may have existed along the overland trade routes.

The evidence suggests extensive trade links with Mesopotamia; in the textual references of the latter the Indus Valley has been referred to as 'Meluhha' which has been given as the source of many valuable commodities including those required to support inter-city wars. Trade was apparently over sea routes through the Gulf of Oman. Dilmun, probably Bahrain, was, it seems, an important staging post along the route. But trade with Elam could have been possible along the land route as well, although movement of goods over such a long distance, over hundreds of kilometres, would indeed have been some achievement of significance. Indus Civilisation flourished during the Bronze Age, and for its trade and industry it collected raw materials from far and wide. It got bitumen, probably even steatite, from Baluchistan, silver from Afghanistan, and gold, silver, lead, tin, semi-precious stones including 'lapis-lazuli' from Iran. It also had plenty of its own resources: semi-precious stones from Kathiawar, copper and lead from Rajasthan, wood from the Himalayan Hills, and so on.

Clearly the Indus trade and industry were backed by a strong merchant community. There is considerable evidence of export of Harappan items to the west, to Mesopotamia, Syria, Elam, but very little has been found in the Indus Valley diggings which might have been imported from other countries. It is quite possible the items of import might have been vandalised at the time of the break up of this Civilisation, or the trade might totally have been under the control of men from the west who colonised the region to exploit its natural resources and labour force. No big palaces were constructed as happened in Sumer, or Elam, Akkad, or Syria all of which existed contemporaneously, nor major temples, nor, it appears, was there a class of domineering priests; there might have been a small number of them to organise worship to satisfy the needs of the small community. The community in its approach to trade and manufacture was conservative, ever reluctant to deviate from the beaten track. It has been suggested that underneath the Buddhist stupa at Mohenjodaro there might be a temple. But this is unlikely, for, as stated, no evidence of any large temple structure has been found; if a temple was a part of the set up, it would have shown during the diggings.

The habitations, it seems, operated as independent units, unfettered by any outside authority, a kind of a situation where no state existed as such; the happy condition the communists want to reach when the state withers away, and there is freedom of action for everyone. Therefore, it is reasonable to assume that there was no empire as such. The uniting factor was trade which ran on the basis of barter or payment in gold or other expensive metals. Trade routes ran along rivers, for case of reference and direction finding, or, maybe, even sailing, and most of the important nodal points were on these routes; for downstream movements. Initially, it appears, only the traders living accommodation was well organised, but with time as the nexus between the traders and their local agents, and the producers/ growers/manufacturers grew and it became necessary for the concerned people to operate closely, the requirement grew to have bigger developed areas. The villages developed and as prosperity visited them they turned into towns, and with time, some of them turned into cities, depending upon the level of trade activity.

It is not possible to state how the village life was organised, but considering the later day villages one can surmise that village council, or 'panchayat', which was elected, possibly on a yearly basis, controlled the social life at the individual and collective level, and sorted out the problems between individuals and at the inter-individual levels; it can be assumed that the later day 'panchayats' followed the pattern of the earlier stages. Indus Valley Civilisation existed, in one form or another, following its ebbs and crests, from about 3500 BC to 2200 BC when it disintegrated under the pressure of attacking hordes from the northwest. During die time that it lasted, the village assumed great importance, and with that the family, and the head of the family, the customs that the family followed. The strength of the family had a lot to do with the governance of the village. The family owned all land and thus controlled the human activity, including that of the artisans. Even though the artisan was the king; he could not have got the better of the land owner. He obviously worked at his command. But since the Civilisation lasted for over a thousand years, it produced workers, artisans, who were masters in their craft—so the diggings reveal, although coordination activity was by higher echelons of traders which included, finalising the quantum to be manufactured of the items concerned, the specifications, the design details and so on. An organisation, probably headed by the village headmen or some other important persons, collected the manufactured items after duly satisfying about the specifications, and bartered them away to the traders, who could be local people or people moved in from other countries, like Sumer. Where requirement was high, or was likely to be high, the interested traders had organised guilds of tradesmen, cooperatives which could ensure a smooth supply.

The goods were transported by bullock carts but this could be done over short distances only. For long distances the movement had to be in stages. Along the river the trade was with boats, and sail boats; both are very slow moving means of communications. Therefore, in those times it was not possible to organise a government looking after large chunks of territory. The spread of any conglomerate of habitats could be barely around a KM or so either way. Which is how it was at Harappa or Mohenjodaro nothing bigger than these two places has been found. The speed of movement for trade as well as general administration was slow, at the rate of the speed of the bullock cart. Although both camel and horse were known, they do not seem to have been extensively used. There is, however, indication that horses were used in Rana-Ghundai for carrying goods and people in that very difficult country. As for the maritime trade movement, the evidence is scanty. But regarding movement by carts, plenty has been found. Any number of clay toy carts and toy bulls have been found in the diggings. Besides, there have been drawings of these on pottery and engravings on seals. But regarding boats there has not been much, except for two representations: one on a pottery shred, showing a rough drawing of a boat with high prow and stern, and another, an engraving on a seal, showing a vessel made out of reed, again with high prow and stern. Both representations resemble vessels from prehistoric Mesopotamia. Bronze models of the present day 'ekka' have been found at Harappa and Chanhudaro. This vehicle was generally used, as now, for conveying a single person. The uniformity in the design of this item and, consequently, of different items of utility in different parts of the Indus Valley, is evident from the identical designs of two models found at two places almost 650 kilometres apart.

The tribes settled around a water source, for existence without water was unthinkable, and since large scale military type movements were not possible, there was no likelihood of finding large dumps of equipment utilised for military purposes. What has been found are chisels, flat axes (without shaft-holes), spears (without the midrib which strengthens the blade), knives, fish-hooks, razors. In fact this variety of tools was produced by the western states, like Mesopotamia or Elam as early as the fourth or fifth millennium BC. In fact whatever was produced, did not constitute a weapon of war, but was merely a tool for day to day work; possibly spears were for self-protection or hunting. In fact what is striking is the complete lack of improvement in the design of these items, even when improved designs were available in countries with which Indus Valley had trade dealings.

Another striking feature of the finds is the rarity of the silver ware, like bowls and vases. There are plenty of bronze items, but even in their case the designs are not attractive, or comparable with those of other contemporaneous cultures. In fact they are dull, like their pottery designs, the emphasis being on utility rather than aesthetics. All this suggests that there was no ruling class as such, a class of aristocrats who lived in big houses and had an extravagant life style, and executed lasting works for the well-being of their less fortunate fellow citizens. None of this has been revealed in the excavations. Both at Harappa and Mohenjodaro one heavy structure each has been located, and the explorers have chosen to call them citadels, but the precise function of these is not clear. These may well have been the kind of secretariates where the merchants guilds assembled to work out their trade strategy and work out the details of items for sale, or to be manufactured for the purpose, or to be imported, and such like matters. That the overall dimension of the Indus Valley Civilisation was limited is vouched by the fact that it broadly comprised just two cities, and a hundred odd towns and villages. One ramp each from the river front climbed to the citadels. The ramps had guard posts, and the level area at the top at Harappa might have been used for some kind of a ceremonial function, on daily basis, or weekly or even annually.

Nothing in the Indus Valley could be called kingly or aristocratic. All that can be said is that a community of merchants, in collaboration with foreigners developed a number of villages and two cities to take advantage of the expertise of the local labour and the valuable raw materials. And these people were intelligent, ingenious and enterprising and surprisingly forward looking for their time, and possessed scientific temper and inclination. No other community matched them on this subcontinent during the time they lasted, nor for many centuries later. In fact nowhere in the world of their time do we see any other community possessing matching competence in all fields, except battle craft. The clock was set back, in the first instance, by the Aryan invasions and vandalism, the establishment of oligarchies and imperialism by them. Its final ruin was perpetrated by Muslim invasions who set the clock back to the days of Adm. With time having been completed dominated by hard core materialism it would be futile to hope to the days of the Indus Valley. In any case in the forward aggressive march of time there is no place for passivity or scope to look back.

The Indus community had a script of about 400 characters which, excluding the variants, could be reduced to about 250 different symbols—compare this with 900 characters in early dynastic Sumerian script, and almost 2000 during the Uruk period, for as the writing and the language develop the number of characters reduce. But the disturbing feature is that throughout the time this civilisation lasted there was no further development in their language or script. The community possibly was under pressure on account of internal problems or external aggressive ingresses. The script can be called pictographic. In this the stylized picture of an item may be used for its indication and to show the quantity; for example, stylized pictures of two bulls standing side by side may be used to indicate two bulls. This may be simplified by having one picture with so many dots to indicate the number. With the passage of time the stylized picture got associated with sound value, and this reduced the number of characters in the script. While Sumerians impressed wedge-shaped marks with a reed stylus on clay tablets—the script is called cuneiform—and the Egyptians did their writing on papyrus also with a script which was essentially pictographic and developed into what is called hieroglyphic, the Indus Valley writing is available only on seals, pot sherds and, rarely, on small copper tablets, and at no place has anything been found exceeding twenty symbols. The writing is done from left to right, but the following line is written from right to left, and then again left to right and so on. No monumental or public inscription has been found, nor anything which might be a business document, or a letter or a historical account. The script is without descendents. Though the script might have developed under Mesopotamian inspiration, it seems to have followed the Egyptian model. A lot of effort has been expended to decipher the script but there has been little success. The assumption has been that it might be related to Sanskrit, or some West-Indogermanic language like Hittite or Latin, or it might be an early form of a Dravidian language like Brahui which is still spoken in Baluchistan. But there has been little success. From time to time scholars have claimed to have deciphered the script, but their claims have been found to be hollow. Some scholars have opined that the script is still being used by the Santhals of Bihar, particularly during their festivals and community prayers, and has words from Sanskrit Hebrew, Arabic and Persian. The sound value of symbols, according to these scholars, is the same as that of the alphabets of the Devnagri script, and the writing varies from left to right then from right to left, and also from top to bottom and vice versa. Every letter is said to be associated with some legend related to Indian deities. It is stated in the findings that even today several script words are used by Santhal tribes in their folk songs; the songs also give an account of their migration from the Indus Valley to Bihar. However, the details of what the writings on the seals and potsherds mean, have yet to be worked out.

The script does not appear to have been used for any proclamations, or drafting rules or laws, or writing down business deals or contracts. It was used to establish ownership of items and commodities and, maybe, record, in outline, the trade transactions. Otherwise, business transactions were oral, as is done even now amongst the business communities of Gujarat and Kathiawar, and the Sindhi, and the Bania communities of the Punjab and Rajasthan. The weights they used were cut in chert and accurately graded in the ratio of 1, 2, 4, 8, 16, 32, 64, 160, 200, 320, 640; the weights were related in multiples or fractions of 16. The system is in vogue even today whereunder 8 rattis make one masha, and 12 mashas make one tola, five of which make one chhatank, sixteen of which make a seer. 16 seers make one kachcha maund while 40 of these made one pucca maund. This system of weights and measures was followed till a change over to the metric system was ordered by the Government in 1958. Even in coinage, the system that was followed was of the Indus Valley vintage till it was also changed at the time of the switch over to the metric system. The weighing scales comprised a bronze bar, having two copper pans suspended at its two ends, and having a central fulcrum device. For heavier weights bigger scales, possibly using a wooden beam, were used, though nothing of the sort has been found in the diggings. As for the measurement of length, the evidence is scanty, but from whatever has been found it would appear they used a measure where a foot was equal to 13.2 inches, a system which was widely used in pre-historic and Roman Europe. The other measure they used was based on the standard cubit ('Hath' in India) of 20.62 inches; this was widely used in ancient world. The accuracy of weights and measures, and indeed the whole layout of towns and cities, suggests not only the existence of a highly organised mercantile system, but also the fact that the system was backed by a sound knowledge of engineering and practical geometry and surveying.

One find that has attracted a lot of attention is the steatite seals. These are actually stamp seals used for marking property. The surface is precisely carved to make figures and letters, and then the seal is heated to give it a bright white face; it is pressed directly on the soft material used for sealing. The figures on the seals are of animals or religious symbols and throw some meaningful light on the religion of Indus people. The sizes vary between 3/4 and 1.5 inches square. Very few seals made out of clay have been found as clay is fragile. Some terracotta seals have been found and it appears those were used for some specific purpose. Every citizen, rich or poor, had them, may be, even to establish identity. Cylinder seals which were fairly extensively used by the people of Sumer, do not seem to be popular here; only three samples have been found.

Very few sculptures and bronzes have been found; only thirteen statues or fragments thereof are on record. They are made out of steatite, lime stone or alabaster, and the biggest is no more than 16.50 inches. Of these eleven are of elderly bearded men clad in a loose cotton garment, having protruding noses like Jews and narrow heads of the brachycephalic, or dolichocephalic, or the intermediate variety. The work is generally of a high quality, and has a mature dimension, more so considering the time when they were made. Amongst the finds are two torsos from Harappa whose arms and heads, which had been fastened with pegs, have since been lost. One of these is of red sand stone and looks like a miniature of later day 'Greek athlete', while the other, in grey lime stone, is of a man in a dancing posture: could be 'Siva Natraja'. The red sand stone figurine later became the 'kayotsarga' pose of the Tirath ankaras of Jain religion; Jainis claim their Tirathankaras (religious guides) go back long years into antiquity. They are pacifists and advocate vegetarianism.

Of the bronzes the most notable is the 4.5 inches statuette of an Austro-Asiatic dancing girl; the model for this was possibly from south Baluchistan. This piece shows a sensitive modelling of the body and limbs, and shows the hairdressing and adornments. Kulli pottery also shows similar figurines and this shows that there existed regular trade between the two areas, but Kulli output is rough in comparison. It also shows that the later day Indian art was purely indigenous in content. It also shows that the naturalistic human sculpture of Harappa was the forerunner of the later day Indian art. But Harappa had no monumental or public compositions. The output is diminutive in scale.

The sculptures do not give much information regarding the clothing the people wore, except that men kept short beards, and wore loose robes, sometimes embroidered, over the torso and the left shoulder, leaving the right shoulder uncovered, and wore ornaments like rings on the fingers and ears. Below the waist they wore a piece of cloth like the present day 'dhoti'. Apparently women were similarly dressed. The garments were of cotton or wool, and often were not stitched, and just wrapped around the body; but some people also wore stitched items, as the needles found at the sites would suggest. The stitched clothing came into use particularly when the weather was bad or it was cold.

They kept long hair with short locks at the back of the head, and parted them in the middle and used a fillet to keep them in place, or they just coiled them in a ring on top of the head; sometimes a part of the hair at the sides were plaited. Fillets could be woollen, or of gold, silver, or copper. Women had their hair 'coiffured' as some of the figurines suggest, though the details are not so obvious. But it can be said that the majority of the women plaited their hair at the back with a bow at the end, as is the practice followed in most parts of India of today, or they had a number of small plaits on either side of the head or woven together into one or two bigger plaits. The ornaments the women wore were of numerous varieties and designs, made of gold, silver, copper or faience, depending upon the status and property level of the family, and included anklets, girdles, bangles and bracelets, finger and ear-rings, necklaces with or without pendants, made of precious and semi-precious stones or beads of pottery or faience, and fillets or head-bands for the forehead, metal or shell cones for the side of the head. No nose ornament has been found.

In cosmetics and toiletries, the vanity case from Harappa has one item which is a combination of a piercer, possibly for use as a tooth pick, the ear scoop for removing wax from the ears, and a tweezer, all of which bear a striking resemblance to similar items found in Sumer and northern Mesopotamia. Also found are toilet jars of ivory metal, pottery, stone and faience. Mohenjodaro women had shell containers for rouge, face-paint, kohl, and lip-paints and other items like shampoos and eye-ointments. They had bronze mirrors and ivory combs of various shapes and designs. Men's razors were made of bronze.

Kitchenware included dishes, saucers, goblets, beakers, cookery-pots and a host of other items, and these were made of pottery, metal, faience, stone, even ivory, depending on the financial status of the family. There were needles, awls, axes, sickles, knives, fish-hooks, and so on house furniture included 'charpais' or bedsteads, reed mats, wicker-stools, lamps of metal or pottery, candle-sticks—apparently wax or tallow candles were also used to light the houses. Marble balls and dice were used to play or gamble; possibly some kind of a board game was played. Men hunted and watched bull-fights, and cock-fights, and fished extensively. Children played with clay-toys for which there was an extensive market, and considering their ingenious designs they were readily accepted in other countries, and were exported in large numbers. Some of the interesting toys bulls made out of stiff fibre and having a nodding head, little clay-carts, pottery rams, monkeys with movable arms, monkeys moving up and down a string where speed could be varied by loosening or tightening the strings, models of men, women, birds, animals, rattles and so on.

Very little information is available about the medicines and the medical system. 'Silajit' was used—the substance was used as a general tonic and for diseases of the liver. Also used horns of animals, cattle fish-bones, coral, leaves of Neem tree: kind of items which are used in the Ayurvedic system of medicine even today. They, apparently, practised the 'Siddha' system of medicine, which is practised today in Tamil Nadu, in South India. They identified 64 herbs which were administered singly or in combination. The treatment is aimed at strengthening the body system: the mind also plays a part in it. Yoga is prescribed, along with other exercises for good health and longevity. The doctors of the system are called

Siddhars. Ther system, it is claimed, evolved after observations and experiments which spread over millennia. It also generates spiritual power.

The trade activity spread to the Nilgiris in South India, and Kashmir in the north, and Sumer, Elam, Crete, Egypt and Iran in the West; there is evidence of Indus people in Sumer. In fact there is so much similarity between Sumer and Indus regarding layout of cities and towns, and the general architecture of the buildings, that it may be concluded that the authors of Indus were Sumerians, or people from the nearby lands. Possibly Mesopotamians, pressed by droughts and floods, or the increasing population migrated here. But not a shred of evidence has been found which might suggest that these people were proud of their achievements, or they were people with grand designs who had ambitions to leave their name for the posterity. They could have been a mix of Mesopotamians, Assyrians, Elamites or Anatolians, and they could have been people riven by class differences and, thus, lived in mutual distrust and friction, and had little interest beyond their trade. This civilisation was at its peak around about 2200 BC.

The founding fathers of this civilisation were traders, that is what the evidence after examining the diggings suggests. A parallel example in recent history is the arrival of the Europeans on the Indian subcontinent in search of raw materials for trade. British were the most successful in India. Other European nations who could not compete diverted their attention elsewhere. The result was that the scientifically advanced nations of Europe divided most of the underdeveloped world amongst themselves as their colonies. They plundered, and it was after two bloody wars that human conscience awoke to the havoc caused by the profligate exploitation. In the past this cycle got repeated every so often, as a study of the human history tells us.

About 100 odd sites have been located, and more and more are getting uncovered every so often. So far the diggings have established the spread of this civilisation from Baluchistan, to North West Frontier, then eastwards to the Indus delta, thence to north-west Rajasthan, Punjab and all the way to the east to western Uttar Pradesh. But there have been sites which do not seem to have been influenced by the Harappan designs. Such habitats either belonged to people already settled prior to the arrival of the Harappans, already engaged in agriculture and raising domestic animals, or they were nomadic tribes, mostly wandering, with cattle and kin, hunting and gathering food and pillaging and plundering the agricultural settlements whenever there was opportunity. How the Indus trader safeguarded himself against this ever present menace is difficult to say, but he might have resorted to aggressive resistance, or made payments in terms of money or commodities to pacify the marauders. But it does not appear there were serious law and order problems.

Not much changed in the customs and habits of the people. The time stood almost still and people followed the same pattern of life generation after generation till almost the beginning of the Twentieth Century, except that the Bronze Age changed to Iron Age and iron implements came into use. Otherwise the potter still turned the same kind of ware, and the people still wore the same kind of jewellery and clothes and lived in the same kind of habitats, living in houses built on the same old pattern—made of mud bricks in villages and baked bricks in towns and cities—following similar pattern of sewage disposal. Mode of transport was still the good old bullock cart, with bronze parts replaced by those of iron.

The Indus people shunned change, more so at a radical rate, and for this reason they avoided contact with foreigners, or their ideas. They were orthodox in outlook. They did follow caste system, and in this the son generally followed the profession of his father. They believed in non-violence and left a permanent mark on the culture and civilisation of this subcontinent.

About the religion of these people, on the basis of the unearthed, semi-nude female figurines, it can be surmised that mother Goddess was worshipped. Bania and the trader (Lala) communities in the Punjab and the contiguous areas in Himachal Pradesh and Jammu are ardent followers of this form of worship. The figurines have been found in many places in West Asia, between Iran and the Aegean sea. She is 'Aditi' and she is 'Prithvi', the benefactress from whose womb emanate all that is essential for the survival of life on this planet. Then there is evidence of tree worship, particularly 'Pipal', the fig tree, which practise continues to this day amongst some sections of the people. Siva, one of the major gods in the Indian pantheon, seems also to have been worshipped. On one seal he sits in a yogic posture, has horns, and has his 'member' erect, and wears bangles on his arm, and is surrounded by wild animals—possibly an early form of 'Pashupati Nath, The erect member, the fertility symbol, is the characteristic of another old form of the god: Lakulisha of the Austric Proto-Australoids; the god is still held in veneration by some tribes in Orissa. Horns are a very common symbol of divinity in Egypt and ancient 'near East'. Legends in some other countries find place on some seals.

It is possible that the concept of Siva was finalised during the later years of Indus Civilisation itself. He is the god of fertility. He is also worshipped as 'Linga' the phallus. Alongside, 'Yoni', the female organ of reproduction is also worshipped; this worship has its base in the Austric thought. A number of animals have also appeared on the Harappan seals, possibly because these animals were regarded as sacred, like, for example, 'the bull', which even today is regarded as the vehicle of Siva. There is no evidence to suggest that water was considered sacred, but the presence of the Great Bath at Mohenjodaro can suggest that water had an important place in the beliefs of these people. They believed in keeping the rivers and other water sources clean. Cow had no sacred status, for even though a number of seals had animal on them, none of them had a cow.

As for the disposal of their dead, only a few burial grounds have been found, and it may be concluded that cremation was the main method adopted. Cemeteries, whatever have been found, indicate three kinds of burials, being complete, fractional and post-cremation. Fractional burial is the internment of the left-over bones after the body has been exposed to wild animals or birds. The urn containing post-cremation ashes was almost invariably buried in a floor of the house or underneath a street. In all burials there were funerary offerings of birds, animals, fish or articles like beads, bangles, and household items like cooking ware and so on. The prevalent concept in most countries of that time was that in the hereafter, for its comfort and happiness, the ethereal spirit needed offerings of those kind of items which provided it happiness and comfort during its human existence.

In some parts of the old world, like for example, Egypt, when a king or a personage of status died, a number of animals, some times even human beings, were sacrificed to accompany him to the next world. The human beings were generally members of his retinue, and other people he was comfortable with, and his wives and mistresses. He also carried treasures, and articles of food and other items of utility so that his needs and those of his retinue were taken care of. How many human beings and animals were sacrificed and how much treasure accompanied as funerary items, depended upon the power and position of deceased person. Whereas a king took a lot, a small-time chief had to be content with, may be, with just his wife(s) and a few animals. The custom of 'Sati' was also from this belief.

The End of the Civilisation

The cohesive form of this civilisation disintegrated around the middle of the second millennium B.C. There are different views regarding the course the disintegration followed, and the causes that precipitated it. Most scholars believe that this was the time when the ancient civilisations in the west were breaking up under the pressure of bludgeoning populations of Central Asia. Tribes fought each other for securing grazing and cultivable lands, and in the ongoing conflicts, the battle field skills as well as the lethality of the weapons systems improved radically, so that when they pounced on the aging civilisations with their new found ferocity the latter just caved in and laid prostrate, leaving themselves exposed to utter exploitation and humiliation. The diggings at the sites at Harappa brings this out clearly. At Rana Ghundai where there has been an almost unbroken occupation from about late fourth millennium B.C., pockets of ashes have been found in the later layers which suggest that there was large scale burning of the place around 2000 B.C. That the place was reoccupied by a different set of people is indicated by the coarser style of pottery in the following layers; the style suggests the new occupants were probably barbarians. The evidence further shows that the place was burnt again and yet again, and every time it was occupied by a different set of people with different pottery style. Similar evidence has been unearthed at Nal and Dabar Kot, in north Baluchistan.

There is similarity between Harappa and the north Baluchi cultures. Both seem to have gone through similar vicissitudes. This suggests that possibly Harappa was approached through north Baluchistan. In south Baluchistan not much evidence of such destruction has been found. But in Shahi Tump cemetry a heavy copper axe with a shaft hole has been found amongst the grave goods, and the pottery, in some cases, has the swastika or a similar motif printed upon it. Clearly a new set of people had arrived. One burial place carried a number of weapons alongside a skeleton indicating that the person buried was a warrior. The evidence also suggests that in the later phases the two cities and some other sites, had been provided with defence works. From this some scholars have concluded that the end of this civilisation was violent, and it vanished from the surface of the earth in one sweep of the pillaging and plundering Central Asian tribesmen.

Even though the possibility of this kind of a demise for a civilisation which had stagnated for the past few hundred years cannot be ruled out, it does not seem likely. To begin with it was not a centrally administered state which could lose its identity after a defeat in battle. As has been brought out, the area was a conglomerate of possibly contiguously located settlements, which followed some basic rules of governance, and some minimum laws, so that they could carry on with their trade and commerce and derive maximum benefits. The settlements were not knit into an empire and therefore, could not have gone out of existence in one swipe. As they existed they could have only faded away, dispersed and scattered under the pressure of violent invaders from the west. The settlements broke up and moved eastwards, to the Gangetic plane, and southwards to the line of the Narbada and beyond, and the areas vacated by them were taken by wild tribesmen from the west, till they too were overpowered by fresh waves of marauding tribesmen and got pushed eastwards. So this process continued till the year 1947, when India got partitioned and the western state of Pakistan was formed. But even after that the process continued, and still continues, except that the movement west of Pakistan is somewhat contained now and very few people manage to get past the Pak boundary into India.

With time better cutting implements came into being these were still of bronze or copper. The area east of the Yamuna, the Gangetic basin, got cleared, howsoever slowly. Likewise the Narmada basin was also cleared for the emigrating populations. An interesting hypothesis has been put forward by Professor M. Dmitriyev of the erstwhile Soviet Union. According to him Mohenjodaro was destroyed in a black lightning explosion which caused it to disappear from the surface of this earth literally in one go. According to him there is an account of this in the 'Mahabharata'. It is stated that there was a powerful explosion over this land, and that was followed by a dazzling glow, and fires without smoke, and the temperature of the water reached the boiling point, and the fish baked. Such explosions, the Professor says, have occurred in various parts of the world from time to time and are caused by physicochemical formations. Under the effect of cosmic rays and electric fields, chemically active particles are formed, which extend over large areas in the atmosphere. These expanses or areas, get compressed by the electromagnetic fields. The atmospheric conditions in which the physicochemical formations appear, activate the formation of toxic agents, and these pollute the air. It seems the people of Mohenjodaro were affected by poisonous gases to begin with, and then a powerful explosion caused the complete destruction. This phenomenon is possible only when a large number of black lightning discharges occur simultaneously; after the first explosion a chain reaction follows.

Whatever the cause of destruction, the end of Mohenjodaro, it appears, was pretty abrupt; it appears there wasn't time to collect even the bare essentials when death struck. The destruction of the city eliminated a vital commercial support system, a loss the Valley could not withstand. Over the time, wandering tribes settled there temporarily, erected dwellings, and moved on after some time. For essentially the place had importance only from the trade point of view, as a trade centre, a nodal point. With time the river receded after the training works had been neglected, and cargo carrying boats could no longer reach the ramps and unload at the marketplace. The land routes fell into disuse on account of inadequate security. The horse rider was ruling, and that had changed the entire complexion of the power equation. The old order was dying. A newer order had firmed up in which there was no place for the old and the outdated.

The civilisation went, but the people who had formed it had left a strong flavour of theirs. During their last days the cities showed a distinct lack of the previous verve and enthusiasm, and the organising capability. The streets had become narrower, and the people preferred to five closer together in order, possibly, to be able to come to each other's help at short notice. Slums sprang up in the middle of the earlier well organised areas; even the manufacturing kilns which earlier were located away from the inhabited areas, were no longer following this rule. The rules were lax, and the order was degenerating into chaos. There was immigration to the east, to the Gangetic basin, or the valley of the Ghaggar in the Thar desert, or to Saurashtra and Gujarat, New townships came up including the very important port town of Lothal in the gulf of Cambay, supplementing the old ports of Surat and Kinnarkheda. The spread eastwards and southwards, continued over a long period, till they had spread far and wide, into all corners of India. Essential left over elements of this civilisation to day live in Rajasthan and Gujarat (Saurashtra).

The Ancient Cultures of South India

About the ancient cultures of South India, not much is record is available. The north-western territory of this subcontinent has been attacked by aggressive tribes since the time the chariot came into being as the war machine. Later the horse cavalry played the decisive role and caused a continuous movement of the population from the north-west/west eastwards. Southern parts of the subcontinent received a large number of the Negritos, Proto-Australoids and the Palaeo-Mediterranean, for being the first to arrive, they were the first to be pushed out southwards by the tribes and communities following them. But the South got other people too, from Persia (Iran), Iraq, Syria, Egypt, who made it directly after crossing the Arabian Sea, or the Persian Gulf, or following the land route along the Makran Coast and thence to Sindh, Gujarat then southwards along the Western Coast, all the way down to the Tamil Land. People from the African countries located along the East African coast have also crossed the Arabian Sea it from time to time and made it to the peninsular India.

The cult of 'Siva and Parvati' is similar to the cult of the 'Moon god' and the 'Lady of the Mountain', which was followed at Ur, the ancient city of Sumer in southern Mesopotamia, including the ceremonial nuptials of the god and the goddess, their palace-temple, the temple slaves, and the 'devadasis'. The South Indian painted pottery often resembles that of 'Tepe Hissar' in Persia (Iran). Egyptian alabasters were discovered in Malabar. There is a lot of similarity in the form of burials and funeral offerings with areas along the coast of the Arabian Sea, or Egypt, Syria, Cyprus even as far away as Breitanny in north-west France. There is also evidence of trade between South India and Mesopotamia, Egypt and neighbouring countries.

Insofar as the population is concerned, the peninsular and South India had a mix, like the northern India, but the majority in the South were Negritos, Proto-Ausraloids, and the Palaeo-Meditarraneans. There were also some Sytho-Dravidians and a mix from Egypt, Syria, Mesopotamia and Persia.

The eastwards and the southwards movements were similar except that during the former there were no inputs of people who might have arrived after crossing the sea, and there was interbreeding with the Mongoloid population inhabiting the northern and eastern fringes. The last major group to arrive at the subcontinent were the Aryans, and they settled in the Punjab and western Uttar Pradesh. They were a dynamic people and synthesised the existing cultures. They had a language, Sanskrit, which was widely used in Europe and Asia, and they evolved a script for it. This went a long way in the development of their social, economic, political and scientific institutions, and brought an era of well-being and all round progress.

As is clear from the evidence dug from the sites, the people of the Indus Civilisation do not seem to have authored any major religious creed; they were not theocratic in outlook. During their time there were any number of ideas about divinity: the Mother Goddess, Siva Nataraja, the ancestors, or trees, or just spots on the ground, or stones. This prevalence of different concepts does not appear to have caused any friction between different sets of people. Praying was recognised to be an individual's choice, and the individual was free to follow his choice.

The ancient tribes professed Yoga and brought in the concepts of Siva Nataraja, the cosmic energy engrossed in the cycles of creation and annihilation, and bringing about order in the system of creation. Of the other facets of this energy, one sustained the creation, and the other annihilated it when it had done its course. Then, at the mundane level, the Creator was visualised as a kind person with all power, to whom one turned in distress for help and succour. They believed that while performing deeds of malice and dishonesty and cruelty and inflicting pain and suffering on the innocent, this power turned in anger and caused hardship that brought sorrow and suffering. They believed in shamans, and magic, including black magic, and believed they could totally control the fate and get over all problems and vanquish their enemies and for ever be happy with the power invoked through the magic chants.

3

Capter-3

Who were the Indo-Aryans, where did they come from and when? Their cradle land has been placed anywhere between Germany in the west and the western border of the Indian subcontinent in the east. Their presence has been dated by some authorities as not later than 2500 B.C. while some have put the date as early as 10,000 B.C. Unfortunately not a shred of evidence has been found anywhere which might throw light on the land of their origination or the time of their arrival in India. Had it not been for the literature of their religion, even the very existence of these very dynamic people would have gone unrecorded. Even the pottery finds have not been helpful because of the semi-migratory life they led for a long time. Some scholars have identified them with the Painted Greyware culture which is dated between 1100-500 B.C. in western Uttar Pradesh. They lived in thatched houses and used copper and with time learnt the use of iron as well. At Hastinapur, on the bank of the Ganges, digging has revealed that around 800 B.C. a part of the town was washed away in floods. This occurrence is given as having taken place in the reign of the seventh successor after Prikshat; the latter was the first king after Mahabharata war; and this would place the date of the war as around 1000 B.C. The evidence of the Painted Greyware culture ends at this stage.

The traditional story the Aryan mythology gives about origination as recorded in the 'Puranas' and the 'Brahmanas' starts with Manu Svayambhu during the flood, which happened in distant past. According to a seventh century A.D. inscription of Pulakesin II at Aihole, the Mahabharata War took place in the year 3102 BC. This is clearly based on the accounts in the traditional history. However during the late eighteenth and early nineteenth centuries evidence based on philology came to be considered more reliable, and for that reason the importance of traditional evidence diminished.

In India the scholars of Sanskrit noticed a close relationship in the structure and sound with Greek and Latin languages. At present these languages are divided in two broad groups; namely, the Satem and the Centum. In the Satem group the velar k became s and labiovelar kw became k, while in the Centum group the velar k and the labiovelar kw have been retained. Most languages of central and western Europe are Centum. The Satem group has two divisions, viz:, Balto-Slavanic and Indo-Iranian. Balto-Slavanic languages are used in Eastern Europe and the States around the Baltic sea. The Indo-Iranian languages have influenced Iranian, Kurd, Baluch, Afghan and all languages of northern India, like Punjabi, Bengali, and so on. From this it can be concluded that originally the Indo-Europeans had a common language, and as sections of them wandered away in different directions, this got modified to accommodate countries and people they came in contact with.

In 1921-22 the archaeological finds at Harappa and Mohenjodaro revealed the existence of a pre-Aryan civilisation in the north-west of India—The Indus Valley Civilisation. This civilisation could have existed between c. 2800 B.C. to 2200 B.C., although it could have been fairly characterized between c. 3500 B.C. and 1500 B.C. This put serious doubt on the 'Puranic, 'history and the records in the 'Brahmanas'. It now appeared that the Indo-Aryans could not have arrived in this country much earlier that 2000 B.C, and in the early stages they could have only been nomads in search of pastures for their animals, and their conquests could not have taken place much earlier than c. 1800-1500 B.C.

As for their cradle land, on the basis of philology, scholars led by Brandenstein have concluded that Indo-Iranian were the first to separate from the main body of the Indo-Europeans, and they believe that the original home of the Indo-Europeans was in the Kirghiz Step, to the south of the Ural mountains, from where some groups, later classified as the Indo-Iranians, moved to the east, and the others, at a somewhat later date, moved westwards.

This latter group split on their way with one part moving to the north to be identified as Nordics, and the other moving to Ukraine and thence to the south and west. Eduard Meyers, however, places the original home of the Aryans in the Pamir plateau. This view is based on the established presence of the Hittites in Asia Minor around 1950 B.C.—Hittites is the oldest known Indo-European dialect. Thus, the Indo-Iranians, on this basis, not only moved to India but also westwards from their common home in the Pamir plateau, or in Russian Turkistan (as suggested by Herzfeld). But if they moved in different directions and arrived in India and western and central. Asia Monor almost at the same time, then the area they moved from had to be equidistant from both places. This would place the original home in Russian Turkistan.

All Centum speaking areas are to the west of the Vistula and the Satem to the east. Therefore, before their final dispersal the Indo-Europeans appear to have been settled on either side of this River. But findings of Tocharian—a Centum language—in Chinese Turkestan during the last century has put a question mark on this view. Another noteworthy fact has been the Lithuanian, most archaic of the Indo-European languages. Possibly the language was brought here by the Indo-Europeans after the Centum-Satem split, and if so then the cradle land could not have been far from Lithuania, or Lithuania itself.

Another view is that German countries—particularly Scandinavia—have not ever been over run by an alien race, and they all speak Indo-European languages. Therefore the home of the Aryans should be in this Germanic region. Penka, the chief exponent of this view, was an ethnologist and believed the term 'Aryan' represented a race comprising people from Scandinavia. However, it cannot be conclusively proved that the people of the interior of the Germanic countries remained totally static over the millennia, in their homeland and did not intermingle with any other racial group. Professor Max Mullar has expressed the view, different from Penka, that term 'Aryan' is language related and signifies only people speaking one of the Indo-European languages and is not applicable to a race. This may be one view in the midst of a number of them, but we know that a language belongs to a group of people who in the initial stages, a majority of them at least, occupy a common geographical location and most of them possess common racial characteristics. Scandinavians could not have been so completely isolated, that no other racial group arrived in their country during their isolation, and there was no interbreeding.

On the basis of the pottery finds, dated to the third millennium B.C., Nehring formulated the view that the cradle land was in south Russia since the place of finds (Tripolje) is located there. Other scholars, on the basis of the age of the languages spoken in various parts of south Russia, also came to similar conclusions. Besides there are similarities between the Indo-European and Finno-Ugrian languages, and it is certain that both groups have influenced one another during the very early times, and since the Finno-Ugrians originated in Central Russia, the possibility of the area south of the Urals being the homeland, is high. It has also been established, by Moller, that there is evidence of similarity between the early Indo-European and Semitic languages, and this shows that the Semites had, possibly, immigrated to Arabia via Iran or Asia Minor, and that there was early contact between the two groups. This, when viewed in the light of the fact that there was contact in early times between the Finno-Ugrians and the Indo-Aryans as well, places the cradle land in south Russia.

Towards the end of the nineteenth century, B.G. Tilak, the famous Maharashtrian leader of the freedom movement in India, published a paper (in Oct. 1893) to establish the age of the Rig Veda on the basis of astrological calculations. He put forth the hypothesis, on the basis of a few accounts and statements contained in the Vedic literature, that the original home of the Indo-Aryans was in the arctic region. Although during the one hundred odd years that have elapsed since he published his findings a lot of other views have been expressed on this issue, but Tilak's findings have not been refuted convincingly. Russian art scholar, Svetlana Zharnikova, has lately expressed the view that Tilak's findings had substance. In the Vedic hymns there are accounts of forbidding mountains in the far north, stretching from west to east, and plains covered with snow for most part of the year, and the tops of high mountains glistening in the golden rays of the sun rotating around them throughout the year, and the Great Bear shining above during the dark nights, and the Pole Star as the centre of the universe. The hymns contain accounts of great rivers foaming down from these mountains, some northwards to the white ocean, and others southwards to the warm sea. The name of these mountains which separate the sea and the blessed northern land is Meru. Mount Mandara is the tallest of them all. The flow of time beyond the Meru is such that a day there lasts for half a year and so on. A similar corroboratory account is found in the Avestan tradition; the mountain there is Hara Berezaiti. The description is, no doubt, of the arctic areas. Greek accounts also mention the northern mountains; they called them 'the Rhipeans' and assumed their location to be in northern Europe.

In Tilak's view the Aryans emigrated from the arctic region of northern Russia. In the view of the Russian scholars, the Indo-Iranian language and culture developed in the third and early second millennium B.C., and their cradle land lay in the South Russian Steppes, while Gornung amongst them places the crale land in the middle reaches of the Volga. Some other Russian scholars believe the home of the Indo-Aryans was in the Russian Steppes in the south of the Urals, that they had emigrated to this area along with other Indo-Europeans, from the north, from around Vologda (east of St. Petersburg) and the lands to the south of a series of low hills (marked on the map as a number of yellow dots) stretching eastwards in the shape of a crescent over a distance of around 3700 km from Vologda all the way to the northern Urals. The small hills are the Meru Mountains. The Indo-Aryans when singing about their original homeland many centuries later, assigned loftier dimensions to these hills under the impact of the fading memory and nostalgic impulses.

But the other details as narrated in the hymns tally well with the ground realities: hills run east-west, the streams are big and foamy and drain north and south, the days are six months long in the arctics and the pole star is right on top of the observer. The names of the places too are almost identical to the ones mentioned in the Vedic accounts even after a passage of thousands of years. The conclusion, thus, is that the original home of the Indo-Europeans was in the Russian plains, to the south of the mountains dotting between Vologda in the west and the northern Ural range in the east, that a long time ago these people wandered off to the south Russian Steppes, and after a very long stay there they branched off in many directions, the Indo-Iranians eventually having made it to Iran. During there wanderings these groups interacted with many other races and communities and ceased to be ethnically homogeneous, and developed cultures and languages and which widely differed from group to group, though retaining some aspects of the original flavour. This concept does not contradict the prevalent view. It states that the south Russian Steppes was not the original home but was only and interim location occupied by them after their emigration from north-western Russia, and before they branched off to different lands in all directions.

B.G. Tilak in his book **The Orion** has concluded that relevant hymns in the Rig Veda show that the sacrificial ceremonies were well-developed during the time of the early Aryans, and, therefore, a reliable calendar to regulate the sacrifices must have existed, for no sacrificial system could have been developed without the knowledge of the months, seasons and the year. The exact nature of this calendars not known today, but a study of the sacrificial literature shows that the phases of moon, the changes in the seasons and the southern and the northern courses of the sun were the principal considerations in the measurement of time. The Aryans originally started their year which was luni-solar and sidereal, with the vernal equinox. Sometimes later the beginning of the year was changed to winter solstice, but the sacrificial year continued to be reckoned from the vernal equinox. Thus, they had two calendars; viz.; one for sacrificial purposes and the other for civil use. This system has been followed right up to the recent times. Tilak's calculations, based on astronomy, have concluded that the oldest period of the Aryan civilisation was when both the civil and the sacrificial calenders started from the vernal equinox. This period lasted approximately between 6000 B.C. and 4000 B.C., During this time the hymns were not in a finished state, and the sacrificial formulae were partly in prose and partly in poetry, and sang the principal names and epithets and feats of the deities invoked. Though the Greek and the Iranian traditions corroborate the Indian tradition for the subsequent period of the Aryan history, they have nothing for this period, for they, apparently, had with them only the calendar which was in force when they left the common home, much after the time of their separation from main body of the Indo-Aryans.

Next according to Tilak's gradation, is the period of what he calls 'the Orion, lasting from 4000 B.C. to 2500 B.C. This is the time when the vernal equinox was in the asterism of Ardra to the time when it receded to the asterism of the Krittikas. This according to him is an important period in the history of the Aryans and their civilisation when many 'Suktas' were composed and many legends were either formed afresh or developed from the old ones. The Greeks and the Iranians left the common home during the later part of this period and have retained most of these legends. This is the period of the hymns.

The next period is classified by Tilak as the period of the Krittikas which starts with the vernal equinox in the asterism of Krittikas and extends to the period recorded in the Vedanga Jyotisha, that is from 2500 B.C. to 1400 B.C. This is the period of the Taittiriya Sanhita and many of the 'Brahmanas'. Hymns of the Rig had already become antique and unintelligible by this time and 'Brahmavadins' indulged in speculations about the real meaning of these hymns and legends. During this period 'Sanhitas' were probably compiled into systematic books, and the Indians came in content with the Chinese who borrowed from them the Hindu 'Nakshatra' system.

The last period of the old Sanskrit literature lies between 1400 B.C. and 500 B.C. or till the birth and rise of Buddhism. This was the period of the 'Sutras' and the philosophical systems.

The beginning of the Aryan civilisation is placed in a time long before the people were able to conceive and formulate the calendar, but how much before, is difficult to decide. Initially the material was passed down by rote, and during this process some variations might have got incorporated, but to suggest that the hymns were composed a long time after the material contained in them was first conceived would be wrong, for by the time of the 'Taittiriya Sanhita' and the 'Brahmanas' the Rig Vedic hymns had become unintelligible. The hymns must have been composed over a long period; calculations in astronomy suggest that this must have happened between 4000 B.C. and 2500 B.C. This means that some Vedic verses existed when the migrants to Iran, Greece and India lived together. According to Tilak, this conclusion is supported by the comparative philology and mythology. He further states that in the Indian literature we have a continuous record of the beginnings of the years, right from the oldest times down to recent years. According to him Zoroaster lived around 1800 B.C. (modern historians place him around the beginning of 600 B.C.), and the Indo-Aryans and Iranians separated during 3000 B.C. and 2500 B.C. This conclusion is supported by the calculations on the basis on Astronomy. However, had Zoroaster lived at a considerably later time, then, says Tilak some Greek writers of the fifth century B.C. would certainly have written about it. In fact Xanthos of Lydia in 470 B.C. considered Zoroaster to have lived about 600 years before the Trojan war, that is 1800 B.C. Indo-Iranian and Aryan split took place on account of the former having accepted a different religious creed. In Aristotle's time Zoroaster was supposed to have lived a long time back, and that would put the Vedic period even earlier. Even according to the general belief of Hindus, the Vedas have a very remote antiquity; in fact it is claimed they came into being at the time of creation.

Some Indian scholars have put forth the view that the home land of the Aryans was none other than the north-western region of the Indian subcontinent itself. The argument is that the Indian Aryan literature does not mention about the Aryan immigration, and the Vedic Sanskrit has the largest number of vocables found in the languages of the Sanskrit family in different parts of India, whereas outside India, in Asia and Europe, where the Aryans are supposed to have settled down prior to their moving here, number of vocables left are only a few. This shows that the Aryans belonged to India, and the Indian languages that developed here had the maximum number of vocables, that the other foreign Aryan languages came about when the Aryans migrating from India came in contact with non-Aryan populations in other countries.

The argument is not convincing, for during those times it would not have been possible for mere immigrants to influence the languages of people spread over such a vast area. The Aryan movement took place over a long time, and gradually. B.K. Ghosh, a philology expert, while writing about the Aryan problem has pointed out, in support of the Eurasian home of the Aryans, that the largest number of the Indo-European languages are found in Europe, while outside Europe there are only scatterings which end up in Punjab in the Rig Vedic age. Besides it is Lithuanian and not Sanskrit which has kept closest to the basic idiom reconstructed by comparative philology. Had India been the original home, the whole of this subcontinent would have been Aryanised. There could have been a case had it been established that the Indus people were Aryans. But there has been no connection between the two cultures. The Aryans could even be older than the Harappans, if one was to go by Tilak's findings, but the language of the Rig Veda suggests its age as around 1000 BC, although the culture represented by it could be older, going as far back as, may be, 1500 BC. Very little evidence is available in support of different perceptions. For example, when the Harappans were flourishing in the Indus Valley, up in the north, in the Punjab, it could have been the Aryans. The two set people might have known each other but might not have interacted closely. It is not necessary that the Aryans should have arrived in India as plundering hordes. There could have been peaceful migrations, and it could have taken some time for the Aryans to organise themselves into kingdoms and push eastwards. It is generally accepted by scholars that the earliest time of the Aryan emigration into India could be around 2500 BC, and the latest 1500 BC, that the Rig Veda could have been compiled around 1000 BC to 1500 BC or even upto 2000 BC. The finds relating to the Indus Civilisation were unearthed in 1921-22 when Tilak was not aware of this. But, nevertheless, on most issues his views are abundantly rational and logical.

The Iranian and Indo-Aryan Split

Today it is difficult to comment on the incidents of a remote past, but a possible reason for the split could have been the different lines along which the religious perceptions of the two factions developed. The ensuing fanaticism could have persuaded the Indo-Aryan faction to migrate to North India; possibly the level of hostility must have made living conditions very unpleasant. The first to leave the Indo-European Group were the Proto-Tocharians, and then were the Indo-Iranians, who moved eastwards to find home in Eranvej, an area coinciding, probably with modern Turkmenistan, with borders with the Caspian Sea, Afghanistan and Iran. They stayed in this area for a long time, at least from late fourth millennium BC to about the middle of the third. During this time they expanded their activities towards Mesopotamia and Syria as well. Iran, particularly the eastern part of it, and the north-western India, at this stage had people of the Austric Proto-Australoid ethnicity, and also comparatively light skinned people from areas south of the present day Turkmenistan. They also had the Mediterranean people, the Orientals, and a host of others, like the Alpinoids, the Dinarics, the Armenoids; these light skinned people were apparently the rulers and the leaders and possibly competed with the Aryans for supremacy. The passive element of the population were the most numerous Proto-Australoids.

Indo-Europeans worshipped deities representing the elements of nature, like sun, moon, sky, wind. With time the Iranians, who, possibly, had been affected by the culture, thoughts, and the religion of the pre-Aryan people in the midst of whom they were living evolved new gods of their own, and on this issue the followers of different pantheons clashed, and so determinedly that they decided to for ever part company. Initially, it seems, the 'Daiva' gods of the Indo-Aryans and the Asura gods of the Iranians coexisted, but by the time of the Avestan (dialect of old Iranian) Gathas, which amongst others laid down strict instructions against the system of animal sacrifice, bitter antagonism seems to have erupted.

But that antagonism was only one factor that contributed to the split. Other important factors were also there, like search for better pastures, and more comfortable living conditions. It hardly matters whether the 'Daiva' and the 'Asura' gods coexisted in Iran before the departure of the Indo-Aryans. The finds of a treaty record at Boghaz-koi show that the two people coexisted. The treaty mentions the Daiva gods, Indra and Nasatya, along side the Asura gods, Varuna and Mitra.

The claim to antiquity of Zoroaster and his Gathas is hardly sustainable. The Gathas were not contemporaneous with the Rig Veda. The date accepted for Zoroaster by the modern historians is c. 628-551 BC which would put him just a few decades ahead of the Buddha, c. 563-483 BC, but nowhere near the Rig, the latest date for which could be c. 1000 BC, while the earliest could go back considerably. The Iranian Zoroasterianism would not, therefore, have precipitated a split. The probable reason for the movement of the Aryans from Iran would be a search for a better life and could have been possible only after the advances in the methodology and technology had been made, like in metallurgy and other related fields; this facilitated travel over long distances and difficult mountains, like the Hindu Kush and the Sulaiman ranges, and camping in the open for prolonged durations, in inhospitable climate and terrain, and surviving in a country bristling with hostility. They do not seem to have arrived in the Punjab as an army on a conquest course; they came as simple migrants, and most likely settled down on whatever land was then available. There is evidence of westward movement too of the Indo-Iranians, to Anatolia and northern Syria obviously also in search of better living conditions. The westward moving people came to be known as Hittites.

In north-west India the immigrating Indo-Aryans gradually organised themselves into small states, probably of the size of a village or a town. By around 2000 BC they were in contact, and, may be, even in conflict, with the Indus Valley settlements. Probably due to poor communications and movement facilities the Indian and the Iranian factions did not develop uniformly. In north-western India it was the Vedic civilisation. In Iran initially it was a country run by tribals on the basis of their own laws, but later it was Zoroasterism. Possibly in Eranvej there was preponderance of the worshippers of the 'Asura' gods and they might have made it difficult for the followers of the Daivas. But in both the countries the migrants had been overwhelmed in numbers by the indigenous people or those who had migrated before them. The cardinal faith was in passivity and non-violence; there was abundant land and abundant produce and there was no need to fight. People seemed to be living in self-contained villages and minimum laws were necessary to get the society organised on productive lines. Aggression in any form was condemned, for it was considered to be the hallmark of a capitalistic system.

The dark skinned Proto-Australoids and their descendents were called 'Nishads' by the Aryans, while the other light skinned people they called 'Dasyus'. In the Vedic literature there is no indication of the Aryans migrating from Iran and that suggests that the process of formulating the Vedic lore started only in India (Punjab), and the lore possibly had literature incorporated in it which was the work of the non-Aryan elite. Of the two important things that the Aryans brought with them, one could be the Sanskrit language, and the other the horse. Both these provided mobility to the pace of the cultural change. Otherwise on arrival they were, at best, only semi-nomadic, and their culture could be rated as below that of the Indus people. Actually northwestern Indian cultures then were ahead of the Aryans in certain aspects: They were urbanised, had a better socio-economic structure, a fairly developed system of medicines, a balanced and defined moral code and a logical and reasoned perceptions of religion. With time as the Aryan immigrations went up in size and frequency, a conflict with earlier inhabitants ensued, and by the middle of the second millennium BC the Aryans were holding a sway over the territory of the present day western Uttar Pradesh, including the hills to the north, and Rajasthan. Getting well organised, using their language Sanskrit, and securing swift movement with their horse, as epic Ramayana shows that, with time, they had managed to colonise or dominate some parts of Central India as well, and extend their influence, perhaps as far south as Sri Lanka. They intermingled with the people already living there and there was intermingling of ideas and lores. Some people they interacted with and whose views had compelling influence, made contributions to the writing of Vedic literature. Those were writings of inspired people, the learned men. The race or sectarian considerations do not seem to have influenced the process. Thus when the four 'Varanas' were formed, it is not necessary that the division applied only to the pure blooded Aryans. Perhaps most fair skinned people, irrespective of whether or not they were Aryans, got placed in the first three, while all the rest were placed in the category of 'shudras'. The offsprings of couples, where one of the parents was a shudra, were classified as 'Chandalas' ; this class did not form a part of the Aryan society. The vocation of an individual also was a factor in deciding the Varna, e.g., all tradesmen got put in the category of the Vaishas, and all teachers as Brahmans. The Vaisyas and the Shudras were, most of the time, bracketed. Kshatriyas generally operated to not only help the king in naming the affairs of the state, but also swelled the ranks of the Armed Forces during the war. This normally gave a big break to the soldiers who bore with grit and determination, the hardships of war. But when war was over and peace returned, these people had very little to do in the army, and they took on whatever profession came their way, and this included all professions where the soldier could make money to support himself and his family. So here we had a Kshatriya who performed the job of a Vaishya, or even Shudra. Later these Vaishyas and Shudras, powerful as they had become, claimed Kshatriya status for themselves, and the situation arose when there were Kshatriyas of all colours and hues, ranging from fair skinned to dark. At this the Bramins of the priestly class, declared that the Kshatriyas as a class had ceased to exist, and they quoted a story from Puranas where in Parshurama, the axe wielding Brahmin sage, an incarnation of Vishnu according to Vaishnava faith lost his patience with the Kashatriyas because they had killed his aged father in his absence and taken away his father's Kamadenu cow which yielded unlimited milk. He decided to wipe out the entire class of kashatriyas whom even otherwise he regarded as too arrogant and unjust, because they possessed too much power for being the custodians of law and order, policemen, the soldiers who guarded the frontiers; even the king was a

Kshatriya. This, the Purana tale says, he accomplished. The only Aryans then left were the Brahmin though they too had dark skinned people in their midst. But, it seems the Brahmins did not want to create dissensions in their own rank and file. And so it went on, till at one stage word 'Arya' had almost entirely lost the ethnic overtones, and come to mean a person of virtue, and of noble and divine thoughts. In earlier stages it had also been used to address a person of noble extraction.

The Way of Life

No evidence is available to show the way people lived in northwest India when the Aryans arrived here. Nor have the Aryans left much material about their life style. Farquhar in his book. 'The Crown off Hinduism' 'has stated that had it been for their religious literature we would have been without any direct evidence about the existence of these dynamic and gifted people. These people first arrived as wandering graziers in search of pastures and settled down in the Punjab and, in course of time took to agriculture like the Indus people. The Hymns of the Rig Veda, the first work of the Vedic literature, were possibly composed, recited, and memorised during this period, which spans over a few centuries.

The traditional accounts relating to these people are contained in the 'Puranas, but these books were compiled between 500 BC and almost 500 AD, over 2000 years after the incidents they narrate. Ramayana and Mahabharata also give some dynastic details and traditional accounts. But there are discrepancies in the accounts, and a lot of mythical material has got incorporated along side the historical detail, the two so intermixed that it is difficult to separate facts from fiction. However, notwithstanding the problems of identifying the historical facts from the traditional accounts, it does appear that at least the royal genealogies as set out in the Puranas bear some relationship to the Aryan antiquity. The earliest record is of Manu Svayambhuva who is given out as the son of Brahma, and who from the female part of his body gives birth to two sons and three daughters. The latter have elaborate legends woven around them connecting them to gods, sages, religious leaders and so on. Svayambhuva is the lord of the first 'Manvantra', which is the period which covers the rule of one Manu on planet earth, and is credited with the establishing of the system of Varnas (the segments of the society and allocating duties to each of these Varnas or segments, like, for example, Brahmans were given the task to teach, and educate society on the correct moral code, the Kshatriyas were to fight and physically defend the integrity of the country and help in the efficient and good governance, the Vaishyas were given to take care of trade and commerce including agriculture, and all manual work went to the lot of the Shudras. The system of marriage and a host of other customs and traditions covering different aspects of social living and communal behaviour, are also credited to him. It is believed that earlier these systems had been ordained by Brahma himself, but with the passage of time they had fallen into disuse. The Brahma then brought forth this Manu to re-establish the world order, the Dharma. Following this there were other Manus, all working to see to the implementation of the Laws of Dharma, till there is Manu Prithu, after whom the earth is named Prithvi. He levelled the earth and introduced agriculture.

Then there is Manu Vaivasvata of the Great Flood. He was informed about the flood by a fish who advised him to build a ship for himself and other species, and the necessary provisions, and when the mighty flood actually struck the fish pulled the ship to a big mountain, and it stayed anchored there for the duration of the flood. The flood caused destruction and swept everything; only Manu survived. This Manu, therefore, is considered to be the originator of the human race, and the first traditional king. He was father of ten sons, the eldest amongst whom had the dual personality of a male IL and a female ILA. The other nine sons founded nine important dynasties, the most important out of which was Akshvaka of the solar line, founded by Ikshvak, the eldest prince; he had his capital at Ayodhya. From ILA, the female personality of the eldest son, was born Pururavas, the originator of the lunar dynasty. The traditional history accounts say that the date of the Great Flood was around 3100 BC, which tallies reasonably with the dates for the flood in the Hebrew and Babylonian accounts. In the Hebrew accounts it is the story of the

Noah's Ark, and that is pretty similar to the account of Manu's Boat, and it is likely that both accounts have come from a common source. But it is also possible that during the receding fourth Ice Age there might have been simultaneous floods in most major rivers of Asia. Whatever the reason, the flood story brings in Manu Vaivasvata. Date 3102 BC is also the start of the Kali Age according to the ancient calendar, though according to traditional history it starts after the Mahabharata war which, after taking into account other detail, could be placed between the years 1400 BC and 1000 BC.

Other important detail from the traditional history suggest dates of Vishvamitra, Parashurama, Harishchandra, between 2550 and 2500 BC, Kings Sagara of Ayodhya and Bharata of Hastinapur between 2350 and 2300 BC, Rama, the king of Ayodhya, around 1950 BC, and Dasarajana war around 1900 BC. These dates have been worked out taking the Mahabharata War in 1400 BC. But if the date of the war is brought down to say 1000 BC, then the dates will change accordingly.

The details in the traditional history suggest that the Aryans were in control of most of northern India during the time of the sons of Manu Vaivasvat, i.e., during the early fourth millennium BC. It is possible that of the kings and dynasties mentioned in the Puranas, all were not pure blooded Aryans, and accounts of non-Aryan kings and lines got incorporated. The details in traditional history suggest that in that distant past large parts of northern and central India were following a distinct civilisation.

From the important landmarks mentioned in the Rig Veda it can be concluded that at the time of writing of the hymns the Aryans were dominant in the land extending from Afghanistan to the western Uttar Pradesh. To the south the line of domination went down to present day Rajasthan and parts of Sindh, while to the north it went up to Kashmir. Saptasindhavah mentioned in the Veda could be the name of the country of seven rivers, i.e., Indus, Sarasvati and the five rivers of the Punjab (Jhelum, Chenab, Ravi, Beas, and Satluj), although it is possible that the western most river could be the Oxus and all the five rivers may not have been flowing through the land under the Aryans.

Bharatas are the most important tribe of the Rig Vedic age. Initially they had the land between rivers Ravi and Ghaggar of the present times. In course of time this land came to be known as Bragmavarta. Their king Sudas fought and defeated a confederacy brought together by Vishvamitra, who was a priest at his court, but had become disenchanted, for he had been demoted and asked to make way for Vasishtha for performing priestly functions at his court. Angry Vishwamitra then conspired and raised this confederacy to teach his erstwhile master a lesson of his life. In Rig Veda this battle is referred to as Dasrajna, the battle of ten kings, and fought on the banks of the present day River Ravi. The Bharatas eliminated their enemy with ruthless ferocity. Sudas later had to take on another united army, this time of non-Aryan tribes under king Bheda. He inflicted a decisive defeat upon them as well. Apart from the Bharatas, after whom India is named today, there were other powerful tribes, named in the Veda. Kurus got formed with the union of Bharatas, Purus, and Tritsus, and later there was an alliance between the Kurus and the Panchalas, basically to safeguard their interests against incursions from the north-west, where there were powerful tribes like the Pakthas, Sivas, and so on, who were for ever straining on the leash to march eastwards.

Apart from the mutual conflicts between different tribes, Aryans had to also face the hostility of the people who were already there, like the Australoids and their admixture with other races, particularly the Palaeo-Mediterraneans. They were almost black, short statured and flat nosed, whom the Aryans called Nishads in contempt. These people served as the under-dogs of the society and gave into the Aryan domination with timidity. The other groups were the Dravidians whom the Aryans called 'Dasyus'. These people were from Central Asia and included a host of tribes, some dark complexioned while others not so dark. These tribes too had been on the move, and on several occasion had fought against the Aryans. But the latter always managed to defeat them; though the non-Aryan states whose accounts figure in the Puranas, managed to survive. After Sanskrit had been adopted as the working language, the Aryanisation of northern India started.

Before arriving in Northern India, in Iran or northwest India both Dasyus and Aryans had lived side by side, sometimes in cordiality and some times in hostility. With time, however, the meaning of the word 'Dasyu' changed to 'servant'. Dasyus too might have had similar expressions of contempt against the Aryans, but there is no record of it. Only the Aryans had a language which was well-developed and had a script. Even today the language gives their way of life. It was with the help of this language that the Aryans developed their administration, state craft, law, trade and commerce, and military sciences. As Farquhar says, only ancient Sanskrit is one Aryan language which has preserved its words in such a form as to make their origin quite plain to the philologist. The linguistic consciousness of the people who developed Sanskrit must have been delicate and analytic far above the average.

No details as such are available of the way of life of the people who preceded the Aryans and whom the latter put in the general class of 'Dasyus, Aryans in their accounts have variously called them demons, 'rakshasas', or evil celestial beings or uncouth barbarians, or people fit to be put in the category of servants. 'Panis' are another set of people whom Aryans considered their enemies and referred to them in disparaging terms in their literature. Of the views about the Panis, they have been put down as Babylonian traders in some accounts, while in others as non-Aryan caravan merchants, and in still others they are mentioned as sea faring Aryans. There is strong possibility that they were Indus traders who had drifted northwards and eastwards during the existence of the Civilisation and its subsequent collapse. 'Panis' are also called 'Vanis' in some accounts and are possibly the Banyas of modern times; they got incorporated in the Vaisya category of the Aryan Varna system. Another important class of traders who arrived in northern India from Syria and Lebanon during 1500-1200 BC, were the Phoenicians. All these communities played a major part in the development of trade and commerce in the northern areas of this subcontinent.

The Aryan epithet for evil gods is Asura. This term was used for worshipworthy gods when Indo and Iranian Aryans lived together, but came to be used in the evil sense after the separation of the two factions. Some opinions suggest term Asura is race-related and is applicable only to people immigrated from Syria, where from some of the founders of the Indus Civilisation had originated. Aryan chronicles have given a low rating to Maghadas of south Bihar who were mostly non-Aryans and who posed a continuous challenge and threat to the Aryan rulers of Kurukshetra-Delhi region. Vangas, non-Aryans of East Bengal, are not mentioned in the Rig Veda but in the later Aryan literature their activities have been amply described. In fact, by the time of the Upanishads (c. 800 BC) the Aryans had under their control the whole of the territory north of the Narmada river, with a few stretches even to the south of it.

Political and Social Organisation

Progressive development of the political and social organisation of the Aryans can be assessed from their legends. When the good and the bad gods were fighting the former reached to their discomfiture that they could be routed unless they had a leader of merit and unquestioned authority running their war. They elected a king for this purpose, and won. Thus was born the institution of kingship. Aryan tribes were organised in patriarchal groups and as the requirement for the security of the grew, the most competent warrior amongst the tribal males was elected to be the chief. With time the rising stakes in the security grew and so did the responsibilities and the privileges. The leader became the king. The king was assisted by a 'Sabha' and a 'Samiti', a council of ministers and a general assembly respectively. These assemblies apart from performing the functions of assisting the king in the process of governance, also ensured that the king did not over step the mandate. Where tribes did not have elected leaders, the functions of the government were carried out by the assemblies, though such instances were rare, for in the highly patriarchal Aryan society monarchy was the preferred system. The Vedic king was essentially a military and defence expert. He could impose no taxes; his assets were built on voluntary gifts. He was, however, entitled to a share in the booty of war, and for that reason he was on the look out for any opportunity to pillage and plunder any other tribe whom, he felt, he could vanquish. He had little say in the matters of religion; the priests ruled supreme in this field.

The Rig Vedic king was addressed as Rajan, which title was also used to address the chieftains of the tribes who ranked above their elders. With time there appeared kings who were powerful enough to not to bother too much about the Sabha or the Samiti. With time the conquests multiplied, and large kingdoms came into being, and there came kings who lived in imposing palaces, granting expensive gifts to their subjects, including courtiers and priests. There is mention of 'samrats' emperors, and Visvasya Bhuvanasya Rajas, the kings of the universe. The pomp and pageantry of some courts and the high life style of their queens and ministers tended to add to their grandeur. The Shastras, the religious ordinances, pronounced that a Kshatriya who had received the sacrament as prescribed by the Veda, must duly protect the whole world. It is also said that the lord created the king in order to protect this world when creatures dispersed in all directions on account of fear. Thus divinity of the king got incorporated in the concept of kingship right from the inception. Special sacrifices were designed to bestow divinity on him and for this the services of the priest became indispensable. Thus grew the interdependence between the king and the religious head. As the power of the king grew with the size of the kingdom, and he had at his disposal an elaborate administrative network and a formidable war machine, the kingship became hereditary. The Sabha and the Samiti still exercised checks on the king but the latter's authority was supreme.

A kingdom, 'rashtra', had tribes, 'Jana', and tribal units 'vish' and villages, 'gramas', where families, 'kulas' lived under the tutelage of their heads, 'kulapas'. The tribal elders and the headmen of the villages assisted the king whose two most important officials were the chief priest, 'purohita' who combined the functions of the court priest, astrologer and advise, and military commander, 'senani' the chief of the battles, though in peace time he generally took on the functions of a general administrator. Then there were the spies, messengers, the department of treasury, the charioteers, and even a superintendent of dicing; the last appointment came into being during later times when gambling had become widespread. The king, essentially a warrior, and his nobles and officials in the army, the 'rajanya', fought from the chariots while the common soldiers did so on foot. They had units and not infrequently marched to the battle on the beat of martial music and fluttering flags which reflected the identity of the units. They used metal or poisoned horn tipped arrows, and lances, axes, spears, swords, sling stones, and wore coat-of-mail and helmets to protect their bodies. Horse cavalry may have been used but there is no mention of it in the Rig Veda. The defences were based on forts, 'pur' which had ramparts of stone or even metal. Hedges of thorny bushes or stakes were used in defended areas. The assailants laid siege and pelted fire balls inside the defence and also used special engines to demolish strong points.

Brahmins imparted education to the people of their own Varna and to the Kshatriyas and the Vaisyas. Shudras and the women were not entitled to this education. However, specialised education pertaining to a Varna remained the responsibility of the Varna itself, like Vedic religion remaining with the Brahmins, or the martial arts with the Kshatriyas, or the knowledge and techniques of trade and commerce with the Vaisyas. However, there also were schools run by Brahmins where all disciplines were covered for all types of students. Since the principal function of the Brahmins was education (and Astrology) they were about the best educated people in the society. They were specialists in the art of state craft and generally held top posts in the government. They also interpreted the religion, and Vedic and other non-secular literature. During the Rig Vedic stage the Varnas division was not rigid and generally indicated only the class of occupation of a person; the varna could change with the change in the occupation; for example, a Kshatriya well versed in the knowledge and practice of the Vedas could well qualify to be a Brahmin. In Muir's view, during this period the hymns could be composed or the sacrifices presided over or other religious functions performed by any member of the three Varnas; during the post Rig Vedic stage, however, functions with strong religious over tones went completely under the charge of the Brahmins.

In the beginning the system of offering sacrifice was simple and no elaborate training was necessary for offering obeisance to one's god. With passage of time it became complex and guidance by well-trained Brahmins became necessary. A lot of emphasis came to be placed on small detail, like how the fire was to be ignored, with what type of wood, with what number of logs, how were the logs to be positioned in relation to one another, and how the words were to be recited and pronounced and so on. Any priest enjoying a reputation with a dignitary of consequence, added his own modifications.

The king and the Kshatriyas of noble extraction, the 'Rajanya' accumulated their wealth through pillage and plunder and taxation, while Vaisya got it through trade and agriculture. As for Shudras, being the working class serving the other Varnas, they had to earn by work; their well-being depended upon how well off the society was in terms of money earnings to be able to provide wage based work to this class. In any case, most of the time, it seems, they made enough to take care of themselves. Ironically the Brahmins, in comparison, were the worse off, more so when the householder himself presided over the religious ceremonies, or himself was well versed in astrology, or trained his offsprings through appropriate coaching, in the professions of their choice. Their work field was restricted, but they were not prepared to pick up work which was performed by other Varnas. Their earning capability diminished, and a lot of them fell into poverty. The well to do Kshatriyas had the leisure. They wondered about the problems the society faced, and discussed them, and evolved systems following which the lot of the common man could improve and he could attain peace and happiness. Gautama Buddha and Mahavira Jain, both princes, disagreed with die Brahmanic religion of caste distinctions and sacrifice.

The Vedic religion was harsh to the Shudras who were forbidden from the study of Vedas; this denial in effect implied denial of education, and resulted in keeping them in the category of the downtrodden. They could be kept under subjugation. Incidentally even the women, of whatever Varna, were denied study of Veda. This policy took away a large segment of the society from active participation and to that extent weakened it. Lack of education deprived them of fair wages and thus of decent livelihood, and self-respect, making them a burden which the society often found difficult to carry.

The Aryan Brahmins were a highly educated community, and not all of them were outright exploiters. They expanded the Aryan sphere of influence and assimilated in their fold non-Aryan people. Their contribution in the field of music, literature, astronomy, astrology, mathematics has been noteworthy. They were generally sanguinely fanatic about the Varna system and got the community to implement it strictly. There are accounts narrated in the epics and the Puranas where Shudras have been punished, even mutilated, for excelling in performance in vocations which were the preserve of higher Varnas.

North-western parts of the subcontinent were wetter during the Rig Vedic age; there was more rainfall, and the streams and the rivers carried more water, and the deserts of the present day had more extensive forest cover. This impeded the Aryan expansion, but with the introduction of the iron implements and cutting tools around 800 BC everything changed. This is the Upanishadic period of the Vedic age, a period marked for religious and secular effervescence; this became possible with better inter-people contact brought about with improved communications.

Family was an important unit of the society, and the 'Kulapa' or 'Kulpati', the eldest male, was its head. Normally people lived in joint families which extended over three or four generations. In a village, grama, in most cases, people were generally interrelated, having originated from a common family a few generations earlier. Land was in plenty; it had to be only cleared and cultivated. In non-joint families, the sons developed the land for their own dwellings; other members of the family group helped. On the father's death or his turning very old, the sons divided the inheritance amongst themselves; looking after the aged parents was their responsibility. The dwelling units during the Rig Vedic stage were mostly wooden structures, but later, as the Aryans got more experience of living on the land and they found the climate friendly enough, mud bricks structures also came into use. The roof was of bamboo, over laid with thatch. The accommodation for animals was incorporated in the main dwelling itself, though where families were reasonably well-to-do such accommodation was laid out alongside. This latter practice, however, exposed the animals to theft, which was not an infrequent occurrence. Cattle raids and lost cattle often led to inter-tribal feuds. Cow was prized and regarded a measure of wealth. With some tribes it was also regarded a totem animal. It was venerated by all. Beef eating was discouraged except on special occasions, when it was considered auspicious.

Horse was what an Aryan was always proud of. It enhanced his status and afforded him superior capability in battle. Amongst other animals, lion was known before the tiger, while elephant was a curiosity. Snake was associated with evil; it was believed to have malevolent power, a possible outcome of conflict with powerful Naga tribes.

Aryans were essentially vegetarians in diet, imbibing milk, 'ghee' i.e., clarified butter, vegetable and fruits of different varieties, and barley. On special occasions, such as the arrival of an important guest, special preparations of non-vegetarian food (meat mutton or fowl) were served, along with locally brewed wines like 'sura' or 'madhu'.

People wore simple clothes, men wearing only a lower garment, or a cloak; clothing was essentially an item related to weather and environment. They also picked up a lot from the clothing habits of the earlier people. Both men and women wore ornaments like the Indus people. Leisure was spent in music, singing, dancing; an idea of the interest in music can be had from the number of instruments in use, like flute, cymbals, drum harp, and other string instruments, and also from the highly developed knowledge of Sound, tone and pitch used in chanting the Sam Veda; they were familiar with a heptatonic scale. Dicing too was a favourite pastime as was chariot racing, the latter being a prestigesport, was organised only on special ceremonial occasions.

The family rejoiced at the birth of a son, for a son not only provided security to the parents in their old age, he also took care of the interests of the community by cultivating food and rearing animals, and, most of all, become a member of the fighting force and defend them. In a highly patriarchal Aryan society he completely eclipsed the girl and was endowed with the status of almost a demigod. His presence was important in all family functions and ceremonies, some which were designed to provide comfort to the already deceased forebears in the hereafter. The girl's position though secondary, was not inferior. In her childhood and during her nubility she was trained by the females of the family to make good housewife. She was educated in any discipline of her choice upto the level she desired, or the family could afford, e.g., music, dancing or other arts and crafts generally in the female domain. Most girls, it seems, did not opt for serious education as their primary interest; only a few works of merit have been found authored by women writers. The belief was that a woman had always to be taken care of, being of the weaker sex; during her girlhood she was in the charge of the father, and then after marriage, the husband, and, if widowed, her sons. As a widow she could marry a brother of the husband, practise levirate, or in his absence, a suitable male of the community. In a society overly dominated by males, this was necessary to protect the interests of the weaker sex. Otherwise the code of conduct allotted a place of honour to the woman. No religious function was complete without her participation, and during such participation her status was equal to that of the male, her husband. Manu the law giver has clearly stated that the women must be honoured and respected by their fathers, brothers and brothers-in-law, for where this happens the gods are pleased, but where this does not, no sacred rites yield any rewards. He further says that a house where women are not duly honoured, perishes completely as if destroyed by magic.

Early marriage was not the practice and the girl had a good deal of choice in the selection of her husband, even though arranged marriages were the custom. Different tribes had their own systems of marriages. Some permitted marriages between consanguine pairs except brother and sister, others forbade between pairs who might have had blood connection as far back as seven generations. However, the latter system was the generally preferred one as it took ample care of any form of inbreeding. Sexual attraction towards females of own community was totally forbidden to safe-guard against promiscuity. Honour of the women was protected stoutly. Some tribes paid dowry, others charged bride-price; this latter practice was followed by lower caste people. Some made a widow go through a symbolic self-immolation, Sati, at the death of the husband, others expected her to actually self-immolate herself, while still others permitted remarriage, generally with an unmarried brother of the deceased husband or with any other male of the tribe whom the widow might appropriately select.

Not much is found in the Vedic literature regarding the practice of Sati. There is a case narrated in Mahabharata, that of Madri, younger wife of Pandu. Vedic Aryans were familiar with the practice but it was restricted to the Rajanya, the ruling class, only, and even they practised it sparingly, mostly when the widow asked for it voluntarily. The practice of widow remarriage varied with tribes. Some permitted remarriage within the tribe, others only within the family; the younger brother of the deceased automatically became the husband, even when he was married. Some permitted 'Niyoga', levirate, when the widow did not have a son, till she got one from another member of the family, or rarely, a person of her choice. Niyoga was permitted in some other cases as well, for example, when the husband could not impregnate the woman, or when was away for a prolonged duration. The permission was valid only till the woman got a son. Most tribes, however, forbade Niyoga or remarriage, except when the widow was very young. Some did not even do that.

Polygamy was permitted during the Rig Vedic age, but was restricted to the high class of Kshatriyas. Otherwise monogamy was the prevalent custom. Polyandry is also mentioned, but was rare.

In the actual celebration of the marriage the bridegrooms party went to the bride's house. The two important events of the marriage were the least and taking the rounds of the ceremonial fire. Beef was the preferred item at the meal. On completion of the rounds of the ceremonial fire the marriage was considered as solemnised. The post-marriage prayers and blessings were for the harmonious and happy life of the married couple. The bride is described as a mistress in the house and is urged to take care of the husbands parents, his brothers and unmarried sisters; it is emphasised that she was not a subservient being.

The sacred or sacrificial fire had an important function in the Aryan household. It is a god, 'deva', the master of the house, 'grihapati', and the guest, 'atithi' a friend, a messenger for the gods. Its high rising flames and smoke, took the offerings heavenwards, and brought blessings resulting in fulfilment of wishes, fertility of cattle and bountified crops, and it took the offerings to the spirits of the ancestors to their abode in the hereafter. The householder performed these rites all by himself, (or he could engage the services of a priest) by making offerings of milk, grain, clarified butter, flesh, while uttering simple prayers. Such sacrifices were offered by all, and this was the beginning of the Vedic religion. With time, however, elaborate sacrificial rituals came into being. Sacrifices by kings and well to do people, were organised around three sets of sacred fires, conducted by a host of priests, with four of them only supervising the proceedings. The idea was to secure the favours of the gods who were also believed to be participating.

The custom of making offerings to the fire is of Indo-European origin and was also followed by the Greeks, Romans and Iranians. The idea was that the gods could be made to yield to grant wishes so long as the correct method, including incantations, and the correct ingredients for the sacrifice were used. Horse sacrifice, performed by powerful kings during their ascendancy, was to please the sun god.

The role of the priest, or the 'purohita', was important. Term Brahmin means one who possesses mysterious or magical power, Brahma, or as some scholars have called it, 'Mana', a term carrying similar meaning during a primitive period. The belief was that during the sacrifice the god, the priest and the offering, became one. The feeding of the priest (during a major sacrifice the feeding of a number of them), was an important requirement. It was equally important to ensure that he, or they, in whom the gods invoked had dwelled during the sacrifice period, left with generous gifts and beneficiently disposed towards the sacrificer. The gifts besides foodgrains and other items of value, included cows, even women when the sacrifice was performed by a king after a victorious battle where he might have enslaved a large number of people.

A sacrifice was a serious and a solemn affair, but it also was a social occasion where people met in cinviviality. At the end there was a feast where 'Soma' wine was served liberally. In time the sacrificial area came to be laid out keeping in view the auspicious time and the position of the stars. A good knowledge of astronomy and mathematics became necessary. Frequent sacrifices led to a good knowledge of the animal anatomy, which became a dominant science ahead of physiology or pathology.

The Rig 'Samhita', as we know, was composed over a long period. Its earlier hymns have nothing to do with sacrifice, although a number of them were chanted for that purpose in later times, when the sacrifice system developed. The later hymns were incantations for sacrifice only. The older hymns were chanted by the householder for simple household ceremonies when he himself, or, at the most, accompanied by the family 'purohita', presided over the ceremony, while the latter were used for major occasion at the level of the village, or tribe, or when sacrifice was performed by persons in high places, or even by kings.

There were no organised legal institutions at the time of the Rig Veda, although after the formation of the states and the institution of kingship, the situation started to change gradually. Law, 'Dharma' got evolved on the basis of customs and traditions, and the king and the chief priest were the arbiters, assisted, possibly, by the elders of the community. In the case of larger states where it was not easy for a complaint to reach the king, most cases got decided at the village level by elders. With time villages formed a body of men for this purpose; in later times such a body of people came to be called a 'Panchayat', i.e., a body of five persons. The main problems in the functioning of this body related to thefts, particularly of cattle, burglary, highway robbery, cheating at gambling. Marriage of brother and sister was forbidden as incest. As punishment the criminals were usually tied to a stake. The punishment for murder was based on wergeld, or blood money, and could be a hundred cows or coins, or something which could reasonably satisfy the aggrieved party. Even revenge was permitted, though it might not have been widely practised. Trial by ordeal was vogue whereunder a person had to prove his innocence by going through some sort of an ordeal, like putting his arm in boiling water, or putting his tongue on a red hot axe-head; there are many variations of this punishment which are placed under the head of water or fire ordeals, the underlying idea being that an innocent person would not feel the pain of the ordeal.

In inheritance the practice of primogeniture was followed whereunder all the property went to the eldest son. It was not the universal custom, however. It was more common amongst the well to do 'rajanya-families.

The going law was tilted towards the wronged person. Gradually the punishments became more stringent and deterrent. The law became more formalised and encoded in the 'Dharma-Sutras', the manuals originally written by the Vedic scholars for the guidance of their pupils, but later accepted as the source of the sacred law applicable to the Aryas. The first of these Sutras were compiled as the Aryan kingdoms expanded and the problems of the law and order became more numerous and complicated and the king was no longer capable to deal with them in a just and equitable manner. The earliest of the Dharma Sutras have been dated 600 BC by scholars, including Professor Max Muller. But these could be older; there are practical problems in dating ancient Sanskrit works.

Indus Valley people had some kind of a script. There is no evidence to prove the Aryans used a script till around 700 BC. To the Aryans the Vedic literature comprised inspired sayings of learned men and seers who had thoroughly understood the mysteries of creation and had passed their knowledge to the common people so that they could lead organised and happy lives. The Vedas contained the ultimate truth, that which was revealed by the creating power itself and beyond which there was nothing to be known. The Vedas were sacred and to put them down in writing, like any other secular literature, would be sacrilegious. Therefore it was committed to memory under a carefully worked out system which avoided error when it was passed down the generations. The ancient literature was either 'shruti' the revealed one, or 'smriti', the traditional one which, even though not revealed, was based on revealed literature and was not to be treated as secular literature, e.g., the 'Dharma Sutras' have been formulated on what has been stated in the Vedas and are not a compilation by any one or more persons based on their experience or assessment.

The Aryans were using Sanskrit for secular purposes soon after their arrival in the north-west of the country. All ancient secular literature of the period has perished, written as it was on tree barks or leaves. Later invaders did their bit to complete the destruction. The religious literature survived as it was committed to memory, though the possibilities of interpolations or editing cannot be ruled out. Thus, a document many have originated in a distant past, but at the time of reducing it to writing the people going through the exercise could have edited or interpolated depending upon their understanding of the subject. For this reason dating of ancient documents has problems.

Veda is a 'Shruti' and not a Shastra, the latter being systematized knowledge in one particular discipline and would contain special terminology and definitions in relation to that discipline. In order to better understand the 'shruti', the Vedic schools systematized and cultivated six sciences which on account of their being closely connected to the Vedas, are called 'angas', limbs—Vedangas: These are (a) 'Shiksha' '(orthography); (b) Vyakarana (grammar); (c) 'Nighantu' (lexicon); (d) Jyotish (astronomy); (e) Chhanda (prosody); and (f) 'Kalpa' (the system of rituals and ceremonies). The schools also evolved the four 'upa' (minor) Vedas, bring (a) Ayur-Veda (The system of medicines and cures); (b) Gandharva-Veda (system of aesthetics); (c) Dhanur-Veda (of defence science) and (d) Artha-Veda (of wealth: the economics of its generation and distribution).

With time as the subsidiary literature developed and the material to be committed to memory increased the Vedic Schools got divided into two categories, being, one, those who committed the literature to memory, and, two, those who interpreted it in the correct sense. Following these came the institutions which worked only on subsidiary literature, like the Ved-Angas, Upa-Vedas or law, and so on. The Vedic Schools, thus, committed the Vedas to memory and correctly interpreted them, and the schools of specialities handled Ved-Angas, Upa-Vedas and other specialised subjects, and worked on the Vedas only where they affected their discipline. The student acquired full knowledge of the sacred texts and for that he had to learn the 'Mantras' as given in the 'Samhita' texts, and the Brahmanas, and also. Tathas' or the method of recitation of these Mantras, and it normally took him four and a half to five years to do the complete course. With time some Vedic schools, or 'karanas' as they came to be called, became schools of special disciplines and ceased to be involved in enquiry and interpretation of general Vedic literature and thought.

The institution of the Vaidics of the recent times performed almost the same functions as was done by 'Karanas'. The former, run on chanty, devoted to memorize the Angas and other similar works and recite them more or less accurately, but they could hardly explain or correctly interpret them. For that purpose there were other specialists, e.g., srauta sacrifices could be performed only by the Sarotriya pundits. Then fields of specialisation further narrowed and the pundits concentrated only on specific angas and committed to memory only that part of the Veda as was relevant to their discipline. His connection with the Veda, thus, became nominal, though he was the authority in his own field.

The system of specialisation aplied to the law schools as well, and with time a number of 'Dharm Sutras' or stings of aphorisms, all based on the Dharma Sutra of the Manava Sutrakarana came up; almost the final work in this field was Manu Smriti; Manu's name derives from 'Man' which means to know (the meaning of the Veda). Sutrakaranas were the schools which first collected the different doctrines scattered in the older Vedic works and arranged them in Sutras for convenience of oral instruction. But with time new institutions came up, developing their subjects as independent disciplines, and claiming superiority over Sutrakarana schools; all this happened over a considerable period. For example, astronomy is connected to the Vedic Sutrakarana school through a few recensions, but jyotyisha, astrology, which is closely connected with it, was developed mostly independently on the basis of work earned out by new institutions.

The first to be compiled were the Dharma Sutras, or aphorisms about religious and social law and observances handed down by tradition, and the rights and duties of individuals, to guide students to lead a life free from sin, in conformity with the sayings of the Vedas. With time these became laws for all Aryans. The metrical Smritis, like Man Samriti, are works of later period and are based on ancient Dharma sutra texts. According to G. Buhlar it can be averred that Manu Smriti, the law book held in high esteem and containing the rules governing the life of the Aryas, was already there at the beginning of the Christian era; nothing more than this can be established. As brought out earlier, there are practical problems in dating old and ancient Sanskrit works because in a number of cases interpolations and modifications have taken place, e.g. in some places the treatise has supported 'Nyoga, in others it has opposed it; in some places it has given an exalted status to the women, at some it enunciates a harsh code for them. According to belief, Manu was the first law giver and consequently the Samriti is of considerable antiquity, probably older than the Mahabharata war. But it was not the first of the law books, and even though it claims authorship by Manu, the descendant of the self existent Brahma, it is intact a recast, in metrical form, of earlier Dharma Shastras and Sutras.

While earlier laws contained in the Sutras and Shastras may have been compiled by Vedic law experts for a limited purpose—for tribe, a kingdom or a republic—the Manu Smriti broadened the scope and attempted to give a law which was above modifications. A number of contradictions within it suggest it has been tampered with. In the Sutras the arrangement of subjects has been haphazard, and apart from the rules relating to inheritance and division of property, their handling of civil and criminal laws is deficient in detail. But that was a time in antiquity when legal cases were settled on the basis of customs and traditions. The

Sutras gave only brief guide lines in terms of what was laid down in the Vedas, while the details were left to the 'Dharmadhikarins', the legal advisers to the kings, the judges and the lawyers. But the Smriti put down the law in greater detail and in a logical sequence, unfettered by religious references and customs, emphasising the moral side of the duties of the administrators of law rather than the legal technicalities. An important work which preceded Manu Smriti is the Manav Dharma-Sutra. This is the oldest property laid out work on Dharma on which subsequent works, including Manu Smriti, have been based. Other works preceding or following Manu Smriti, are those authored by Bhrigu (mythologically one of the ten mind-born sons of Manu), Narada, and Yagnavalkya. Dharmashastra of Vasishitha is also an important manual covering the laws of the Aryans.

The Vedic Literature

Rig Veda

The core of the Vedic literature is the Rig Veda, a collection of over a thousand hymns (Sanhitas) of various lengths, set out in more than ten thousand stanzas. Many recensions of this Veda are known but the one which has come down in almost complete form is the Sakala recension. This has happened because only the hymns of this recension were used in the rituals by the priests of the Sakala school. A number of them became irrelevant after the change of rituals but were retained nontheless because they had become sacrosanct.

Rig Veda has hymns dating back to the Indo-Iranian period, and some of them throw light on the geography of the area inhabited by them, their way of life, the kind of opposition they encountered during their eastward move, the people they had to overpower. The hymns were composed by a number of priestly families in the language that they had been using for their sacrificial rituals for a long time. The authors are called the Rishis, the seers, the people with illumined minds who had understood the working of the universe and who, consequently, could compose hymns or incantations, Mantras, which when accompanied by a specified ritual, could force the gods concerned into fulfilling the wishes. A person could perform the rituals himself or a priest could do so on his behalf. The recitations were not only for personal gains, often these were in praise of gods or God, just of love for the divine being.

The Rig Sanhita has been organised in ten systematic Mandalas, parts of which the middle six, second to seventh, are believed to have been composed by six different families of priests, Rishis, being Gristsamada, Vishvamitra, Vaindeva, Atri Bharadvaja and Vasishtha. The eighth Mandala is ascribed to Kanvas and Angirases, while the tenth appears to have been a later addition. In all Mandalas the opening hymns are addressed to god Agni, followed by one to Indra. Then come the hymns to other gods in keeping with a prescribed system. In the eighth Mandala the hymns have been arranged authorwise, while in the ninth they are meterwise. Some hymns, like those addressed to Ushas, the goddess of dawn, are fine examples of lyrical poetry. The whole of the Rik Sanhita (the term Rik is used for one stanza of the hymn or one mantra), including the later added tenth Mandala, were existing before the Sanhitas of other Vedas came into being.

Max Muller has divided the Vedic literature period into four, being of the Chhandas (prosody), mantras (incantations), Brahmanas (where elaborate details of the sacrifice rituals have been worked out), and the Sutras (aphorisms). As Tilak has said, by the time of the Brahmanas, the hymns of the Rig had already become antique and unintelligible, and the institution of the Brahmavadins had come into being to study to find out the real meaning of the hymns. The language of the hymns was the old Sanskrit which was scarcely understood then, and this became even more difficult later.

Distinguished Brahmavadins wrote commentaries from time to time about what they thought were the direct or implied meanings of the hymns. They were helped by etymologists and grammarians. Patanjli wrote his commentary, Mahabhasya, while Panini wrote Astadhyayi, both authors based their work on common and Vedic Sanskrit, quoting extensively from the works of renowned etymologists. In recent times, Dayananda (1824-83) and his followers have believed that only the Mantra portion of the Vedas can be relied upon. Brahmanas, being only commentaries, can be relied upon only where they agree with the Vedic revelations. Sayana, the Brahmin scholar and Vedic commentator of the last quarter of the fourteenth century, from the kingdom of Vijay Nagar, has called the hymns as formulas of mysterious efficacy, designed to perform rituals which he believed to be part of the divine knowledge. He believed hymns invoked gods for the good of man and society if the prescribed code of conduct was followed. In the nineteenth century, however, the western scholars did a reappraisal of the Vedic literature and questioned Sayana's views.

Dayanand, the prominent Vedic scholar, disagreed with the ritualistic interpretation, and took on the task of writing his own commentaries on the Rig and Yajur Vedas, but barely had he covered the Yajur Veda and just the six Mandalas of the Rig Veda when his detractors poisoned him. But a serious enquiry was already underway amongst the European and Indian scholars to investigate the impact of Vedic literature on the evolution of the Indian culture and civilisation. Vedic influence in shaping the philosophy as contained in the Upanishads, and language and grammar as taught by Panini and Patanjli, and astronomy, mathematics, surgery and medicine, was recognised. Neo-Vedantists believed that the Vedic religion was monotheistic, that Agni, Soma and various gods sung about in various hymns were the facets of one God and that all names given in the hymns were in fact references to the one Exalted Being. The concept of monotheism has also been advocated both by Ramanuja and Madhava, during the twelfth and thirteenth centuries AD.

The earliest hymns of the Rig Veda are in praise of gods named after the elements, like fire, earth, clouds and Soma. India is the lord of the gods in the later hymns, and in still later ones the concept of one omniscient and omnipotent God has crystallised. In the ultimate vision (Vedanta) the concept has shifted to one creating energy, the power, of which all that we see, or do not see, are constituents. God as a separate entity has ceased: He is all, and all is He. It is monoism.

Within this vast spectrum of concepts many different ideas have been propounded. But Vedic religion accepts only those concepts which have been revealed and are contained within the Veda. The belief is that this revelation is as old as the creation itself, that the Vedic religion is 'Sanatana', without beginning, and is beyond the scope of any modifications. It is a religion of 'Homa', sacrifice to fire, of chanting of hymns to suit different occasions, of faith in the divine origination of the Veda (which is its most important aspect), of gods who may or may not be considered to be the facets of one almighty God, of sacrifice which initially included slaughter of animals, depending upon the occasion but in later times, particularly in India, got restricted to offerings of grain, flowers, leaves and the like and where the priests played the cardinal role in its conduct. The followers believed that their way was the surest road to happiness in this world and emancipation in the hereafter.

But the Vedic religion did modify with time. It was a religion unencumbered by complicate philosophy and laid stress on the practical process of living, emphasising the pursuit of happiness and achievement of excellence as the principal objects of human existence. With time, however, here simple concepts of heaven and hell moved to the thoughts of karma and rebirth, that is there is no separate existence for the good and the bad souls in the hereafter. All that is there is the rebirth on the basis of karmas, the deeds performed during the existence of the soul while in the human body. From the simple galaxy of gods who could be prevailed upon through the medium of mantras and jantras, that is, recitation of incantations in a prescribed manner, they accepted the concept of the universe being a cosmic whole, run by Dharma, the Law, which among other things, places the soul in the interminable process of births and deaths till release is secured through righteous thoughts and actions.

By the time of the Atharva Veda a regimen of complicated charms and spells had come into being; this had happened essentially because of the influence of the earlier thoughts and pre-Aryan inhabitants who constituted the major part of the population. The Vedic religion sang the praises of nature and had no temples as such. The Aryans were conquerors, and although initially they had arrived as emigres but had later organised and established themselves as rulers. They had a developed language, Sanskrit, and horse driven chariot which, amongst others, served as their vehicle in war. They were fair complexioned and good looking and bore contempt towards dark skinned earlier inhabitants of the Proto-Australoid/Dravidian stock. They divided the inhabitants into four categories (Varanas) being Brahmans, Kshatriyas, Vaishas and Shudras. Of these the first Varna took care of the religion, its philosophy and everything connected with it, the second got concerned with the affairs of the state, its governance, and defence against external aggression, including soldiering for it, while the third category, the Vaishas took care of the trade and commerce including cultivation and the last one, the Shudras, were responsible for everything other than what was done by the first three categories. Generally they performed menial types of jobs. The lowest class were the Chandalas, the offsprings of Shudras from women of higher classes.

The males of the first three classes were regarded as the twice born, the Dvijas, and wore the sacred thread, the second birth being when they were given the thread (the thread has three strands woven to form a loop which is worn across the body over the right shoulder). Only the twice born could study religion and the Vedas; the women and the shudras and other lower classes were forbidden this facility. Generally only marriage within the Varana was approved, but even inter-varna marriages between three higher var-nas were tolerated. This brought into being two cultural streams, one born out of the Dravidians and earlier inhabitants including the Australoid group, and the other based on the Vedas. The two cultures flowed side by side through the time, and now and then made contributions to each other, although the non-Aryans dominated, being in majority. But they maintained their separate identity. The non-Aryan culture has stressed pacifism, peace and non-violence. Buddhism and Jainism are a direct result of this thought.

The Rig Vedic society was patriarchal. They worshipped no female deities other than, may be, Ushas, the beautiful Goddess of Dawn, and Sarasvati, the Goddess of Learning. During the days of the early Aryans River Sarasvati flowed through the present Rajasthan, and the Aryans composed a lot of their religious literature while they lived along its banks. The River's flow diminished in later times because of the tectonic changes in the upper reaches of the Himalayan foothills, and whatever of it remained has been lost in the sands of the desert. The woman in the Vedic society enjoyed a status although she was always placed below man. In later days the caste and the Varna systems became more strict and to ensure purity of the stock and discourage sexual promiscuity, stricter control over her was exercised. Besides, the rebirth theory postulated that she was born a female and not a male, because of her inferior performance in earlier lives. In some communities even the basic education was not considered right for her, for it was considered that would broaden her mental horizon and loosen her moral discretions. Lack of education kept her ignorant and not only kept her dependent on man, but also accentuated her apparent inferiority. However, in spite of this attitude widow remarriage was not uncommon during the Brahmana period.

The view that the deeds of the past births were the direct cause of the problems in the life of an individual, considerably influenced the attitude towards fellow human beings, for it came to be believed that person's station in life was the result of his/her own doings and no consideration was due on this count. In fact higher castes considered it their privilege and tight to exploit the lower castes. One Brahmana text states that if so required a Shudra could be killed. Woman was given as the epitome of falsehood. The Varna system placed the Brahman group at the top, followed by the Kshatriya and then the Vaisha. But with the passage of time the system tended to be dogmatised, and flowed into narrow groves and stagnated. The later day Vedic literature in the form of Brahmanas did not possess the spontaneity and loftiness of earlier times. Any attempt to improve the living conditions was deprecated: it was blamed on the past deeds and thus was considered unnecessary. Under the same argument conversions to Hinduism were, not accepted. The individual was asked to bear his circumstances with equanimity and perform his duties appropriate to the station of his birth and improve his merit and strive to secure better life in the next birth, and so go on improving till securing the final deliverance from the cycle of rebirth and attain Moksha. People other beliefs were held in low esteem, because they did not have the access to the Veda, the only revealed literature.

The Brahmanas emphasised pious and truthful living, and the five daily offerings (to gods, beings, fathers, charity and the study of the Veda) became the corner stone of the orthodox Hindu sociology. These works contained literature of high intellectual content concerning religious order, philosophy and the speculative aspect of the religion.

The Shudra society comprised the workforce and they were well organised in communes and guilds from the time prior to the arrival of the Aryans and they ensured that their interests were well protected; in fact they, the performing hands, often were better off economically as compared to the Mantra reciting Brahmans.

In the case of women too any number of cases have been cited in the Vedic literature where they have excelled in learning and the knowledge of the Vedas. But she has been always below man. In Ramayana, Sita, the wife of Lord Rama, has this to say about the status of women (translation, J.N. Farquhar):

The woman who on this earth below,

Her parents on a man bestow,

And lawfully their hands unite,

With water and each holy rite.

She in this world shall be his wife,

His also in the after-life."

The Hindu woman, thus, marries not only 'for better or for worse' but for this world and the next; the marriage cannot ever be broken. She is asked to treat her husband as her lord yet enjoys a status which adequately matches that of her husband. Most of the time she is well respected and is considered the symbol of honour of the community. She has a mind and will of her own. It would be wrong to assume women were not respected during the later Vedic age. They had reckonable status amongst the well-to-do upper strata of the society, through amongst the poorer sections their position was, perhaps, not so comfortable.

The Vedic religion believed that after death the soul travelled to the world of Yama, who commanded the world of the souls, and there it was rewarded or punished on the basis of its deeds performed during its life time. Yama, was not a god, but only a human being who had attained that status on the basis of excellence he had achieved during his living days on the earth, and was a twin brother of Yami, and together they made the primeval pair; he had discovered the nether world after his death and had established his rule there. The forefathers lived in his company in immortality, in the midst of joy and plenty, having attained the objective they had cherished during their days on the earth, which was attainment of god-like status in the hereafter; to attain this they had performed fire worship and sacrifices. In this process the offerings from relatives, particularly sons, also added to the merit.

Sharadhas are a worship performed for the departed relatives, under the guidance of the family priest, the Purohita. The belief is that during this worship, through the invocations by incantations, the gods are made to merge with the priest. All prayers are, therefore, addressed the priest, who also becomes the legitimate recipient of all offerings, which comprise, food, grains, clothes, sometimes, depending upon the status and means of the family, even cows. The Vedas are essentially concerned with life, its vitality, energy, its capacity to provide pleasure and joy. They were not overly involved with the hereafter. They postulate that the spirits of the dead travel either along the path of the fathers, or the gods and the mortals and in the paradise of Yama they have the best of the foods and drinks, and all other joys that the gods have. But all this is achieved by performing good deeds during life time; among the deeds the performance of sacrifice has a pre-eminent position. Souls of evil people go to hell which is dark and suffocating miserable. After expiation the soul moves on to higher world.

Rig Veda also has writings with sexual symbolism, like Yama-Yami poem where Yami expresses sexual desire for her twin brother, or the poem of the Virile Ape and Indrani in which the latter seeks the sexual favours of the former because of Indra's deficient virility. In the latter Vedic period it was difficult to appreciate the esoteric meaning, if any, of these poems; they are not considered Tantric literature which is replete with sexual symbolism. However, because of the Old Sanskrit of the Rig and the thousands of years that have elapsed since their first writing, it is not possible to comprehend the exact meaning and purpose of such compositions.

The Sam Veda

Word stands for knowledge, and Sam for devotion, and also for melody, while Yajuh stands for Karma, action. The Vedas have not been arranged subjectwise, though most of the hymns are related to the topic indicated by the name of the Veda. Sam Veda is a collection of melodies which are designed to be used while chanting the verses of the Sanhita. Theoretically any melody could be chanted for any verse, but in actual fact the procedure was fairly developed. The verse on which a melody is chanted is called Yonti The source, which suggests that the verse itself was regarded as the source of the melody. The dore of this Veda, Archika, is a collection of 585 Yonis. Additionally it has other literature forming the text part, the basic function of which is to assign melodies to the verses. Vedic chants played the essential part in the Sam rituals.

The Yajur Veda

Like Sam, this too is a ritualistic Veda, and forms the guide book for the Ardhvaryu priests who perform all the functions in the sacrifice except reciting Mantras and chanting melodies: reciting is done by the Hotri priests and chanting by the Udgatris. Thus, while the Sam Veda laid down the melodies for the hymns of the Rik Sanhita, the Yajur prescribed the actions to be performed during the recitations, like pouring the clarified butter or other ingredients of the sacrifice, into the sacrificial fire, or drawing signs or symbols at or around the place of sacrifice, or going around it, and so on. Six complete recensions of this Veda are available today, being two of the White and four of the Black Yajur Veda. The latter is the older of the two and is preserved in the Taittiriya, Maitrayani and Kathak recensions, The White Yajur is preserved in the Vajasneyi recension which has around forty chapters; the last twenty-two appear to have been added later; the basic text comprises the first eighteen chapters only. The formulas given in these chapters are found in the Taittiriya Sanhita as well, while of the last twenty-two are contained in the Taittiriya Brahmana. Chapters 19 to 21 are for expiation of sin of excessive indulgence in Soma, and 22 to 25 are for horse sacrifice.

Actually in the Veda itself there is no instruction, Viniyoga, regarding the verses to be recited at the various occasions. This has been left to the discretion of the priest though with the passage of time a fair degree of uniformity has evolved on this aspect.

In the Black Yajur Veda the Mantra and the Brahmana are mixed throughout the text, and, thus, the Sanhita is more like a Brahmana than a Sruti. The sacrificial prayer has not only the hymns taken from the Rig Veda but also original prose formulas for the Ardhvaryu priest.

The Atharva Veda

Originally the three Sanhitas, Treyi (three fold knowledge) were recognised as the canonical scriptures. Much later Atharva Veda, the book of magical formulas, also got included in this category. In this book many hymns are of popular rather than priestly origin, and could be as old as the earliest hymns of the Rig Veda, or, maybe, even older, of the time even earlier than the arrival of the Atrayns. It is a book of songs, spells and incantations against disease, dangers from any source, enemies, designed to bring evil to those who are hated. The book has a large number of what are called the *khila* hymns, that is hymns which do not have a high sacred status. These apparently were included under popular pressure, suggesting adulteration of Brahmanical religion with non-Aryan literature; after all the majority of the people of the land were non-Brahmans. But Sanhita does have hymns of rare beauty, in the non-*khila* category, some extolling the power and omniscience of God, others beneficence of Mother Earth. Generally it is the Saunakiya recension which is in use, although the other recension, Paippalada recension too has a lot of relevant material. Both recensions have a lot of chapters which have been added later.

The Brahmanas

By the time of the Brahmanas, the hymns of the Rig Veda had become quite unintelligible, and the Vedic scholars had differing views regarding the meaning of the hymns. Brahmanas texts were compiled a few centuries after the last of the Rig Vedic hymns had been composed—according to Tilak the interval could have been even a millennium, though this view has not been accepted. Brahmanas contain detailed instructions on the procedure to be followed to perform a sacrifice, and since these are based on the understanding of their authors of the meaning of the Vedic hymns, these may be regarded as the commentaries on the Rig and the Atharva Vedas. Each of the Veda has its Brahmana: Rig has Aitareya, Sam has Jaiminiya, Yajur has Satapatha and Atharva has Gopatha. Although most Brahmanas have been assumed to be works handed down in the form in which they were first composed, it does not appear to be so. They appear to be works of many authors and edited and re-edited many times. Apart from the details of the Brahmanical sacrifices, the works also have duties of the priests, the Mantras to be recited and other essential detail considered essential for the sacrifice. They have tended to mystify the ritual with illustrative stories to emphasise the importance of the ritual, and the benefits the sacrificer would draw from it, sometimes dealing with speculative aspects, like how the world came into being and the part the sacrifice would play in the scheme of things. The modification of the texts continued long after Brahmanas were first composed.

The literature of the Brahmanas had a beneficial effect, leading to a more polished and forceful writing and speech, with more attention to the rules of grammar (mostly Paninian). Besides, a disagreeing opinion also got evolved amongst other educated sections of the society, particularly the Kshatriyas, who were gradually getting disenchanted with the complexity of the ritual. This led to the Aranyakas and the Upanishads.

Shrauta-Sutras

The prolix and complex jumble of detail of the Brahmanas often lacked coherence. This was overcome through Shrauta-Sutras wherein sacrificial detail was arranged concisely and systematically. Shrauta means according to Shruti, the revealed knowledge. A Shrauta sacrifice is performed strictly in accordance with the Vedic injunctions. Sutras are aphoristic texts, most of the time expressed so pithily that to understand them separate commentaries have become necessary. Brahmanas defied proper understanding of text because of a lack of coherence, but the Shrauta-Sutras are equally difficult because they are just too brief and assume too much of the sacrificial detail to be already well-known and understood to need any mention. They have, however, separated the common and the special features of the sacrifices and expressed in digits, in a kind of a coded manner, computer-style—a remarkable arithmetical achievement.

Each Veda has its Shrauta-Sutra and they bear relationship with the corresponding Brahmanas, i.e., Brahmana appended to the particular Veda. Normally Atharva Veda which has nothing to do with the Shrauta rituals, should not have had its own Shrauta-Sutra, but it has; possibly this has been done by its followers who believed in its being of canonical status, though it is Shrauta-Sutra anyway for its twentieth chapter which has a Sanhita status. A considerable time elapsed between the compiling of the Brahmanas and the Shrauta-Sutras.

The Aranyakas

These are sacred "Forest Texts" which contain secrets which could be taught only in the seclusion of the forests. Though considered to be extensions of the Brahmanas, they, in actual fact, were not stressing the sacrifice or explaining its detail. They were more concerned with its mystery and the meaning of the symbols used during its conduct and unfolded a philosophy which stated that sacrifice was not the only method of realizing Brahma; meditation without any sacrifice, was an equally if not more effective method. They advocated meditation instead of ritual, for securing Moksha and thus initiated a new thought; meditation was an important ingredient of the pre-Aryan worship. In order to secure the acceptance of the new thought over the importance of sacrifice it was, painstakingly, established that it was based on the sayings of the Veda. Actually the Brahmana sacrificial ritual had become so complex, time consuming and expensive that it had gone out of the reach of the common people.

The sacrifice required a minimum of four priests, namely, the Hotri who invoked the gods by selecting the relevant verses of the Rig, the Udgatri who sang the hymns as laid down in the Sam, the Adhvaryu who performed the sacrificial acts with appropriate recitations from the Yajur Veda and, finally, the Brahman, the supervisor who ensured the ceremony was conducted in accordance with the Brahmana texts. Shiksha, education in phonetics and correct pronunciation and so on, while reciting Mantras, played an important part. Though the Vedangas, the limbs of the Veda (and Shiksha is one of them), are not a divine revelation—these have been written for the proper understanding, recitation and the sacrificial use of the Veda. The Shrauta sacrifice was so complex that it required three fires going at the same time and employed sixteen or more priests. The number went up when more than one god was invoked at the same time or the invocation of one god was required to be emphasized. Such elaborate invocation ceremonies were expensive and could be possible only when conducted jointly, like invocations to the rain god by the people collectively, or by rich traders or by the Rajanyas. At the level of the common man the requirement was for simple and affordable procedures. The authors of the Aranyakas were basically concerned with the argument that sacrifice was the only way to realize happiness in this world and the hereafter. Aranyakas have stressed the importance of the development of the spiritual self to reach the Brahma lok (the abode of Brahma), a place higher than what is attainable through sacrifice and ritual. The Upanishads have taken the refrain further and stated that this is the way to the freedom from the birth and death cycle and ultimately unity with Brahma. As stated already, Aranyakas are extensions of Brahmanas and are their appendices and are attached to particularized Vedic schools, e.g., Aitareya Brahmana of the Rig Veda has an Aranyaka of the same name as its appendix.

Kalpa Sutra

These oldest works systematized the sacrificial procedures by dividing them into three classes, namely, (a) elaborate sacrifices based on Brahmana and Shrauta texts as explained above, (b) simple domestic rites, like marriages, births and deaths, (c) rites to regulate the conduct of a person to purify him morally and make him worthy to receive the benefits of sacrifice. Works in (b) and (c) are in Grihya Sutras. The details of the five sacrifices prescribed for the house-holder are also contained in these Sutras. In fact, details of all sacrifices for the house-holder are given in these Sutras, including house building or digging of a well, or for effecting a cure from a disease, and so on are there in these Sutras. Shrauta-Sutras are so called because they are claimed to be based on Shruti, the revealed knowledge, but Grihya Sutras are Smarta, that is, based on Smriti, tradition.

The instructions regarding the responsibilities, duties, conduct, behaviour of an individual as a member of the family, society or citizen of the state are contained in the Dharma Sutras which form a part of the Grihya Sutras. Broadly, Dharma is what holds together and is the basis of all order. It is also understood as religious merit for securing good for the future, including the hereafter. The rituals of the Dharma Sutras are for securing wealth, children, particularly sons and whatever else that secures happiness. The instructions are put in two categories, viz., (a) general, meant to improve the character of a person, like self-discipline, kindness, consideration towards others—not only towards fellow human beings but even animals and plants—speaking truth, altruism, and such like qualities, and (b) people in the four Varnas, and the four Ashramas, their duties and obligations. Even though the society had been divided into four Varnas, namely, Brahmans, Kshatriyas, Vaishas and Shudras, it is not clear how rigid the divide was; it does not appear to have been so rigid as it became during the second millennium AD.

The Ashrama System

By the time of the Brahmanas the Ashrama system had taken firm roots. The system applied to the male population only and presumed a total life span of one hundred years and divided it in four parts, each of 25 years. The first 25 years were called the Brahmacharya Ashram, the period of celibacy, when the Aryan male devoted himself to education, training in religion and profession, including arts and sciences. The second 25 years were the Grihastha Ashram when the individual performed the functions of a householder. He raised a family and guided his children to be positively productive and be useful members of the society. He devoted himself to (a) Dharma, as has been explained above, (b) Artha, the art of generating wealth to secure personal and family's welfare, (c) Kama, enjoying arts, beauty in general including sex, and Moksha, indulging in activity, like prayers, meditation etc. which might lead to deliverance from the birth cycle. As for the women, they were enjoined, if married, to lead a chaste, and noble life and tend to the family with loving care.

The next stage was the Vanprastha Ashram, i.e., the stage of the forest dweller. The individual during this stage devotes himself to the study of religion, and ponders over issues confronting the society and teaches and preaches, having broadened his outlook through intermingling with people of other thoughts and beliefs. A lot of revolutionary thought concerning all aspects of the society developed during this stage. New ideas, like Buddhism and Jainism and the Upanishadic literature evolved due to the effervescence in the religious and secular thinking engineered by the activities of this group of people. Finally, there is the Sanyas Ashram, when the individual is enjoined to lead the life of an ascetic, when he lives unconcerned about the family and retires from all worry and care and just spends his time meditating and praying. He is now prepared to depart from this world and has little energy to take care of himself, and since he has little utility for the family, they too tended to ignore him. He faced the danger of perishing on account of neglect. For this reason some Dharma Sutras have denounced asceticism and have enjoined the family to take care of their old and infirm.

With the sacrifice becoming more complex by the day, and open discussions regarding sacrifice, its mode, utility and its beneficial effects on the development of faith, a trend developed towards the need to understand the older religions of the land;

meditation was accepted. As we have seen from the Indus Valley seals, the pre-Aryan culture stressed meditation. Thus, the Aryan religion was being intermixed with other thoughts.

The four classes of activities a person performed were: Dharma, Artha, Kaam and Moksha. These activities he performed as a member of the society with a view to benefiting the society. Dharma is what binds, as explained earlier, and Artha is generation of wealth. But Artha has to be performed within the ambit of Dharma and not through indulging in dishonest practices or subterfuge. Likewise, Kaam is artistic activity, including sexual, and also has to be performed keeping Dharma in view. Illicit activities under this head are strictly forbidden. Essentially, this activity is permissible only to bring forth children.

The Upanishads

These are the last works of the Veda, and for this reason their teachings are referred to as Vedanta, that is, Veda's 'Ant', the ultimate revelations. Their teachings which have vastly varied from the Brahmana teachings, stresses the importance of realizing the goal of seeking unity with Brahma, the self-existent, omnipotent and omniscient God, that the whole Universe is a reflection of the manifestation of Brahma and each part of it, howsoever small, is but a constituent of the whole, i.e., Brahma. It further postulates that the human soul is stuck in the Sansara, the phenomenal world, because of the ignorance about this truth, that this truth can be realized through Gyana, knowledge, and once it has been realized the soul is freed from the Sansara. True Gyan is realized by meditation and contemplation upon the self. The Kshatriyas played a leading role in the development of this thought, for important sections of them had grown disenchanted with Brahmanical ritual. Likewise women, and the traders' community and the Shudras, all together forming a large segment of the people, were unhappy with the low priority Brahmans had allotted to them. All this led to the drop in the importance of Brahmanism and ritualism and spread of the contemplative religion.

4

The Creation

The Word

The Upanishad religion, Vedanta, postulated that the power that creates is eternal, that there is nothing that caused or causes its coming into being, that all that exists, including the human being, is but an inseparable part of this power, 'Tat Tvam Asi' 'that thou art!'.

The Veda is the revealed text, the primordial word, Vak, of which no human being can be the author. In fact, the word itself is an aspect of the Supreme Being. It is closely connected with the life-force, the senses, the mind, and is like an ocean—deep, endless and unfathomable. The Veda is not to be regarded as having been authored by God, or as a kind of a message from God communicated through some sage or holiman. It is the Word itself, which, in essence, is the phenomenon of creation and pervades it like a dimension, like the dimension of time, Kaal, and gets revealed through intuitive minds when these minds are attuned to the process of creation. Even the Supreme Self becomes visible through the medium of the word. According to Atharva Veda the manifestation of the Supreme Self takes place in four stages and the people with insight know them: three are dormant and hidden, and the fourth appears in the form of speech. Sayana, while commenting on this, explains that the Original Word is the inner Immortal Light and when this is realized all frivolous activities of the body and mind cease. In the middle stage it becomes an object of the intellect and takes the form of thinking and brooding, and in the final stage it is just speech. The Rig Veda gives the four stages as: Para (the original and the highest); Pashyanti (the visible); Madhyama (the middle) and Vaikhari (the articulate). The words have vibrations which generate beneficial or harmful effects. The words of the Mantra came down to man to create a desired effect; those words have power. The Vedic Seer, the Rishi, discovered the word after practising rigorous austerities, after he had discovered the working principles of the cosmos and become conversant with the universal order and become a part of the divine speech. The words then came to him which when arranged in the proper Mantra form, and uttered in a specified metre, and accompanied by an appropriate sacrifice, endowed him, and subsequently any person who followed his directions, with the desired power. The word, thus, is a facet of God, and when turned the right way round, it is God. It is Naam, the name of God, and generates sound current, Vibration, which is the essence of creation, anexperience which is transporting, and could eventually lead to union with God. Humanity communicates with its help and transacts its work with it and uses it to pray. Life would have little meaning if it was not supported by word.

Om

The word most effective for good sound vibrations is Om, which has no meaning as such in a literary sense. The sound, it has been stated, it generates is believed to be a combination of A-U-M, where 'A' is for Brahma who Creates, and 'U' for Vishnu, the sustainer and 'M' for Siva, the annihilator, all together forming the Hindu Trinity. Siva is also connected with all knowledge—the three thus standing for Creation, Desire and Knowledge (Kriya-Ichha-Gyana), the three facets of the Supreme Being. Thus as the sound emerges, it is Creation, and it goes through the process of sustenance during the second stage with sound flexing to 'U', till with 'M' it is all over and it is the end. Then there is a long silence, Shunya, when the Primordial atom has completely withdrawn into itself, till once again the process of Creation starts with the utterance of sound 'A'. The word thus represents the Creation and the Annihilation processes. However, even though the word makes no grammatical sense, the sound it generates is regarded as the most helpful during meditation. Its vibrations are beneficial in all situation in all kinds of situations a human being might face. Buddhist Lamas believe that the word generates vibrations even on a fluttering flag. It is the original sound that comes to a person when he meditates and concentrates on the Self. It has a mystical impact and is used at the beginning and the end of all sacred recitations.

Rta

Veda is not a Shastra where the subject-matter might be arranged logically for ease of reference. It is a record of the transcendental experience of the seers (Rishis), and different ideas like those about the Creator, or the Creation, or how it came about, or which way is it heading, and so on, lie scattered all over the literature. Besides, the literature so old that now it is difficult to even understand it. The Vedic scholars have understood Rta to mean the Truth, but that does not cover this expression entirely. Some European scholars likened it to Universal Order, but this was opposed by the likes of Luders who argued that the Vedic people at no stage spoke of the Universal order. He said the word stood for Truth, i.e., non-lie, which is how it has been understood in the earliest reference in the Rig Veda. It is cosmic power which is expressed in a variety of ways, both at the cosmic as well as the terrestrial levels. Rta is energy that enlivens faculties like will power, perception, urge to action and so on. If Rta is harnessed, control is achieved over the Creation. This the Mantra does, and achieves the control, and bends the energy for the well-being of the people including fulfillment of their cherished desires. Most essential phenomenon of creation are born out of Rta, including Brahma, the Creator of the Universe. Agni, the cosmic fire, resides in its womb.

What controls Rta? The belief is that by Rta is Rta controlled, although Mantra should influence it in whatever way the Rishi to whom the Mantra came, wanted it influenced. In certain hymns there is a suggestion that the visible aspects of Rta have invisible counterparts, e.g., the invisible part of light or fire has been given as water. The assertion is that there is double Rta, implying that there is no visible entity which does not have its invisible counterpart. The hymn talks of the balance, equilibrium, reached by the interaction of the visible and the invisible entities: Sun and its movements, right speech, even right conduct, are the visible aspects, which are being held in the perceptible by the corresponding invisible constituents.

Rta has also been described as cosmic moisture which brings rain and water to the earth, and the seer who, with his Mantric power gets into the guts of the cosmic process, so to speak, is considered to possess the capability to get a favourable response from this power, like, for example, the precipitation of rain. Possibly for this reason, the tradition gives it the meaning of just water. Sayana who sees nothing in the Veda beyond ritual and sacrifice has also given it the same meaning. This view has been considered rather restricted. European scholars have had different views: some have understood it as 'the holy power' while others have called it a 'ritualistic formula' for exciting the cosmic power in favour of the person performing the sacrifice. Some have understood it as the absolute power in the whole nature which amongst others also constitutes nature, for Brahma's origin is in Rta.

According to some scholars Brahma is 'a mysterious fluid', or potence, that fills the Universe. It can be made to manifest itself in a particular substance or situation, through charms, incantations or with the help of scientific or magical movements. It is also for giving expression to thoughts that arise in the mind leading to speech (vak). It pervades the cosmos and is its inner core (that sustains it). The concept has a broad meaning that covers, amongst others, 'Mantra and Prayer', or the 'inner power', or the results that the Mantra can produce, or the complex activities of the nature which constitutes the Universe. But Brahma's abode is in Rta.

The Vedic Content

Veda has been considered as the literature of rituals, though, in actual fact, it is more than that. It is also speculative, and literature of contemplation. The Vedic seer, while contemplating, went through certain intuitive experiences which gave him insight into the process of creation, how it sustained and wither was it heading and such like questions. He was so overwhelmed by the experience of his thoughts that he just did not have the vocabulary or the words to express. So he designed some esoteric expressions for this purpose, which came to be known as the Tantric language. This form of language described meditative and contemplative experiences freely using sexual symbolism, which though appearing brash at the face of it, comprehensively explained the method of getting to them. Tantras are treatises wherein, in some cases, highly learned men of religion and philosophy have described intricate and difficult aspects of rituals and their own meditative and contemplative experiences, in a manner to make them comprehensible to their selected disciples. For this purpose they used even sexual symbolism. With time, however, some people adopted what had been written literally, without bothering about the intent behind the writing. This set in motion a process of degeneration which took the ritual to an absurd level, making a mockery of the ancient religion.

The knowledge about the Creator, it is stated, is attained through the Veda and the Tantra; the latter is considered to be an elucidation of the Vedic experience. Tantras explain the process of Creation by a diagram called the Chakra, the Circle. It could also mean the Universe, or the Cosmos. The centre of the diagram is a dot, Bindu, which has two triangles around it, one with apex upwards and the other downward and this arrangement is contained within a circle which has eight lotus petals along the circumference; each petal has two filaments. The dot in the centre stands for absolute consciousness, Chitta, the all pervading Universal Force, the Supreme Being; its nature is absolute joy, the supreme bliss, and it expresses itself in the form of knowledge, desire and action. These are represented in the figure by three points around the central dot, and when these points are joined they form a triangle of which the dot becomes the centre and this triangle as referred to as Yoni, the place of origin, the source of all consciousness in the Creation. Immediately around it are the static force, Sthiti, represented by the triangle with apex upwards, and the dynamic force, Gati, represented by the other triangle. The two together form one unit and are not separable.

Somewhere in this matrix is the primordial atom in repose, that which is the potential Universe(s), and beyond this is the abode of the Absolute Being, represented by the Dot. The Creation process is activated by the intense heat in the womb of Rta, which is a characteristic of the Absolute Being, and a stage is reached, maybe after an explosion (The Big Bang) or otherwise, when it propels into action the static and the dynamic forces (the two inseparable opposites), and expands; the expansion is represented by the circle. This is Mula Prakriti, the Primordial Matter. This is also the Hiranaya Garbha, the Golden Germ, the Primordial Egg or Seed. Hiranaya means heat, light, brightness, splendour, energy, effulgence, the fire-ball of the universe immediately following the activation of the static and the dynamic forces, and it is the Garbha, the Womb, for the Creation in the form of primordial matter and the consciousness comes out of this. For simultaneously with the explosion of the primordial atom, the source, Yoni, comprising knowledge, desire and action, also gets activated and pours forth consciousness in an unending stream. Rta, the ultimate dynamic and harmonious structure of the Reality, which operates alongside the creating energy, controls this process. Though Agni, Heat, the visible aspect of Rta, resides in Rta's womb, its non-visible aspect is water out of which is born Brahma, the mysterious fluid which pervades the Universe and is the cause of its creation. Things pick up because of the static and dynamic aspects of Rta, that is, the static and the dynamic aspects move in opposite directions, or the matter and anti-matter particles interact till stability is reached and shapes and forms are discernible in the unidirectional flow of energy. That is how 'by Rta is Rta controlled', and it is established that for everything that is visible there are those which are not visible. Thus is Rta, the abode of Brahma, the Creator, canalizes the creating process along harmonious and dynamic lines, and thus is Dharma, the Law, born. This Law governs each entity created, including the functioning of the human beings. Rta ensures the proper functioning of the static and the dynamic forces once the matter has been projected into time and space—which are also the aspects of Rta—and it goes along its projected course, till the time when universe folds up and collapses into the Primordial Atom. Rta ensures the orderly flow of creation and its collapse without any chaos, Thus, Rta is the force of creation while Dharma is what sustains it, though the dividing line between the two is hard to see, for in all non-volitional activity Dharma appears to be the same as Rta: it has its modes of creation, sustenance and annihilation. It assumes significance essentially in the volitional human activity. Violation of Dharma would surely lead to annihilation.

Universe is governed by unbreakable laws and this has been covered in detail in the later Vedic thought. Karma philosophy and the idea of the transmigration of soul takes firm roots in course of time. What it implies is that there is no superior agency that take control of your destiny; it all happens on the basis of the deed performed during ones life time. Some deeds show their effects during the life time in this life itself, while others influence the fate in the hereafter. There is no escape from the shackles of the Karmas, for the law takes over to award punishments or rewards on the basis of these Karmas. The law is applicable in the sphere of thoughts or speech as well, these are constituents of the Word, a dimension of the Creator, one amongst many known and unknown dimensions. Bad or evil speech or thoughts will precipitate bad results while reverse is true of good thoughts and speech. Prayer has effect, as also meditation, contemplation or singing of hymns or devotional songs. The system of Vedic rituals is based on the same idea. The rituals and invocations in the form of formulas as designed to influence the gods, representing different aspects of the energy, Rta, are, strictly speaking, not prayers as understood in the normal mode of worship.

The come back to the Chakra. In the beginning it is pure consciousness and pure primal matter, Mula Prakriti, and the two have not intermixed and therefore there is no form. But as the process expands, a stage is arrived when the conditions are right for the Mula Prakriti to split; in this split state it is Bhinna Prakriti, i.e., split up primal matter. This splitting is in eight elements, five being earth, fire, water, air and *akaasha*, and the three are *Manas*, mind, the seat of all emotions, *Buddhi*, intellect, including thought and understanding, and *Ahankaar*, ego. The term Akaasha means space, ether, vacuity (emptiness); it is all penetrating and infinite, like the Creator. On the diagram this split is shown by eight petals of lotus. The two filaments in each lotus petal represent sentience and insentience. This is the time name and form come into being. With continued expansion the conditions become ripe for further split of the primal matter, and the eight lotus petals increase to twenty-four, representing new evolved elements in nature, like sensory and motor organs, and subtle and gross elements, all of which combine to evolve life. The Creation Hymn in the Nasadiya Sukta of the Rig Veda states as follows:

Then even nothingness (Asat) was not, nor existence (Asat),

There was no air then, nor the heavens beyond it. Who covered it?

Where was it? In whose keeping there then cosmic water,

In depth unfathomed?

Death was not then, nor any sign of day or night.

That One-Thing, breathless, breathed by its own nature, Svadhaya;

Apart from that there was nothing whatsoever.

Darkness, Tamas, there was.

At first concealed in this darkness, this all, Sarvam dam, was indiscriminated chaos (plasma, Aparketam Salilam)

All that existed then was void and formlessness.

By the great power of warmth, Tapisah Mahina, was born that unit, Tat Ekam.

Thereafter rose desire, Kama, in the beginning;

Desire, the primal seed and germ of spirit, Prathamam Retah.

But, then, after all, who knows and who can say,

Whence it all came, and how creation happened?

For gods themselves are later than creation.

The expansion process of the universe goes on and a stage is reached when what till then appeared as chaos, gradually starts showing orderliness and movement towards stability. Chakra diagram shows that through knowledge and right experience can the understanding of the Reality be possible and get past the web cast by Bhinna Prakriti (the web of ignorance) and understand the truth in its most magnificent form, and reach the Reality, DOT, Bindu, and merge with it and be freed of the birth-death cycle.

The Chakra has influenced the design of the sacred structures of the Hindus, including temples and sacrificial altars. Even Sivalingam is representing the same idea. Buddhist Stupa is a magnified form of the pillar.

All the while when Brahma the mysterious fluid, which is pure energy and consciousness, is causing the expansion of the Universe, what remains unmoved is the Dot, the ultimate source of everything, including Brahma; it reposes in its pristine purity as absolute consciousness, embodiment of Ananda, pure bliss. Time is born when, impelled by the infinite heat in the womb of Rta, the primordial atom begins its expansion, along with the pouring forth of knowledge, desire and action; like Rta these too are constituents of the Absolute Consciousness. Time *Kaal*, is a constituent, or an attribute, of the *Mahakaal*, who is also referred as *Akaal*, that which is not bound by time, which creates time but is not affected by it.

The Universe of Brahma expands, and, as already stated, the Mula Prakriti, the primordial matter, breaks into Bhinna Prakriti, the broken down constituents of the primordial matter, and the conditions become right for the evolution of life. According to Vishnu Purana, this activity of Brahma, from the time of the first stirring, starting the process of creation, to its reaching the zenith, and then its final collapse into absolute consciousness and the primordial Atom (which is an attribute of the former), lasts for the duration of one Kalpa, which is one day of Brahma. Thereafter it is the night, Pralaya, when it is the non-existence, more or less. With the rise of the next day the creation begins again, like it did the previous day. In this manner Brahma functions for one hundred years, and at the end of this another Brahma is born, and the process is continued unabated. However, at the end of one Kalpa only the finer, delicate, fragile constituents of creation get eliminated. The gods, sages and the substance of the universe stay intact. It is only at the end of the life of a Brahma that there is complete annihilation, when the elements merge with the primary substance, 'besides which only one spiritual being exists'. A Kalpa comprises Manvantras and Mahayugas. A Mahayuga has four Yugas, time cycles, comprising, firstly, of Sat Yuga, the time cycle lasting 17,28,000 years, when only absolute virtue prevails over the universe, Treta Yuga of 12,96,000 years when the virtue element has been reduced to about 75 per cent, Dwapara Yuga of 8,64,000 years with the virtue element gone down to 50 per cent, and finally the Kali Yuga, the time cycle in which we live, of 4,32,000 years having virtue element of around 25 per cent. This means the human being has evolved in the final Yuga when the enquiring intelligence is at full play and has a role in the evolutionary process. The inert morality has limited relevance in the human existence and in the existence of everything which is influenced by human existence.

The total of these Yugas , 43,20,000 years is one Mahayuga, and seventy one Mahayugas make one Manvantra; during this period different worlds of the Universe are under the care of one Manu. Planet earth came into being during the time of Manu Svayambhu. 14 Manvantras plus six Mahayugas together make one Kalpa; this works out to 1000 Mahayugas, i.e., a day of Brahma is equal to 4.32 billion years. His night, Pralaya, is of the same duration. Thus, the creation and the annihilation of the finer and fragile constituents of the Universe, Bhinna Prakriti, takes place after every 4.32 billion years and this is followed by a period of repose. Process springs up into action with the start of a new Kalpa, and so this process goes on till the stage is reached of complete annihilation at the end of the life of a Brahma, which is 4.32 × 2 × 360 × 100 billion years; one year of Brahma has 360 days (Kalpas), and an equal number of nights.

What has one to make of these Yugas and Mahayugas? There have been various thoughts, some as naive as suggesting they represent the four seasons in the year, ending in the deluge—the Monsoons—after which the cycle begins again. Traditional history based on the accounts recorded in the Puranas, states that the four ages, namely Krita, Treta, Dvapara and Kali, flourished during the times of kings Sagara, Rama and Krishna respectively, and not counting the Kali age, being the current one, the first age covers roughly 40 generations, Treta, the second one, covers 25 generations, and Dvapara 30 generations. Clearly this is being given in a context different from the one dealing with the age of the Universe. Other accounts in the same history give the beginning of the Dvapara age with the coronation of Rama after his return to Ayodhya, and its end and the beginning of the Kali age with the end of the Mahabharata War. This too could not have borne any direct reference to the age of the Universe. However, some accounts place the end of the Mahabharata war and the start of the Age of Kali in the year 3102 BC. There is some confusion here, for, obvious reasons the Mahabharata war cannot be placed much earlier than 1400 BC. But it can be inferred that some event of historical significance took place at this time. By the accounts of the traditional history this period is of the Great Flood and the start of the period of Manu Vaivasvata, the seventh Manu of the current Manvantra, who is believed to be the originator of the human race, although the legend about the flood would suggest that Vaivasvata was not the originator of the human race but was one of it, who after the entire of his clan had perished in the flood, restarted the process of raising the clan along with Ida, the female. He has been held in great respect by his following generations, and was reputed to be a man of great character, wisdom and foresight. He is thus of the present age of competitive materialism when dialectical, achievement oriented activity has overtaken activity based purely on virtue and religious ethos. Thus year-3102 is about the time for the start of the Kali Yuga. This is also supported by the figures based on astronomy as worked out by Aryabhatta.

In the calculations about the age of the Universe, one Mahayuga has 4.32 million years, and 71 Mahayugas make one

Manvantra, i.e., the period presided over by one Manu for taking care of the Universe. This period would be 306.72 million years. A Kalpa, i.e., a day of Brahma, has 14 Manvantras and there are six additional Mahayugas during which the collapse of the Bhinna Prakriti takes place; this is referred to as the evening of the Kalpa. A Kalpa, thus, has a total of 1000 Mahayugas, and is of 4.32 billion years. Thus while total annihilation takes place after every 100 years of Brahma, the annihilation of the finer constituents is once in every 4.32 billion years; subtle variations in the creation pattern occur during each Manvantra. The creation process is highly dynamic and changes are taking place all the time; there never is a time when any of its constituents is static. But Manvantras differ from each other, even in terms of flora and fauna and some other aspects. Yugas and Mahayugas too signify stages of changes in the structure of the Universe. Evolution is gradual but continuous process. To begin with matter (Mula Prakriti) and consciousness are floating side by side. With the evolution of Bhinna Prakriti the interaction between Prakriti, or matter, and consciousness begins. This interaction leads to the evolution of three subtle attributes of matter, namely, intellect, mind and ego. In the beginning these attributes are almost dormant, but gradually they become defined and definitive, and get mixed with consciousness, and there is the evolution of life which has all the three attributes pretty well developed. The ultimate development of this process appears to be the human being. We are in the period of the seventh Manu, in the seventh Manvantra, which is almost the mid-point of the Kalpa. The earth has already gone through the first three Yugas of this Mahayuga, but of the Kali Yuga of 4,32,000 years, we have done only around 5000; there is thus a long way to go. The typical characteristic of this Yuga is the continuous sharpening of the subtle attributes, namely, intellect, mind and ego. Vishnu Purana says that towards the end of the Kali Age an incarnation of Vishnu in the form of Kalki shall appear on this earth and rid it of rapacious, self serving tyrants, and the people shall be awakened from the wrong concepts and shall become as pure as crystals.

The life was first formed in water is borne by the concept of the Dasha Ávtaras, the ten incarnations of Vishnu. Avtaras of

Vishnu appear from time to time to rid his creation of the inimical elements which crop up from time to time. The first time he came down as Fish, indicating the origin of life in water, then as tortoise, when life moved to dry land, then as boar, when herbivores were evolved, and then as a lion when carnivores came into being. The remaining Avtaras, namely, Vaman, Parshurama, Rama, Krishna and Buddha, appeared to rid the humanity of despots, and show it the way of peace and happiness. The last one, Kalki, has yet to appear, towards the end of the Kali age, to rid the earth of rapacious materialism.

The Creation is a manifestation of a mysterious power, energy, which, in a matter of speaking, pours out of the Hiranaya Garbha, the golden germ—golden because it is absolute heat—, and which has two constituents, namely consciousness and matter. Pure energy no form or name. It is just energy, invisible like, let say, electricity flowing through a conductor. But the two attributes of energy that manifest as matter, namely, Stithi, the static aspect, and Gati, the dynamic aspect, finally combine together to precipitate name and form. The function of the former is to interact with the dynamic force and create the illusion of static forms, Creation, and impart name, form, shape, to things that appear created on the infinitely vast canvas of the Creator.

Absolute Creator is the reality comprising absolute Bliss, the ocean of consciousness. One of its attributes is the creation of the Universe, and that is the Brahma characteristic of the Creator. The aspects of sustaining and the annihilation of the Universe are represented by the Vishnu and the Shiva aspects characteristics respectively, and together the three form the Trinity. But the core idea is the ocean of creation wherein the Creator is visualized as sea of Bliss in which mode he is free of Karma, i.e., of the need to perform, and that of the Creator when He is energy manifested as the working universe. The Blissful mode is represented as the male symbol while the Creator mode is represented as the female symbol, or Shakti, the absolute power or the creating energy, which also takes care of what it creates. The blissful mode is the infinite sea of consciousness and peace and tranquility, the very core out of which everything comes, including the Creator mode. This is the abode the soul attains after it has been freed of the birth-death cycle of the matter in which it has been trapped. Iconography as evolved depicts God as a male-female pair, the male aspect representing absolute God, the abode of peace and bliss, above the disturbance caused by Karmas, while the female aspect representing creation; the examples are Radha-Krishna, Vishnu-Lakshmi, Sita-Rama or Shiva-Parvati. The Saivas, the devotees of Shiva visualise Him as Ardhanarishvara also, i.e., half male and half female, to emphasize that what creates (the female aspect) has its roots in the abode of bliss and tranquility (the male aspect) and though that part of Him (the male aspect) though not directly in the creation process, or of sustenance or annihilation, is ultimately, is the very source and the cause of it all, this Creation, that while one attribute of it all, this creation, that while an attribute of Him is the activity of creation (the female aspect), the whole of Him is just actionless tranquility (the male aspect). Visualizing the creating energy as female is particularly helpful in the devotional form of worship. Here God is the Mother, and it is much easier to love the mother than the father or any other relationship for that matter. Basic idea of loving the Mother is the paying obeisance and thus recognizing the active principal of the Creator, the aspect which it is believed is concerned and involved with the well-being of the creation, including the human beings. If in deliverance, the soul merges with an agency other than the eternal Creator, then its merger is with a Force which is in intense activity, a Force not sitting in the sea of Tranquility. Deliverance, in fact, implies getting freed of the agitation caused by the effects of Karmas. If the soul has to face intense, or even less than intense activity, it is not in the kind of peace categorized as Moksha. The concept of Buddhist Shoonya is almost the same.

The Dynamic and the Static forces combine together to produce the impressions of thing, and this can happen only after the things have attained some kind of a static status. But the things being in a static state is only an illusion, an impression; otherwise there is nothing static as such. It is the interplay of the two forces which is what the manifested creation is all about. And where such interaction has not taken place, and it has not in the case of a fairly large percentage of the energy that emanated out of the Hiranaya Garbha, the phenomenon of the name and form is missing and no creation is visible.

The power that creates, Brahma, the unknowable and incomprehensible, is understood to be Nirguna, without attributes or qualities, transcendent Absolute. In Bhagti, or devotional worship, however, God has been assigned attributes, for it is not possible to develop devotion for anyone or anything that cannot be conceptualized. For this purpose the being of devotion has to be visualized in human, or near human form, for being worthy of respect, even awe, for its great power, and for its being omnipotent, omniscient, beneficnt, kind and merciful. It has to have appealing looks, and be visualized as the destroyer of the oppressors, is mighty, and can fulfil the wishes of the devotees, and generally look after their interests. This is Brahma with attributes, Ishvara, the personal God. But this is only a modification allowed essentially to help develop devotion and love in the heart and the mind of the worshipper. Otherwise the Creator is only Nirguna, without attributes, and the followers of the Bhagti mode have no doubt that as the intensity of devotion develops, the object of devotion gently and gradually changes from the Saguna to Nirguna.

Brahma, the force, power, energy that creates is the cosmic fluid, and the myriad visions of the human being, or for that matter, of all created beings, from the smallest germ to the stars and galaxies, and much more that is not perceived, is a phenomenon precipitated by the interaction of Stithi and Gati, the static and the dynamic forces. Where the interaction is successful, it is manifestation, but where there is no interaction, or it is not successful, nothing gets perceived, and the cosmic fluid, matter and consciousness, flows on, unseen though in full potency. Is the flow of energy for the purpose of creating a manifested universe. It may be so, but the entire flowing energy does not express into manifested universe, like all the seeds which grow on a plant do not convert into plants. Nature does possess super abundance when it comes to producing the seeds, or progeny, but all the seeds do not translate into plants because so much else has to go into to achieve it, and all that is not provided for. But why does this great fluid spill out in the first instance, for whose benefit?

Vedas are silent on this. Puranas state that all this is a divine play, the Lila of the absolute consciousness. He seems to have been conditioned to these cycles of creations and dissolutions, and may be, He enjoys the play. Otherwise there does not appear to be any reason which might suggest to the infinitesimally small human mind as to what that he experiences and witnesses, is all about.

The consciousness that spills out of the divine source, an attribute of the absolute consciousness, and which has knowledge, desire and action, as its constituents, mingles with the Bhinna Prakriti, the split up primordial matter, at an appropriate stage, and we have the seeds of evolution which ultimately bring forth the sentient beings. The process in the form of the birth-death cycles, with all the pains and rewards and the intense struggle that goes with it, with ego assuming a distinct identity for itself, proceeds at a feverish pace, generating perpetual restlessness, from inception to dissolution, in cycle after cycle of creation. There is one place where there is complete serenity, peace, and, consequently, absolute bliss, and that is the seat of absolute consciousness, and that is where the freedom is from the febrile agitation which the Bhinna Prakriti inflicts upon the elements of consciousness trapped within it. The role religion is to guide the individual towards this seat of absolute consciousness.

The belief in the continuous life-death cycle is fundamental to the Hindus. Like matter which is indestructible, consciousness too cannot be destroyed. What form the soul takes at each birth depends upon the Karmas, the sum total of the deed it performed while in the mundane world. The resultant impact of the thoughts and deeds gives the soul an identity, which, no doubt keeps changing with the accumulation of fresh Karmas, and soon the lustrous soul gets trapped in the muddied deeds. The rebirth is dependent upon the residue of the Karmas. The process continues even after the creation has ceased, for in the following cycle the process starts from where it left off during the preceding cycle. Only after the influence of the Karmas has been neutralised is the spirit set free in absolute bliss.

Buddha, who did not believe in the existence and identity of individual souls, has said that it is the collection of Karmas alone which decides about the type of body which comes into being in the next birth. The final aim in both traditions, Hindu as well as Buddhist, remains the securing of freedom from the stranglehold of Karmas and secure Moksha for the Hindus, or Nirvana for the Buddhists; the latter is the deliverance for the consciousness in general, while the former is for the consciousness in the form of individual soul.

Another issue which is fundamental to the Hindus, essentially to the Vaishnavas, the followers of Vishnu of the Hindu Trinity, is their belief in Avataras, the descent of Vishnu on this earth to eliminate negative influences. Rta and Dharma together ensure smooth movement of creation through time and space. The mechanism which fine-tunes the survival process for the created beings is through the Avataras.

Whenever, in any age, there is fall in righteousness, and unrighteousness increases, then I incarnate myself, so as to protect the good and destroy evil, and re-establish righteousness.

Geeta IV, 7,

Dharma is what holds together. It is the basis of all order and in its ambit includes all religious and moral merit.

It is the essential nature of a being that determines his or her behaviour. So long as our conduct is in conformity with our essential nature, we are acting in the right way. Adharma is non-conformity to our nature. If the harmony of the world is derived from the conformity of all beings to their respective natures, the disharmony of the world is due to their non-conformity. God does not stand aside when we abuse our freedom and cause disequilibrium. He does not simply wind up the world, set it on the right track, and then let it jog along by itself. His loving hand is steering it all the time.

Radhakrishnan

Avatara belief is prevalent amongst the followers of Vishnu. Saivas do not have any such concept. For them Shiva is the lord of the creation and the system automatically takes care of the negative influences; such negative influences might exhibit temporary success but eventually get overtaken by the system and eliminated.

Other Accounts of Creation

In one account in the Vedic literature the creation came into being with the sacrifice of Prajapati, the primordial God, who dismembers and immolates himself to create the Universe. The point to note is that Prajapati is Himself the sacrificer and the recipient of the sacrifice, for apart from Him there is no other existence. The Creation comes into being on account of Kaama and Tapas, i.e., desire and primordial fervour; the latter is the supreme concentration, the ultimate energy, the creative force that initiates the whole cosmic movement. The desire is the birth of consciousness, which is born alongside Tapas, and which gets incited to the point where creation is initiated, or spills out of the Hiranaya Garbha. This has been projected as the dismemberment of Prajapati.

The Hiranaya Garbha hymn (rv. x 121) describes God as the effulgent being, the Creator of everything, the Almighty who has established the order and the laws of movement. Hymn Rv x 190 states that from Tapas, or fervour, or heat, kindled to its extreme, Rta, the eternal law, or the cosmic order, and Satya, the Truth, were born, and then came night, Ratri, Tamas, and thence the ocean of cosmic intelligence, from where came the time, the days and the nights. The Great Creator, Dhata, then as in the previous creations, formed the sun and the moon, the celestial heaven and earth, the regions of air and the Svar, the regions beyond.

The Change in Emphasis

The earlier portions of the Vedic literature comprises the Mantras, the incantations, contained in the form of hymns in the Sanhitas of the Rig and the Atharva Vedas. Then come the Brahmanas which have emphasized the importance of ritual, laying down even the small detail for the performance of sacrifice. They also had the roots of the earlier Upanishads in the form of Aranyakas, the forest treatises. This literature was not based on the sacrifice, but bordered on interiorization. Both Brahmanas and Aranyakas are appendices to different schools of the Sanhitas.

And finally came the Upanishads, forming what is called Vedanta, the end of Veda, and contain the mystical and the philosophic thought which was considered to be the essence of the knowledge contained in the Veda.

In the early stages the Mantra with prescribed ritual and sacrifice was all that was required to urge the gods to grant the wishes of the sacrificer. This is the phase when the reincarnation theory was not in vogue, and the belief was that after death the soul travelled to the abode of the Pitris, the forefathers, and lived in joy and equal power, in their company and in the company of gods. Gods were the natural elements, like rain, fire, earth, sky, and the prayers were addressed to them, essentially for good crops, sons, and general well being. In later hymns the idea of reward after death for good deeds has been emphasized, The hymns talk of the journey to Svar Loka (the abode of joy and plenty) for good deeds and Narka Loka (the abode of pain and suffering) for evil deeds. Only in the tenth book of Rig Veda, which contains later hymns, are there two passages which suggest the idea of rebirth. It seems the idea is from some earlier civilization.

In the later Vedic literature, i.e., the Aranyakas and the Upanishads, the importance of sacrifice has diminished and its place has been taken by love and devotion to the deity, as is clear from the later Vedic hymns and the Brahmanas. Aranyakas almost completely forsook sacrifice and emphasized prayer and devotion, Bhagti, while Upanishads stressed knowledge, Gyan, about the Absolute Reality, without which, Upanishads argued, even Bhagti was not possible.

In the later hymns of the Rig Veda and the Brahmanas, the attributes of all gods—they were earlier identified with the elements of nature—have become similar: they are devas, luminous, and maintain the world order, are omniscient, omnipotent, friends of the virtuous and so on. From here evolved the idea of one God, though He is not the God of monotheism: He is just that Power that works behind all gods, a Being who possesses the qualities of all of them, Prajapati, the Father god, who has created all beings as his children. The concept of Rta, the power that maintains the world order, has Prajapati born out of it. Later, with the

Upanishadic thought, Prajapati has been relegated to a secondary place, though sometimes he is also referred to as Brahma of the Hindu Trinity.

There are many Upanishadic compilations, though only twelve or so are considered as authentic Vedic literature. Their emphasis is that the Ultimate Reality is of the Spirit, and everything exists in it and through it. Everything created has this Reality as its integral part; in fact, everything of the creation is just a manifestation of this reality, an aspect of it, a facet, a version maybe; there is nothing outside of it, be it the spirits of the sentient beings or the physical universe; all this is one whole that expands when it is creation, and goes back to the Bindu, the dot, when it is dissolution. And this process of expansion and contraction goes on interminably. This Reality is Sat, Chit, Anand, i.e., Existence (the Reality), Sentience and Bliss. This is the monoism of the Upanishads.

5

Systems of Philosophy

There are six orthodox systems of Indian philosophy, Astika Darshanas, which believe in the authority of the Veda, and are called the Vedic schools. In addition there are three heterodox systems, Nastika Darshana, which do not accept the authority of the Veda and are classified as Avaidic. The Vaidic Schools are:

(a) Nyaya,

(b) Vaisheshika,

(c) Sankhya,

(d) Yoga,

(e) Purva-Mimansa, and

(f) Uttara-Mimansa or Vedanta

The three Avaidic systems are:

(a) Charvaka

(b) Buddhism, and

(c) Jainism

Out of the Vedic systems Purva-Mimansa and Vedanta are strictly Vedic. The other four accept the Vedic Authority only conditionally; they are not dependent upon it, and expound their doctrines without reference to the Veda, i.e., the authors of these systems have given their own interpretations of the Veda which do not necessarily coincide with the commonly held beliefs, and possibly have some dilutions from the pre-Aryan doctrines. While discussing these systems Nyaya and Vaisheshika have been clubbed together for their similarity of views on most points. Likewise Sankhya and Yoga have been put in one group.

The generally accepted period of the Vedic is 1500-1200 BC. A revised view of the Indian as well as the Western scholars puts the period as early as the 2500-2000 BC. The Systems came into being a couple of centuries after the Vedic age, i.e., after a dozen odd classical Upanishads had been compiled. During this time, regarded as the period of prolific intellectual activity, many philosophical treatises were authored, and in an attempt to systematize and preserve them, their Sutras or aphorisms, had been compiled. Each system has its Sutra; in the case of Sankhya, however, the Sutra was compiled much later. Even the non-Vedic Systems have their Sutras.

The Systems have argued their cases on the basis of Parmanas, or the means of knowledge. The empirical Parmanas are perception (Pratyaksha), inference (Anumana) and verbal testimony (Sabada). This last Parmana implies acquisition of knowledge from others, since it is not possible to get the whole of it through personal study or experience. The literature of study could either be revealed, Sruti, like the Veda, or it could be man-made. The latter could be open to errors, depending upon the capability its author to critically analyse the acquired knowledge, and cannot be fully relied upon. The knowledge obtained from Sruti, though more reliable since it has come from inspired minds, could also have faults, since the person to whom it was revealed could possess defective understanding. Therefore, even such a knowledge could be accepted only if it had the approval of learned persons having good knowledge of Sruti, and having personal experience in this field of knowledge. Both Purva-Mimansa and the Vedanta accept this and for verbal testimony have taken the support of the portions of Sruti, which the illumined minds have found to be totally acceptable.

Mimansa means enquiry, and Purva Mimansa means enquiry into the earlier portions of the Veda, while Uttara-Mimansa (Vedanta) means enquiry into its later portions; Uttara means later or subsequent; the widely used expression is Vedanta, for Uttara-Mimansa, and just Mimansa for Purva Mimansa. According to Mimansa, action in the form of ritual, Karma-Kanda, is the means to Moksha, while Shankra in his expositions on Vedanta, has been of the view that the way to Moksha is through knowledge, Gyana. What is Karma?

It visualizes a soul, that it transmigrates and takes on another body after the one in which it is housed, has perished, that the type of body it adopts after its reincarnation depends upon the deeds performed during earlier existence. The soul is eternal but is trapped in matter which assumes name and form depending upon the deeds of the previous lives. The forms of sentience vary between vegetation at the lower end (grass is the lowest) and the human being at the highest end (Brahman male is the highest because he studies Veda and teaches it too).

The term Karma-Kand means ritual action, i.e., recitation of Mantras with the sacrifice as laid down in the Veda and the Brahmanas. The basic assumption in all systems is that deeds cause rebirth and hence suffering. The systems have defined the deeds which do not contribute to rebirth, for it is accepted that all sentient beings have to be active; ceaseless activity being one of the most important attributes of the power behind the creation.

He whose understanding is unattached, who has subdued his self and from whom desire has fled, he attains, through renunciation, the supreme state, transcending all work.

Geeta 49/18

Thus renunciation, absence of desire, are essential to spiritual perfection, which destroys the effect of deeds promoting rebirth. In the highest state of perfection there is complete absence of desire: this is described as the state of Naishkarmya, the state which transcends all work. In fact mere renunciation of the fruits of action is enough, as given in verse 47 of Chapter 2 of Geeta. The verse says:

As being of action your right is only to act but not to the fruits of this action. Therefore, let the fruits of action not be your motive nor should there be in you any attachment to action.

Giving up the fruits of action implies the giving up the ego, for ego makes a person believe that he is the author of the deed, because the soul wrongfully identifies itself with the physical mind-body complex, and that causes the bondage. Thus a deed has to be performed as a duty towards the Creator, a sacrifice, and not an achievement of the mind-body complex. Thus a deed is performed implementing the designs of God; mere renunciation of the fruits of action is not enough.

The other aspect to which the systems have devoted attention is Moksha, liberation from Samsara, the birth-death cycle. For Samsara is sorrow: Sarvam Dukham—all misery, as Buddha observed. This sorrow, however, is not the relative sorrow that human beings experience alongside the relative pleasure or happiness. In fact, there cannot be experience of pleasure unless there has been an experience of pain. A state of continuous pleasure ceases to be pleasure; it possibly becomes a monotonous continuum. All pleasure have roots in pain. So, the systems believe that the entire life of the soul in the body, as conditioned by the mind, is of sorrow. This is because of the bondage. Freedom means where there would be no further embodiment of the soul, a state when body will no longer condition it. In this state it is all bliss. This freedom is variously called Moksha, Mukti, Kaivalya, Nirvana.

Nyaya-Vaisheshika

Vaisheshika system is based on the earlier non-Vedic systems, some aspects of which, particularly regarding Dharma, were accepted by the Vedic authority; hence, it became Vaidica. Its views are very similar to Nyaya and is considered along with it. Author of Nyaya Sutra is Gautama and that of the Vaisheshika is Kanada. Nyaya is based on logic and dialectics. Together the systems believe that there is no identity between the material cause and its effect. This they call as the theory of new beginning, Arambhavada. The effect is not pre-existent in the cause, like, for example, a weaver weaves from threads, but once the cloth has come into existence it ceases to be threads, or potters wares cease to be clay from which the potter makes them. The universe comes into being through the interaction of matter, time and space; all the three are independent entities. Matter comprises Akaasha (space), Prithvi (earth), Vayu (air), Apah (water) and Agni (fire or heat). Except space, all the rest are made up of atoms, and different combinations of these atoms produce different objects, like hills, trees, and so on. Akaash is infinite and all pervading, a substratum of the quality of sound. Time is also infinite. The physical universe, thus, comprises an infinite number of atoms, or whatever is the smallest particle of matter which cannot be further subdivided or reduced in size, of air, water, fire, and of two pervasive entities of time and space. Though ordinarily Akaasha should mean space but its philosophic connotation is somewhat mysterious; it is perhaps the equivalent of another mysterious entity called ether. It is often identified with Brahma, and can be regarded as another infinite entity making up the physical universe. Atoms are indestructible and are different for different elements, though in same element there is difference in atoms; but qualitatively they are alike. In all cases they are indeterminate and above perception by the senses. The difference in the atoms of different elements is based on their qualitative nature: air has only the quality of touch; fire of touch and colour; water of touch, colour and taste, and earth has smell in addition to touch, colour and taste. One quality of each element is considered to be its principal quality, Vishesh Guna; air has touch, fire has colour, water taste, and earth smell, Sound belongs to Akaasha. God is not considered to be the material cause of the creation of the universe, but only the efficient cause. The force that causes the manifestation of the physical universe by the interaction of atoms and the infinite entities is Adrshta, the unseen potency, and the power that guides the unseen potency is God. In other words, just like a potter makes pots out of clay, God make the universe out of the pre-existing atoms. The constituents of the world, the atoms and the infinite pervasive entities have not been made by any agency; they have always been there, and, therefore, the question as to who made them, or whether they will cease to exist at the time of dissolution, is just not relevant: they are eternal. God is like potter; the clay has always been there.

The combinations of atoms produce binaries and triads—they could be called molecules—and at a certain stage there is interaction between molecules of different elements, and thus starts the process of creation of the universe. At the end of the cycle the process is reversed till finally the atoms are separated into individual entities, in which state they remain till the start of the next cycle. God does not create the atoms; they are eternal like Him. He only organizes them into visible universe. In support of the view that there is the existence God, the systems say that there has to be a Being to bring this vast and diversified universe into existence, and from the evidence of the design and the purpose and the method of the working of the universe, it is clear that God, the efficient cause of the creation, is not only a prescient and a just Being, but also of infinite wisdom and power. The variety in creation is attributed to the past deeds, and the purpose is to afford the opportunity to reap the fruits of those deeds, Karmas, and make available to the human beings the occasion to secure release from the birth-death cycle.

The next important element in the creation is self. It is the soul, Atman, plus Manas, (heart, mind, intellect). The souls also, like the atoms and the infinite entities, (time and space) are eternal. They acquire knowledge, feeling and volition (psychic capability) through their association with Manas; this is their characteristic, i.e., they have the vulnerability to get trapped by Manas. Individually and collectively both the soul and Manas are non-spiritual. The self with its inbuilt physical element, experiences only through the physical organs it possesses at the time of the experience. Selves are not identical, and this difference shows in the circumstances of the living beings. Even after release the selves maintain their distinctions, like the atoms; each of them has its own distinctive Manas, which stays with it till it has secured release. Manas is atomic, but does not produce new products. Because of its association with Manas (except during deep sleep) self acquires knowledge and that generates feelings of love, hate, pleasure, pain and volition. These feelings are specific to the self like colour to fire or touch to water. To these are added Dharma (moral merit) and Adharma, (morally incorrect activity). These are not felt directly like love, hate etc., but are inferred from the effects, like the pleasure and pain they cause in keeping with the Karma doctrine. (For good deeds the feeling shall be of pleasure and vice versa for bad deeds). Love, hate etc. are perceived through Manas only. But this knowledge cannot reveal itself and needs another kind of knowledge for this purpose. This is called after-knowledge. In any case knowledge is not the essence of the self. It comes into being (existence) when certain external factors—all non-spiritual—cooperate. Like God, self also has infinite bliss or happiness. The systems are pretty close to the concept of materialism.

The things are of two types: (a) Derived, which are mere aggregates of atoms, a variety in objects, and (b) new creations, like the weavers cloth woven out of threads: a totally new and different thing has been created out of the parts which were threads, and this new creation exhibits totally different features. The causation is thus creative. The system enunciates two theories here, that of new beginning, Arambh-vada, and that of the effect not being pre-existent in the cause before it comes to be produced, called Asatkarya-vada. But the cloth cannot be woven by, let us say, mere juxtapositioning of bamboo sticks and yarn. The mutual relationship between the threads is intimate, Samvaya or closeness, while for bamboo sticks and yarn it is a case of just conjunction, Samyoga. It is Vishesha or quality of each atom that will decide whether any two or more will combine to form a new substance.

The movement can be effected only by atomic and finite objects—which is what action means in this system. All-pervading primal entities cannot move, for they have already filled up whatever space there was, their spread is infinite. Movement of other things is initiated only by sentient beings; by themselves they just cannot move. Movement like that of wind can be given as having been caused by some supernatural agency. Since the atoms cannot move by themselves, the creation of the universe requires a competent, conscious agency to initiate movement in them; this is the cosmological argument in support of the existence of God; the other is the universality of the belief in Him, i.e., He is there because it is universally believed that He is there. Substance, quality, action, Samyoga and Vishesha are five of the six positive categories of the system. Samyoga is one and eternal, Visheshas are many but also eternal, characterizing eternal things like atoms of the same class, or selves, which cannot otherwise be distinguished.

The sixth positive category is the 'Universals', Samanya. The system believes that the eternal substances, like the four elements, selves and Manas form the basis of the universe. Add to these many finite objects derived from the four elements, and we get fundamental and derived objects each of which possesses certain characterized features which provide shape and size to the object like a ball, knife or earth or water atoms or selves. These characterized features which provide shape etc., to the objects, like a ball etc., are the universals. They are considered to be real and eternal, and like atoms and the selves, are the fundamental aspects of the universe. They characterize not only substances, but also action and quantities. For example, a particular shape, or colour, seen in many objects is not just one thing but many, as many as the objects in which these characteristics are seen, though all of the share the distinguishing feature, colour or shape; this characteristic is eternal and unchangeable. Samvaya and Vishesha have no universals. The means of cognizing universals is perception where corresponding particulars are perceptible, or it may be inference or other testimony. The system also accepts one negative category called 'non-existence', Ahava. But it is not absolute nothing. A thing not of one particular shape just means it is not of that shape—it may have some other shape. Absolute nothing is just not within human thought and is a false concept.

Non-existence can involve a reference to time, suggesting a thing has already happened, or is likely to happen in the future, with reference to a particular moment in time, mutual exclusiveness, like we say a bowl is not a plate, this last aspect is eternal. The cognizance of the eternal is through perception where it correlate is perceptible, and in other cases it is either inference or verbal testimony. For example, absence of an item can be perceived when we do not find it where we expected it to be, but absence of a thing like germ can known only from the information given by another person.

Self acquires knowledge through Manas which is in contact with the objects about which knowledge is being acquired through the sensory organs. But in a case where existence of fire is being inferred from the past presence of smoke, it is the experience which comes into play. Perception is what enables the senses to know and then pass the information to Manas where it gets transformed into knowledge for the self. There is an involved argument to illustrate how perception can err, like, for example, mistaking a length of rope for a snake. The error is attributed to some past experience where an individual has actually seen a snake. Thus, a snake is a fact, though it is not a fact for this situation of the rope. The conclusion is that the basis of all error is objective, and error precipitates when some experience of the past, or the present, gets transferred to a situation under examination.

For the validity of knowledge, the system believes that truth or otherwise of all knowledge should be ascertained by appropriate tests, unlike some other schools which believe that all knowledge is correct, and only when there is doubt is there need for verification. The system emphasizes the cognitive capabilities of the means of knowledge, Parmanas. Error means ignorance of the true character of the object, hence the need for validation by appropriate means. Vaisheshika accepts only two Parmanas, namely perception and inference, while Nyaya accepts two more, being verbal testimony and comparison.

(a) Perception (Pratyaksha)

This has already been broadly covered. The only addition is 'transcendental' perception, which can be achieved only by mystics or Yogins and covers such diverse subjects as selves, atoms, moral merit (Dharma). Mystics develop capability to perceive super-sensuous entities through their mystical powers; this is developed with moral purity and meditation.

(b) Inference (Anuman)

Fire can be inferred from smoke. This is an inference which will benefit an observer. But when it comes to satisfy another person regarding the incidence of fire deduced from seeing smoke, the information has to be put across logically. But information by speech is not the main element that convinces the other person. The language puts a thought in his mind, and it is this thought that eventually makes him accept or reject the inference. This method of deriving an inference is accepted by this system.

(c) Verbal Testimony (Shabada)

Only Nyaya system accepts this Parmana. It traces it to the omniscience of God and views Him as its author. Veda too has come from God in the form of Shabada; its authority, therefore, is unassailable. But the system extends this means of knowledge to secular matters as well, like the testimony of a trustworthy person who knows the truth and communicates it correctly, though this kind of testimony cannot have the same authority as that of the Veda, for obvious reasons.

In essence Nyaya-Vaisheshika accepts God who with the help of the 'unseen potency' (Adrshta) puts eternal elements comprising the atoms, and the infinite pervasive entities and the non-spiritual selves, together to create the world after his design. To begin with atoms combine to form binaries and triads and then the universals give shape, size, numbers and movement. At the end of the cycle the process is reversed and dissolution takes place. Self experiences through the Manas which is in contact with the sensory organs which communicate the knowledge to it.

The systems have worked out the procedure to ascertain the truth closely and accurately regarding the coming of the world and its final destination, and the role of the sentient beings in this and have suggested that the essential requirement for a human being is to secure release from the cycle of rebirth, and thus, from misery. The emphasis is on misery, and deliverance from it. According to some systems, this state of freedom has inbuilt bliss. Gautama, the author of Nyaya Sutra is of the view that bliss cannot be experienced unless it preceded by pain. Moksha, according to him is achieved after the self has departed from the physical body, and in this state there is no pain, pleasure, thought, feeling or will. So how is bliss visualised. If it is a state of eternal happiness, then that brings in comparison which could be only with unhappiness; unless unhappiness has been experienced it is not possible to make out happiness. But if it is something in built in the state of perfect repose, then it is a different matter for that kind of bliss cannot be conceptualized by the human mind. Nyaya visualises a kind of a repose as it exists, let us say, in a rock, a kind of a repose as it exists, let us say, in a rock, a state in which every part of the subject is bereft of any trace of animation; that, according to this system, would be the state of the self on being delivered. However, some systems believe that the perfect state of repose for the self is no other than the state of absolute bliss. This is not like the happiness of the sentient beings on this earth which comes only after pain and misery have been experienced. Heavenly repose is different. It is perfect peace, which in effect is perfect bliss. The system accepts perfect repose, but not the aspect of bliss inbuilt in it.

Mention has been made of terms like Parmana, Vishesh-Guna, Samvaya, Samyoga, Samanya, Universals and so on. It is not within the scope of this work to dwell upon these terms and to show how these have been used to develop this branch of philosophy. The idea is to show that the theory has taken a number of factors into account and examined the issues from many angles before arriving at the conclusions.

According to the system, the cause of evils is the association of the self with the body-mind complex, and this association has been brought about by the merits and the demerits gathered by the self during the past lives. At death the physical body gets destroyed, but Manas, being eternal, remains connected with the self and leaves it only after the latter has secured freedom. Merit or demerit is acquired by the deeds depending upon whether they can be classified as Dharmic or otherwise. In some areas the concept of Dharma or Adharma is purely moral, but on the authority of the Veda, the system classifies the deeds as those which are commended (Dharmic) or condemned (Adharmic).

The cause of bondage (Sansara) is attachment (Moha), which breeds desire and ego, and hatred and aversion; love has a strong element of self interest. Therefore, to secure freedom, detachment has to be cultivated, and there has to be intense moral training to overcome ego and selfishness. Simultaneously there has to study of the Vedic literature, and a lot of reflection to pursue the philosophical ideal. In the final stage it is meditation and Yoga to get the direct experience and banish all ignorance and realize the ultimate truth.

Sankhya-Yoga

These two philosophic systems are considered together because their broad metaphysical views and concepts of ideal life are similar. They do, however, differ in their approach to realizing the goal of Moksha. While Sankhya emphasizes the role of knowledge and reflection, Yoga lays stress on meditation. The author of Sankhya is Kapila, and Yoga, Patanjali, not the grammarian of the second century BC. In importance the doctrines are next only to Vedanta. These appear to be based on the Upanishadic thought, though some scholars believe them to be totally of independent origin. Not much background literature is available about Sankhya; Ishvara Krishna's work on this is of 5th century AD, while Sankhya Sutra was compiled as late as 14th century AD.

The arguments and conclusions put forth by the systems are based on logic and reasoning and are not given as revelations. The systems regard both matter and spirit as real and accept the plurality of the selves, whom they term as Purushas. They believe the universe originates from a single, all-pervasive substance, Prakriti, the primordial matter, and evolves through transformations within this substance; it is not creation as such. Causation is just a transformation of what was latent into what becomes visible. In other words, unlike Nyaya-Vaisheshika, the view here is that effect is always there though in a potential form and becomes visible when the conditions like the efficient cause, like the weaver in the case of cloth, get into action. This is the doctrine of 'the pre-existent effect' (Sat-Karya-Vad). Evolution is change of form and not change of place as postulated by Nyaya-Vaisheshika: the latter thought would imply involvement of time and space, the infinite pervasive entities, in the process of evolution.

It is not possible to perceive Prakriti; it can only be inferred, like atoms in Nyaya Vaisheshika. According to Veda, it is devoid of all attributes, but has an eternal existence with the potential material causality as its only characteristic. In its existence it is eternally real, but when it is non-manifested and devoid of name and form it could appear as unreal. It has three Gunas (qualities) as its constituents, being: Sattava (goodness, purity), Rajas (action, activity) and Tamas (inertia, that which offers resistance). These have no beginning and are eternal like the former. Although Gunas may be referred to as qualities, but in actual fact these are constituents which possess certain characteristics. During the state of no creation the three Gunas are in a state of equipoise, and though somewhat antagonistic in their nature towards one another, can and do act in concert, and though essentially distinct in their nature, they are mutually interdependent. This prevents their mutual separation ever, and, thus, break up of Prakriti by such a separation. However, Prakriti just not these three qualities. It is much more, and while it is dependent on them, they are also equally dependent upon it; dependence is mutual. The evolution emerges from these Gunas; i.e., the Gunas cause the change of form and create the diversity in things after Prakriti gets into creation mode. In this mode the equipoise of Gunas gets disturbed and this causes the transformation of the latent into the manifest diversity. Unlike the Nyaya-Vaisheshika, the Sankhya system believes that, as stated above, effect is not something different from the cause; it is the cause only that gets transformed into effect. This is the theory of transformation (Pariniamvada), which in effect is the same as Sat-Karya-Vad. Prakriti in this system is not visualized as a static entity, but a dynamic force which does not need any other power to make it evolve into this universe. Thus God has been done away with; Prakriti evolves on its own and produces the diverse universe. Diversity is caused by the varying proportions in which Gunas enter into the make up of the things created or manifested. Prakriti is changing continuously, and as stated, is all pervasive and complex, forever in agitation, never static. In its creation process the need for the presence of an intelligent being or beings is met by the individual souls, Purusha (s). Prakriti evolves in their presence. All things born out of Prakriti have the three Gunas ingrained into them, and these gunas, like Prakriti, are complex and continually changing. The fact that the three qualities have the capability to operate in concert, shows that the universe is an orderly whole and there is no contradiction in it, though each of these qualities may possess ingredients which may be hostile to some ingredients in other qualities.

Every period of evolution (Shristi) is followed by a period of dissolution (Pralaya) when the entire diversity of the universe, caused by the Gunas, becomes latent and comes to rest in Prakriti; these cycles of creation and dissolution are endless. In the state of dissolution too Prakriti is not still; to stay in agitation, in motion, is its one essential characteristics. In this state the Gunas, instead of acting on one another, because of loss of equipoise, now regain it, and reproduce only within themselves; during the state of imbalance they generate heterogeneous transformations resulting in visible universe. The belief in Nyaya-Visheshika is that matter has no activity beyond what has been communicated to it from outside.

Prakriti produces three kinds of substances—firstly, to adjust to the needs of Purusas or selves, it evolves the organs of thinking (Mahat), which in turn produces ego (Ahamkara), the feeling of individuality in the self. Then comes the mind (Manas), which has the five sensory organs for hearing, sight, smell, touch and taste, and five motor organs of speech, handling, walking, evacuation and reproduction. Then there are subtle elements of sound, colour, touch, taste and smell and these combine to produce gross elements: sound from akaasha, air from akaasha and touch, fire from akaasha, touch and colour, and water from these three and taste, and from these four and smell there is earth. Akaasha, thus, is characterized by sound, and air by touch and sound, fire by these two and colour, water by these three and taste, and earth by these four plus smell. Nyaya-Vaisheshika does not recognise division of elements into subtle and gross. Sankhya system visualizes continuous evolution, starting from intellect and evolving into things that ultimately form the universe.

Gross elements are the ones that get transformed into things, like rocks, trees and such like natural objects. But these objects do not produce any new category of items which might contribute to further evolution. They only interact with one another, and also with subtle elements and Manas or mind, and intellect, and make their contribution to the variety which is the hallmark of creation. But otherwise they are at the lowest rung of evolution; beyond them there is no evolution, e.g., intellect will not turn into egoism, or sound into Akaasha. Things constituted out of the gross elements do not last throughout a cycle of creation; once they have run out their life they just break up into constituents and are not reduced further. The subtle elements and other evolutes, on the other hand, last throughout the cycle and disintegrate only at its termination. Manas, the sensory and motor organs have mostly the Sattava aspect of the ego, while the subtle and the gross elements, the Tamas aspect. Rajas cooperates both with Sattava and Tamas.

By itself the spirit, or the self, is passive and unable to have any knowledge; it acquires knowledge through Manas or mind, ego and intellect; collectively they are called the internal or the psychical organ. The constituents of the organ receive impressions from outside and respond to them. In this they are assisted by the sensory and motor organs. In other words the internal organ and the total nervous system, both psychical entities, operate together to impart experience to the self. This constitutes the 'subtle body' which, less the sensory and the motor organs (which perish with the gross body at the time of death) stays with the self throughout the cycles of rebirths and cast off only after the self has stained the freedom. The gross body, constituted as it is from gross elements, perishes at death and disintegrates and has nothing further to do with the self or the subtle body. Thus, in this system apart from the self, everything else that makes up the universe is materialistic, a manifestation of Prakriti, which is primordial matter.

The doctrine allots independent and equal status to Prakriti and Purusha. While the existence of Purusha (self) has been established on the basis of logic and reasoning, the existence of Prakriti is postulated on the principle that effect presupposes a material cause. There are complex and tedious arguments in support of this contention; this is beyond the scope of this work. The selves are believed to be many while Prakriti is just one; this is the doctrine of pluralism. The plurality of the selves is proved by the difference in the temperaments of the sentient beings, though this difference is restricted only to that in which the selves and the primordial matter appear, duly integrated in their Sansaric or worldly manifestation. Otherwise in their liberated state there is no difference between the different selves. Nyaya-Vaisheshika stipulates that each self has distinguishing peculiarity of its own.

Purusha is a simple, non-dynamic entity (Prakriti is dynamic), and does not have the capability to know or will anything, unless assisted by the internal organ (Manas, Ego and Intellect). It is a mere onlooker, the one to taste whatever knowledge or experience is passed on to it; it is not an agent of precipitate action. But it is the essence of sentience though its psychic life springs from its association with the evolutes of Prakriti (which make up the internal organ). Since internal organ activates mental life, it is dominated by Sattava qualities; most things of the material world, as well as a large portion of the human body, have Tamas predomination. Prakriti evolves for the selves, for the benefit of the sentient beings, and self and Prakriti operate in unison most of the time; the fact of their coming together is verified by the day to day experience of every individual. But the consciousness is not a product of matter—it is considered by the materialistic schools like Charvaka, something through which the spirit manifests itself Purusha is spirit in its pure, unadulterated form. But in the empirical sense is a contaminant of Karmas. Therefore, it is not passive like the Purusha, but is active and reacts to external objects, depending upon the limitations imposed upon it by the past Karmas; i.e., the universe is richer than what is perceived by the self, because the latter cannot sense the full richness on account of its limitations. When the path of Dharma has been followed and the human weaknesses have been totally banished, and delivery from the cumulative effects of the past Karmas has been secured, the self begins to shine like the Purusha and freedom from the bonds of Prakriti is secured even though the person still has a balance of life to live through. Thus, the character of a person and his perception capabilities depend on the hold the

Prakriti has on the self on account of the past deeds. For this reason no two persons can be identical in character, intellect, perception and so on. However, the visible universe is common to all and is real in its own way, and to that extent, at the physical or visible level there is not much difference amongst individuals. But when it comes to non-physical, emotional or intellectual issues, there are prejudices because of differences in personalities which are conditioned by the deeds of past lives; these differences breed conflicts within the same person at different times, or different persons at the same time.

It is the knowledge of truth (which is intuitive and based on synthesis and is not so much a result of physical experience), that makes a person identify Prakriti and see it is different from Purusha. It helps him to identify the empirical self, and then the Purusha appears in its own lustrous self. This is Release. Thus the knowledge has to first identify Prakriti, and then the empirical self, and once this has happened, the pure radiant form of Purusha comes into comprehension. Attainment of this truth is the goal of life, and belief is that Prakriti is ever helping the individual in attaining this goal, for, after all, the reason for Prakriti's evolution is to fulfill Purusha's purpose. It takes form and structure in keeping with the need of the self, e.g., eyes see because it is necessary for Purusha to see, and not just because the organ has the capability.

The experience of knowledge is temporal as well as eternal. The former is through common worldly or secular values (Bhoga) falling under Arth (acquisition of wealth, and Kama (enjoyment of pleasures), while the latter comes through self realization or escape from Prakriti, under the head of Dharma (religious and moral merit) and Moksha, the final release from Prakriti-Apavarga. It implies that the way to the goal is through worldly life; the duration depends on the moral and intellectual level of each person. Thus, man turns to the way of spiritual freedom after he has learnt of the futility of secular values.

Knowledge is the key to identify Prakriti and realize its distinctive existence vis-a-vis the Purusha. This knowledge can be direct, which is not likely to be much use when the quest is for the metaphysical entities like the Purusha or Prakriti. The system accepts the knowledge acquired through the psychic perceptions. It accepts three Parmanas, namely, perception, inference and verbal testimony. There are two types of reasoning which the Indian philosophic systems recognize, being (a) syllogistic, like inferring fire from smoke, and (b) analogical—deducting the existence of a potter from the presence of an earthen jar; a good jar with intricate and delicate work proves the existence of a competent potter. Likewise the world, assuming it to be an effect, is brought into existence by a competent force, Purushas, or, since they are identical in their pure, radiant forms, collectively they can be taken as one force, i.e., Purusha. The other way to look at it is to visualize Purushas collectively as one sea of consciousness from where individual Purushas, as constituents of this force, depart to mingle with Prakriti to effect creation. This is an inference based on likeness. Since the inference is about transcendental matters, the Vedantins feel such reasoning can give only probability and not certainty.

Like in Nyaya-Vaisheshika, in this system also the goal is to secure release from Prakriti, attain Kaivalya, solitude, detachment, the state of supreme freedom. And the way to achieve this also is the same as in other system: cultivate detachment, acquire knowledge of the ultimate truth under proper guidance, and then reflect upon it and practise meditation. In essence Sankhya covers the theoretical details of the system while Yoga deals with the practical side of it. In the Upanishadic expositions Yoga unites the self with the creator, but this system which does not recognize any absolute self, leads to where the individual self separates or extricates from the hold of Prakriti and comes to be on its own, be by itself. The system recommends an eightfold path of discipline, which includes (i) self restraint, (ii) observe Dharma, (iii) practice the correct posture for meditation, (iv) regulation of breath, (v) withdrawal of senses and cultivation of detachment, (vi) steadying the mind, (vii) contemplation, and (viii) meditative trance (Samadhi). This takes an individual to a broader vision which finally brings freedom.

Under self restraint and observing Dharma the systems cultivate discipline so necessary for yogic training. To begin with the focus is on attaining physical and mental goodness and purity as distinct from truth. There has to be purity of thought and deed, contentment, right aspiration, study of philosophic texts, and devotion to the power which is the cause of all creation. It is not the God of the Upanishads, but a superior Purusha of the Yoga system, or a collective of the spirits or Purushas, the sea of consciousness, or a combine of Prakriti and Purushas: the power the causes creation and sustains it. Again there has to be no cause for injury to others, and always speaking the truth and not lies, and no stealing and having possessions, and there has to be celibacy. These are restrains, meant to rid of ego which is the cause of much evil, and awaken spiritual will to develop impersonal attitude. This is lower stage (apara) of detachment; higher (para) detachment is about the same as enlightenment.

Once the spiritual will has been awakened, the person is ready to practise posture, regulation of breath, withdrawal of senses, and control of mind by controlling physical posture. The next three stages, i.e., steadying of the mind, contemplation and meditative trance (Samadhi), lead to revelation of truth-bearing knowledge. During the Samadhi stage the desired knowledge is attained: initially the experience is that self and Prakriti are two different entities, but eventually this feeling is transcended and the person becomes oblivious of the world around, and then even his own existence, and is face to face with the effulgence of untainted Purusha. The operations of the internal organ are now suspended and the spirit returns to its own pure form. The person practicing self discipline and living in total (para) detachment has now secured release and become Jivanmukta or liberated, during his lifetime itself.

God is integral to the doctrine of Sankhya. Prakriti, the primordial matter, is self creating, and the fact that the creation is orderly and follows a pattern or design, is because it creates for and adjusts to the needs of Purusha. Thus, the orderliness and design get evolved for the self; the doctrine denies any conscious designer. Yoga, however, accepts God (Ishvara), but not of the Upanishads. He is visualized as a super Purusha, eternal and omniscient, but not all-comprehensive. He is not the God of the

Nyaya-Vaisheshika, cause of a creation, but is unique and perfect, and the liberated Purushas do not match his greatness. Disciplines like posture, regulation, right upto meditative trance, are designed to effect complete surrender to this God. He is not visualized as the great God of the Upanishads, but he great enough for the sentient beings. According to Patanjali (of Yoga), mere devotion (Bhagti) to God can secure freedom; in His abundant mercy He grants the wishes of his devotees. This path of release is easier than that of knowledge. But Sankhya considers knowledge of the ultimate truth as important. The belief in a supreme God is not organic to the doctrine.

Prakriti secures secular values, like wealth (Artha) or pleasures of the senses (Kama), or it secures self realisation through moral merit (Dharma) or final release (Moksha). It adjusts its activity differently to meet the needs of different Purushas. For this it requires mental or spiritual capability, which could be provided by Purushas, but these are conceived as totally passive and external to Prakriti. Thus, in this concept insentient Prakriti exercises choice like it is done by beings in possession of sentience. May be this comes about under the power of Dharma, the law, which is the basis of all order and which is the essential ingredient of Prakriti. This suggests a spiritual content in the inert Prakriti which content completely guides from within its evolutionary course. The doctrine, like the Upanishads, believes, that the main aim of life is to secure freedom from the cycle of rebirth, that a person pursues lower values initially because of the ignorance of the ultimate truth. Purusha and Prakriti have been considered separately. Intellect (Mahat) and ego (ahankara) have been given as evolutes of Prakriti. As cosmic entities they represent the psychic organs of the universal self, though by itself the psychic organ is a product of Prakriti. The thought that spiritual content is latent in Prakriti has been dropped from the doctrine, possibly after it had been freed from the influence of the Upanishads.

Dharma gives Prakriti the capability to provide secular values to the self, or the values which lead to self realization. Take the insentient planet earth. Its substances, singly or collectively, react in certain predetermined patterns to ensure its continued functional efficacy, e.g., when floods are eroding the soil the damage is contained by way the silting takes place. The blowing winds, the flowing waters, the shifting sands; all these are continually engaged in the process of restoring the balance, equilibrium. The activity is triggered under the effect of Dharma, the law.

The choice to bestow secular values to self gets actuated on the basis of the needs of the psychic self, whether the self is ready for it. This, no doubt, is conditioned by the deeds of the past lives, and the depth of desire risen in the present life, and the training the person has received in this direction.

It could be that originally the doctrine was totally naturalistic and the spiritual element was brought in later to match with other doctrines. Yoga has its origin in the Indus Civilisation—it could be of even earlier times. It being Yoga based suggests that it could have developed during pre-Aryan times, and the Aryan thinkers adopted it after appropriate modifications. The Sankhya-Yoga systems believe that Prakriti took care of the entire evolutionary process and all else that got the universe going and made it functional. For the sentient life the Purushas played their part. But Prakriti is self evolving and self regulating and needs no outside assistance.

Purva-Mimansa

Mimansa means enquiry and Purva refers to the earlier portion of the Veda which deals with rituals (Karma-Kand). The system is thus based on the instructions contained in the earlier part of the Veda, and originated during the Brahmana period; Brahmana means considered opinion of a priest of recognized authority. The works were systematised in Kalpa Sutras, which means aphorisms dealing with Vedic rituals. The primary source of the system is Jaimini's Sutra compiled 300-200 BC. It is the biggest philosophical work of its time, and the oldest. The earliest known commentary on this is from Sabara Svamin (400 AD), which has been explained in two different ways by Kumarila Bhatta and Prabhakara. Their works were compiled around 700 AD and have given rise to two schools, which though agreeing on fundamentals, have differences in smaller detail. Like Nyaya-Vaisheshika the systems believe in the plurality of souls and the multiplicity of the fundamental elements comprising the physical universe, i.e., the ultimate reality is many and not one. Originally the system gave heavenly happiness as the goal of the human endeavour; this, it was believed, would accumulate merit during life time, and secure a place in heaven after death. Belief was that if the rituals as given in the Veda were performed correctly, then the accumulated merit would get heaven for the soul. Later, after the theory of rebirth on the basis of Karmas was accepted, the attainment of heaven ceased to be considered as feasible on the basis of the Vedic rituals; such an attainment was considered as temporary, only for the duration for which the accumulated merit lasted; the idea is of the later Brahmana period when the idea of rebirth had been accepted; this idea got consolidated during the Upanishadic period. It was stressed that the final goal of life had to be freedom from the cycle of rebirth, Sansara, and that this could be achieved by correctly performing the Vedic rituals.

This system classifies the Karmas (of the Karma-Kand, the Vedic rituals) into different categories, being (a) Kamya, the optional rituals performed to attain heaven; the Karmas for this task are called Kamya-Vidhis; they are also called Jyotishtoma sacrifices; and (b) the Nitya-Karmas, the obligatory rites; their texts are called Nitya Vidhis. These rites, like regular prayers in precise texts and performed at the prescribed times; these are compulsory; the non-performance would attract demerit. Then there are the Naimittika-Karmas, occasional rites, which are performed during specified occasions, like birth, death, marriage and so on; these are obligatory and have to be performed as laid down; their non-performance would attract demerit as well. Finally, there are the Pratishidha-Kamyas, the prohibited acts, the performance of which would attract only demerit.

The system believes that if the deeds performed are good then one is born in good circumstances, in human form maybe, but bad deeds cause birth amidst lower species, like animals or vegetation. But life, brought about by birth, is the germ of all suffering, no matter whether it is of a human being, or a beast, or vegetation. For absolute freedom there should be no Karmas, which means that the Karmas have to be such as would leave no residue which might cause rebirth; it is accepted that Karma (activity) is the essence of creation and cannot be avoided.

The system believes that state of no-Karma can be achieved by following the Vedic injunctions regarding the different categories of Karmas. By following the Karmya-Vidhi and performing the optional rites, merit is gained. But this will cause rebirth. The system suggests that such actions can be performed if the requirement is for heaven or for worldly gains like getting rain for the crops by performing Kariri sacrifice, for getting a son through Putra-Kameshti sacrifice, or conquest of territory by performing Ashvamedha. Through optional rites reward is secured, but there is the risk of rebirth. Therefore such rites are best avoided.

Prohibited deeds, Pratishiddha-karmas, definitely cause re-birth and have to be avoided. The Nitya and Naimittika-karmas do not afford merit but their non-performance causes demerit. Therefore, obligatory and occasional rites have to be performed meticulously to the very end of life in order to avoid rebirth. The way to the final release is through performing Vedic rituals. The expression Karma here means Karma-Kand, performance of Vedic rituals. It also stands for activity other than Karma-Kand, i.e., general activity during the course of a life time. Both meanings are relevant to this doctrine.

The system covers the whole gamut of the ingredients of creation as covered by the Nyaya-Vaisheshika and recognises all of them, like substance, quality, action, universals and non-existence. But it discards Samavaya and vishesha. It considers the latter as arbitrary assumptions acquired by Nyaya-Vaisheshika to put forth its case. There are differences in the understanding other detail. It does not accept that particles of earth, water, air and fire are super sensible, i.e., beyond the perception of the senses. It believes they are finite, and not atomic. The conclusion by Kumarila is that relationship between these particles and the whole that manifests out of them is like a relation between substance and attribute—the identity in difference: the whole and the parts are absolutely distinct, but distinct while being the same. He also differs regarding the precise magnitude of the ultimate material of the universe.

In respect of self also the viewpoint is similar to that of Nyaya-Vaisheshika, with some minor differences, however. The qualities of the self are similar though Dharma and Adharma are not there. The remaining six qualities, i.e., knowledge, desire, hate, pleasure, pain and volition, are accepted as internally perceivable, as in other two systems. But the knowledge gained through introspection is regarded as inferred and not direct. Unlike the other systems the existence of an omniscient, super excellent God is not accepted; otherwise how do we account for such abundance of misery in the world? This is explained by the past Karmas, and according to Kumarila, if Karmas are the cause even after accepting the existence of God, then it is only the Karmas where full explanation can be sought. Thus, a Creator and cycles of creation and dissolution are not accepted. The physical universe is considered to be without beginning or end, self existent; it was never any different from what it is now; origin, growth, decay are attributes of the things of the universe, but not of the universe itself. The system believes in the selves and the Karmas and lays stress on the ethical order of the universe.

Like Nyaya-Vaisheshika this system also postulates 24 qualities for matter and spirit, but with certain modifications. It omits 'sound'—puts it under 'substance'—and Dharma and Adharma. Of the new qualities one is Shakti, potency, casual power, like burning capability of fire. This power is not visible, but its existence can be inferred from the effect it produces. Kumarila's views on universals too are a little different.

Like Nyaya-Vaisheshika this doctrine too rejects intuitive perception. It accepts six Parmanas, or the means of knowledge, including perception, inference and verbal testimony. The other Parmanas are (a) comparison, (b) presumption; for example, the Veda says the rewards for performance of rituals come in a future life and the Karma doctrine says rewards are reaped by the doer—conclusion: self survives the body, (c) non-apprehension (an-Upalabdhi). Nyaya-Vaisheshika ascribes the knowledge of non-existence to perception and all else to inference. But Kumarila says perception can come through contact with a sensory organ and it is impossible to think of perception when the thing is just not there. Hence the need to think of non-apprehension as a Parmana.

The doctrine has expressed opinion regarding the validity of the Veda, but before that there is an exposition on the nature of knowledge. Nyaya-Vaisheshika suggests that if the practical activity to which the knowledge leads is a success, then that knowledge is valid, not otherwise, i.e., knowledge can be validated only by more knowledge. But this can lead to an unending chain of bits of knowledge, each bit validating the one preceding it. However, there is little requirement for this, for normally one or two tests should suffice, and for things of every day experience no tests are required anyway. Purva-Mimansa states that knowledge by its very nature is valid. Verification becomes necessary only when knowledge has strayed from truth, like, for example, when correct position may not be visible on account of poor light, or some other outside interference, or when an element of contradiction is detectable in one bit of knowledge on account of another bit of knowledge.

The system expresses its view regarding the validity of knowledge contained in the Veda. The view of Nyaya-Vaisheshika is that this knowledge is valid because it is a word of God, but the system does not rule out its being questioned. Kumarila, who does not recognize God as such, has suggested that this knowledge is valid because all knowledge has the aspect of validity built into it. He believes that error at the source is not possible because Veda, not being work of any person, human or divine, has no source. Nor is Veda in conflict with any other knowledge, as it refers only to the super sensuous matter which, in any case, is beyond the reach of human experience. But Veda does contain material of ordinary, mundane experience, and whenever there is conflict between what has been stated in the Veda, and the knowledge gained through personal experience, it is the latter which has to be considered more authentic. It will, however, be seen that if such contradictions are given liberal interpretations, their superficiality will become apparent. The need, therefore, is to interpret the Veda correctly. The aspect of correct interpretation is as important to this system as that of rituals or philosophy. The system believes that the purpose of revelations is to impart correct knowledge regarding Dharma and Moksha, which are two supreme values of life; it, however, mainly concerns itself only with Dharma. In essence its view of the Veda is that (a) it is self existent or eternal, (b) it is concerned with super-sensuous matter, and it has portions which require liberal interpretation.

Kumarila and Prabhakara schools differ in matters of some detail. The latter does not accept non-apprehension as a Parmana, and explains every form of non-existence positively. It accepts the remaining Parmanas and adds four more, making a total of eight. Differences are also there regarding concepts of knowledge, error and truth. There are other points too where the two schools have their own views. But all that is beyond the scope of this work and the inquisitive reader shall have to locate the details elsewhere.

Since the schools do not recognize God, their views on world activity are based on Dharma/Adharma. In general Dharma implies Vedic rites and religious duties, including ethical conduct and activity taken on for the good of others. In the five daily sacrifices (Maha-Yajnas) hospitality towards the guests is also prescribed. Adharma is the opposite. Dharma/Adharma do not produce results directly, but only serve as vehicles. The actions produce unseen effects, invisible potency which abides in the self till appropriate results in terms of pleasure or pain has been produced. According to Kumarila, Veda promises heaven and other pleasant results for those who perform the Vedic rites and rituals. The guidance provided by the Veda is not available from any other source and should, therefore, be valued and followed strictly. Prabhakara, on the other hand, says that to view Dharma as the means to secure heaven or other pleasant results, is to deny what it actually is or what it stands for. Dharma, therefore, has to be followed for its own sake, and not for rich results or for securing heaven; it should not be viewed as a ceremonial act, but an intrinsic value.

Original the goal prescribed by the system was to secure heaven, which later got modified to securing Moksha, absolute freedom from the rebirth cycle. Kumarila's schools believes Moksha is not just freedom from misery; it is positive and unending bliss. But the emphasis is on Karma and not Gyana, self-knowledge, or even Bhagti, devotion. To achieve the ideal, natural impulses have to be purified and selfish inclinations curbed, and social and religious duties performed as taught or implied in the Veda.

Vedanta

The system is also called Uttara-Mimansa, i.e., enquiry into the later portion of the Veda, which are the Upanishads; even amongst the Upanishads the enquiry is directed to the final portions, and the term implies the 'settled conclusions of the Veda taken as whole' : Ved-Anta. It also covers the Bhagwad Gita and the Vishnu Purana, both of which are considered to be amplifying the Upanishadic doctrine. The Sutra which systematised the doctrine is by Badarayana; it is called the Vedanta Sutra. This Sutra, the Upanishads and the Bhagwad Gita, are the three pillars which support this doctrine. The Sutra, aphorisms, is too cryptic and is not clear on many details resulting in many interpretations and viewpoints. However, the schools agree on the eternity of the self, and the need for Gyana, knowledge, to attain Moksha. The principal schools are: Absolutist, which expounds Advaita, non-dualism; it accepts Brahma as the impersonal principal; Shankra was the main exponent of this school; (b) Qualified non-dualism—Vashishtadvaita—the principal exponent is Ramanuja, and (c) Theistic, Dvaita, dualism; accepts Brahma as the personal principal; Madhava is the author of this doctrine.

Different views of the ultimate reality have emerged, primarily because, firstly, the Vedanta Sutra is too cryptic and lends itself to different interpretations, and, secondly, even the Upanishads have not defined in clear terms, the nature of Brahma, the self and the physical universe, and their mutual relationship. Bhartraprapancha, who was about the first person to have written a commentary on the Vedanta Sutra, has postulated that Brahma is one, but that oneness includes variety which has been caused by infinite number of selves included within Brahma and numerous distinctions of the physical universe. This variety which is implicit in Brahma, became explicit at the time of creation. This creation in not a new origination, like making something new or for the first time, but only an articulation of distinctions already subsisting in Brahma. The thought is almost the same as that in Sankhya, except that the evolving principal is not the insentient Prakriti, but sentient and all comprehensive Brahma. The liberated soul is not lost in Brahma but retains its individuality. To achieve liberation a person has to acquire moral and religious merit, essentially to eliminate selfish impulses and develop detachment, and, having achieved this he has to acquire the right detachment and dispel ignorance, Avidya, about the oneness of the ultimate reality. The commentary commends Karma-Kand as the direct means of liberation, almost like Purva-Mimansa; other Vedic schools also emphasise the positive role of Karma, but not this extent.

Shankra, however, did not accept this viewpoint, and so down graded it that it could never again be revived. His Min objection was Brahma, self and the physical universe cannot be identical and different at the same time; the presumption is self-contradictory and, hence, incorrect. According to him, the teaching of the Upanishads is only about the unity, and the stream of thought which talks of the reality of diversity is only at a superficial, something experienced at the initial stages of contemplation. He is an exponent of non-dualism and not of monoism since he accepts the existence of variety; the question of unity would arise only if there is variety in the elements.

Shankra, a great thinker from South India, lived barely for 32 years, and in this time he wrote Bhashya or commentaries on Bhagwad Gita and all the important Upanishads, and the Vedanta Sutra (also called the Brahma Sutra). These Sutras are aphorisms, short sayings which need to be explained or interpreted; they are like paragraph headings. To write commentary on the Vedanta Sutra, Shankra moved to Varanasi in Uttar Pradesh. Shankra travelled extensively and spread his Advaita (non-dualism) Doctrine, and monastic institutions in all the four corners of this country: Sringery in Mysore in the south; Badrinath in the snowy Himalayas in the north, Dwarka on the Arabian Sea in Kathiawar in the west, and Puri on the Bay of Bengal in the east; he visualized the people of this vast land as one nation. And all this he achieved in a short life span of 32 or 33 years. Tradition places Shankra in a period before the birth of Christ, but the according to scholars he was of the late eighth century AD. It has not been possible to pinpoint the time when he lived and worked, but the generally accepted period is 788-820 AD which scholars suggest may be accepted within limits of a 100 years. He was born in a Nambudiri Brahman family of Kaladi village on the west coast of Kerala in South India. His father died when he was still a small boy; he was brought up by his mother. He was a precocious child and learnt fast and sought to renounce the world when he was just eight. At last he turned to philosophy and travelled north to the bank of river Narmada, where he sought the renowned Guru Govinda and received the initial grooming under him.

The basic thought of Shankra's Advaita is that self is not the body, nor Manas (mind), or Ahankar (ego). It is eternal and non-dual; it is the absolute spirit: Tat Tvam Asi, that thou art, i.e., you are Brahma. Only Maya, the cosmic illusion, comes in the way of recognizing this fact. Otherwise this universe is a reflection of Godhood itself. He is the creator and the created, the sole essence. The matter exists not independent of perception; the substances appear real because of the ideas of the mind. Otherwise all that we see is Maya. There no two things in existence. Only the spirit exists and not the matter. The universe is not God, but there is nothing but God in this universe.

Shankras views on Karma are in agreement with other impressions; that Karmas, put the self in the cycle of rebirths, but he does not agree with Purva Mimansa that Karmas can be eliminated simply by performing some rites, or not performing some others. He believes Karmas are caused by ignorance and nascience. These can be eliminated only by eliminating the effect they produce, namely the cycle of rebirths, Sansara. Only knowledge of Brahma, the non-dual self—which is the same as the Atman, the individual self can dispel ignorance, and once that happens, the final truth is realized and freedom attained. In the final truth, the ultimate state of perfection is not something which is created afresh, for if it were so then it would not be eternal, because whatever can be created is prone to destruction. Release cannot be non-eternal; if it is prone to destruction, it would not be much different from Sansara. But even Sansara need not be destroyed, for it is just a false appearance; destruction of ignorance destroys Sansara. In the oft-quoted example of a rope mistaken for a snake, the person taking the rope for snake is distressed and frightened and urgently moves to destroy the danger. But soon he realizes his mistake and feels relieved and happy. Likewise, if the truth about Sansara gets realised through right knowledge happiness is achieved: this state is comparable to freedom, Moksha. When this state is achieved during a life time itself, it is referred to as Jeevan Mukti, (and the person is Jeevan Mukta). According to Advaita, this state of freedom or bliss was in fact never lost, for the very essence of self is bliss, but the self, having got entangled with the body-mind complex (Called Jiva in this state, i.e., the soul in its individuality) becomes confused and ignorant and forgets its real nature and, consequently, plunges into pain and misery. But no sooner does it realise its true nature and the veil of ignorance is lifted, it is in Moksha, freedom, bliss. Jiva, attains this by shedding limitations imposed by the internal organ (mind, intellect, ego) which being of matter is unreal and illusory. But Jiva is not illusory, only the internal organ wrapped around it is. By itself Jiva is Brahma.

According to Shankra, all diversity is illusory, Mithya. Reality Sat has to be eternal, and since only Brahma is eternal. He is the only reality. Non-reality (Asat), is absolute nothing. The physical universe is neither real nor unreal. It is not real because it is not eternal and because it is constantly changing. Born out of Tapas, the heat, or the inner energy, or the spiritual fervour, and Kama (the god of love), or the creative power of desire, it grows from the primordial atom to its full stature, and then undergoes the process of dissolution till it is back in the stage it started from. But it is not unreal (Asat) either, for it has an appearance which cannot be regarded as nonentity, or be classified as absolute nothing. It is a non-permanent appearance which in the flow of time when viewed at a particular instant, has an appearance which is a reality at that particular instant, but the moment it has gone past, it becomes an illusion in relation to that moment of reality: it was but is no longer there. That appearance has been reduced to an illusion: it appeared and then vanished out of sight, for in the next instant what is visible is a totally different form of that momentary phenomenon, impression. In the rope and snake example, for the person undergoing the experience the snake is neither there, nor is it not there. To a certain impression in the mind, which is born out of some experience of the past, it is there, and has impact mentally or psychologically, but on close examination the snake is not there and the person feels relieved and his mind restored to the original state; he has been rid of the feeling of fear. In this situation a complete illusion turns into reality for a while.

But the things of the world though not real ultimately, because of being non-permanent, follow certain patterns which suggest reality. For example, a tree does not grow with its roots in the air, or the pull of gravity always follows prescribed laws. These patterns and laws are for ever applicable, till as long as the universe lasts, and this suggests reality. It is these laws which make Rta and Dharma, which hold the universe together. But the universe itself, being non-eternal, is not a reality. We thus have a situation where a seemingly real thing exists within a non-reality: thus, what appears to be a reality, is in effect a non-reality. This is the situation where reality turns into an allusion in the very next instant. Only Brahma is eternal, Sat, changeless. Prakriti, the primary matter, is unreal, for it is for ever changing. Whatever reality may be ascribed to the manifested universe, it is derived from Brahma; it is not a part of him, but since it is changing constantly, it is Maya, illusion, the primary essence of which is ceaseless change, while that Brahma is changelessness. He transcends all empirical attributes (He cannot be described as this or that, and so on; he is Neti, Neti (not this, not this), and is Nirguna, without features or attributes. How ever for the humanity. He is Saguna, with attributes or qualities, very much related to Maya, although still of the self.

What is true of the part is also true of the whole. Jiva is trammelled by the internal organ; which is the cause of Avidya, nascence or ignorance: the trap is Avidya. In dreamless sleep the self is not involved with Avidya, or the internal organ. But during dreams it is. During waking hours its association is chiefly with the physical body (matter), which is derived from Avidya. In dreamless state the self is in its original, pure form. Likewise Brahma also, when viewed in relation to the created universe, is not absolute consciousness. He is Apara, lower and not Para, the higher power—this latter is eternal, unchanging and the abode of absolute peace, tranquility and bliss and is untouched by Maya. Thus Vishnu, the Para Brahma, lies on the cosmic waters in absolute tranquility and bliss and the myth has it that it is out of His naval that Apara Brahma is born; the latter is, in effect, the active principle and has Maya as an inbuilt part. The manifested universe is the creation of this force, the Apara Brahma. Thus, just as Brahma has Maya, the individual self has the internal organ. In fact the Maya of the Apara Brahma at the level of the individual self is the internal organ; the quality and nature of this would depend upon the Karmas of the different selves. Thus, though Maya is an essential part of Apara Brahma, it is lodged only in pure consciousness, i.e., Para Brahma, and as one view holds it, both Apara Brahma and the Jiva, the individual soul, are reflections of pure consciousness in Avidya and mind respectively. Another view is that reflection of pure consciousness in Maya is Apara Brahma, while its reflection in Avidya is Jiva. Some scholars are, however, not happy with the concept of reflection, for, according to them, the attribute of reflection cannot be assigned to Brahma who is formless. Advantins say that if the redness, which is without form, of a flower, could be reflected from any reflecting medium, Brahma's formlessness could also be, and this could not be an argument against the reflection concept.

Maya is indeterminable. It is not real, and if it were it would not be removable. Yet it is not unreal either, for then it would not serve as the transformative material cause of the universe. Since it is real and unreal at the same time, it would violate the law of contradiction. Likewise it cannot have parts for that would suggest it had a beginning. But its not having parts means it cannot be transformative material cause of the universe; only objects with parts can serve as the cause of the effects. Hence Maya cannot be partless. But it cannot be partless and with parts at the same time, otherwise it will violate the law of contradiction. Thus, Maya is indeterminable.

The Saguna Brahma is the Ishvara, or the God, of the Advantins. The universe as we see it, is dependent upon Brahma; it is not a mental fiction, but is as real as the individual perceiving it. But it is not the ultimate reality. Self, Atman, is the same as Brahma, the essence of self which is the deepest part of our being; it is one with the essence of the universe. The universe cannot exist by itself, it is wholly dependent upon Brahma. The changes in the universe, however, do not affect Brahma. While the universe depends upon Brahma, Brahma depends upon no one. Ignorance, Avidya, affects the self, it is removed once the truth has been realised. But nothing happens to the world when ignorance is removed; only the person's view of it changes. Moksha is not the dissolution of the universe, but only a change of false outlook, Avidya, by wisdom, Vidya.

As for the means to valid knowledge (Parmanas), the system accepts all the six of them, being perception, inference, verbal testimony, comparison, presumption and non-apprehension. Regarding the Veda, unlike Mimansa which believes it to be self existent and eternal, the system accepts its authorship by God, but unlike Naya, which also believes it to have been authored by God, it believes that at Pralaya, the end of each cycle of creation, the Veda too goes, and reappears only at the next cycle. The content of the Veda may thus be taken to be independent of God, but its re-appearance is caused by Him. The belief secures self validity for the Veda.

As in other systems, here too the ultimate aim is to remove sorrow and secure Moksha, freedom from the cycle of rebirths by acquiring knowledge about the truth of the reality. The requirement is to realize that the individual self, which is the inner core of a human being, is Brahma, that the self drifts away from Brahma because of Avidya, ignorance, which is caused by the association of the self with the internal organ (because it forgets its true identity). Self sees it pure and true nature once this ignorance is removed.

However, it is not to be presumed that mere dispelling the ignorance of the Jiva, soul, about its true identity, is all that secures freedom. The knowledge has to be from a learned man, a Guru, and it has to be experienced, and for that certain discipline has to be followed, which include non-killing, cleanliness, correct posture for meditation, control of breath, restraining the senses, learning to fix the mind on meditation, meditation and finally Smadhi, or attaining the stage of super-consciousness. There has to be reflection on whatever is learnt, for unless there is conviction progress cannot be made. But once there are conviction and ardent desire, the person achieves Jeevan-Mukta, i.e., freedom while still living. He rises above the internal organ and is beyond the reach of ego and is full of spontaneous love and after he leaves the world he is finally free. This is achieved in one life or over a number of life times.

As in other systems, here also there are expositions on the elements that constitute the material world, including the sentient beings, and how the gross and the subtle bodies are formed; universals, means of knowledge (Parmanas), valid and invalid knowledge, and result of all the arguments and considerations is the system of the Advaita philosophy.

Vashishtadvaita

The Upanishads have not been categorical in explaining the relationship between Brahma, self and matter. It has been asserted that the self and the physical universe have their identity in Brahma, and yet it has also been stated that Brahma is distinct and supreme. Advaita has tried to get past the problem by stating that self is a part of the whole which is Brahma, and that matter is only appearance, Avidya, the trap where self is ensnared, till it has secured true knowledge and attained freedom. In the year 1100 AD, Ramanuja, a renowned Brahmin from South India (near Chennai), a follower of Vishnu, wrote a commentary on the Vedanta Sutra, entitled Sri-Bhasya. He postulated that relationship between Brahma and self on the one hand and Brahma and matter on the other, is of very intimate nature, and it is not possible for the self or matter to exist without Brahma or vice versa. According to the teachings of the Upanishads, Brahma, and the self, and the physical universe are mutually inseparable, but at the same time they are real and eternal and are totally different from each other, unlike Advaita of Shankra where physical universe is not real, is only a reflection, Maya, and the individual self is a part of the whole which is Brahma. Ramanuja has given the three entities as different, but they are together in a close relationship. The doctrine is referred to as Vashishtadvaita, implying that the physical universe and the individual selves have existence only in the body of Brahma, though these are different from Brahma they have no existence or purpose to serve apart from him. The doctrine as also called qualified non-dualism: one Brahma has two forms, i.e., selves and matter. The concept of matter is almost the same as of Prakriti of Sankhya, except that it is not independent of God, and Satva, Rajas, Tamas are its attributes and not constituents; it is described as the garment of God. According to Sankhya, Prakriti is a dynamic force and does not need another dynamic agency to set in motion the process of evolution; it can evolve on its own. There is thus no need to regard God as the prime mover in the evolutionary process of Prakriti. There is requirement for an intelligent being or beings for the evolution of sentience, and that need is amply fulfilled by the individual selves; Prakriti evolves in their presence. God is out. Ramanuja has also said that Prakriti cannot evolve on its own into such a complex universe which has so much diversity and is so rich in content. There has to be an intelligent being—and not beings—for the becoming of the universe. God, thus, is not only the efficient cause of the universe, as is affirmed in Nyaya-Vaisheshika also. He is the material cause as well; the universe is a transformation of God. The essential difference between the views of Ramanuja and the Sankhya doctrine is that while the former believes universe is a transformation of God, the latter holds it as the transformation of Prakriti. Shankra's Advaita also considers God to be the efficient and material cause of the universe but does not regard it as a transformation of God; transformation implies change and only non-eternal entities change, not God who is eternal. According to this doctrine, universe has to be only an appearance, even though this appearance is only in God.

In Vashishtadvaita salvation is defined as release from limiting barriers imposed by the internal organ. Self cannot be dissolved into God, but the released self has a permanent intuition of him; self continues to retain its identity and individual existence after release.

Doctrine accepts only three Parmanas, viz., perception, inference and verbal testimony and gives equal importance to both sections of the Veda, i.e., the earlier portion relating to ritual and sacrifice, and the latter one which is concerned with Brahma. Its view is that the former deals with the worship of God and the latter with His nature. Shankra also gives equal importance but his view is that the former portion is for those who are trying to acquire Brahma knowledge and the second for those seeking Brahma realization. Vashishtadvaita relies heavily on Puranas for support; advaita also does so but to a lesser degree. In Tat Tvam Asi, that thou art, Tat is for God with the entire universe as His body, and Tvam with the individual self as his body. Individual self is a part of the highest self just as the light issuing from a luminous body, such as fire or sun, is a part of that body, i.e., fire or sun. Although the distinguishing attributes, and the thing distinguished thereby, stand to each other in the relation of part and whole, yet they are different in essential character.

Ramanuja laid stress on devotion as the primary means of securing release, and attaining the world of Narayana (Supreme God as designated by Vaishnavites) and enjoying complete freedom and bliss there. For this a person has to completely surrender to Narayana and have complete faith in his mercy. This has to be done under the guidance of a Guru, for, as stated in the Upanishads, knowledge is the essential, if not the only method of securing release. Alongside, correct posture, control of breath, restraining the senses, reflection on the day's learning, and belief in the correctness of the course adopted, has to be there. This is accompanied by study, learning and reflection, and follows meditation and, finally, direct experience of the ultimate reality. This course is open to every one.

The course of devotion (Bhagti) meant exclusively for higher castes, progresses through the stages Karma and Gyan Yogas. Karma Yoga means performing duties with the best of ability, unmindful of consequences; the duty is performed only to please God. Karma here means more than just performing good deeds and gathering religious and moral merit, or merely performing Vedic rituals and sacrifices. It also implies following Dharma—

performing in keeping with the station in life is Dharma. Thus even a householder can secure liberation. Renunciation, Sanyasa, as advocated in the Upanishads, assuredly secures release, but following the path of Karma Yoga does it equally effectively.

Gyan Yoga is the realization of the true nature of one's self in relation to God and the physical world, and involves meditation in an attitude of complete submission to God. This Yoga is a way to God realization. Bhagti Yoga is constant meditation on God, not in blind faith, but in loving devotion based on highest knowledge. It demolishes ego and the rest of the internal organ, and the soul has a direct vision of God as it own ultimate essence. It cannot be called a direct perception, for operation of sensory organs becomes unnecessary at this stage. It is a unique direct experience.

Doctrine does not recognize Jeevan Mukti, i.e., liberation during the present life itself.

Dvaita

Dvaita is dualism. Madhava (1199-1278) who lived in a village near the coastal town of Udipi in the present state of Karnataka in South India, was its exponent; he has also written commentaries on important Upanishads, the Bhagavad Geeta and the Vedanta Sutra, and has left several other works as well. Like Vashishtadvaita, the doctrine is theistic and Vaishnav in content. God, Narayana of the Vashishtadvaita, is referred to as Vishnu here. It is pluralistic and believes that God, selves and the universe exist permanently and are separate entities, though the latter two are subordinate to God. He directs the universe, is transcendent to it and is immanent in it. He is the ruler of all selves. Self by nature is blissful but gets subjected to pain and suffering because of its association with the material body; this happens due to Karmas. No two selves or two material objects are alike. The doctrine claims the support of the Veda which, being revealed, cannot be inconsistent and should teach the same truth as the Upanishads. The exponents of the doctrine claim that it is as old as the Upanishads and that Madhava was only its exponent.

The doctrine postulates that God is beyond the reach of unaided faculties of man. He is the efficient cause of the world while Prakriti is the material cause, as in the Sankhya doctrine. Everything exists, knows and functions at God's will. To support this it quotes the Upanishadic statement: Sarvam, Khalvidam, Brahma (all this indeed is Brahma). Everything is dependent upon God's Will but nothing is derived from Him; He exists in his own right. Essential characteristics of an eternal entity are eternal, while of a temporal entity are temporal. God possesses all excellencies, but it is not possible to know him even with the aid of revelations, though, as in Advaita, He is not beyond the reach of the mind. He is above Sattav, Rajas, Tamas which are products of Prakriti (and not its attributes as in Vashishtadvaita). He is infinitely powerful and has infinite mercy. He is the essence of all knowledge and joy, and is the creator and terminator of the universe, and entirely controls its every aspect. Individual selves, matter, time, exist by his grace and would come to nothing if that grace were withdrawn. The complex and multifarious activity of the universe only reveals His perfection. He can assume any form, like incarnate form, Avatara, and is the significance of all words.

Souls are infinite in number and are different from each other. Each has its own imperfections which put it in ignorance and suffering. It is atomic but has some features which are common with God, like sentience and a degree of bliss. The Upanishadic statement Tat Tvam Asi (that thou art) does not imply identity of self with God, but only resemblance. There are three types of souls, being those which are bound but may become free, or those migrating from life to life within the mundane sphere, and then those permanently doomed to the miseries of hell. Madhava's thoughts seem to have been formulated more on the basis of the Brahmanas than Upanishads. He is pessimistic. Even though he places reliance on divine grace, he does not believe in universal redemption. He is of the view that evil will persist—for ever and scope for human freedom and divine grace is limited.

Prakriti, the ultimate source of physical universe is eternal but insentient. Sattava, Rajas, Tamas are its first products (Gunas), and from these come intellect (Mahat), ego (Ahankara) and mind (Manas), and five sensory organs and five motor organs, as postulated in Sankhya doctrine as well. The effect of the cause of the universe is both existent and non-existent; in material causation a thing may exist as a cause, but it may not exist as effect. To properly understand the ontology of the doctrine a good understanding of the Visheshas i.e., special characteristics that distinguish things, is necessary. The doctrine explains knowledge as a transformation or a mode of the internal organ and, therefore, as characterizing it and not the self. But the self initiates the process of knowing and is not unconnected with the knowledge gained. All knowledge points to complex or qualified objects and there is, thus, no reason to admit any attributeless. Knowledge in respect of something is with reference to something other than the thing about which knowledge is to be gained. Anything which comes into relation with time and space, is necessarily real, no matter for how long and to what extent. There is no distinction between the real and the empirical, or the empirical and the unreal. Ontologically the difference is between the real and the unreal. Advaita explains the absolutist stand of the Upanishads by accepting only one reality; it accepts the universe only as an appearance of this reality. Dvaita postulates God as the supreme reality and everything else as totally dependent upon it.

Truth corresponds to reality—this is the realism of the doctrine. The object is perceived as it is. Dreams and recollections are also taken to be true, but that part of the dream is an illusion in which the dreamer is not involved directly; dreams are real because they are not contradicted later. Recollection is also real, and right knowledge. The doctrine accepts three means to valid knowledge or Parmanas, being perception, inference and verbal knowledge. Valid knowledge itself is a Parmana as it points directly to a fact, though that fact by itself is not the means to valid knowledge. There are primary and secondary means to valid knowledge, the former indicating a fact directly and the latter mediately; inference as Parmana indicates fire mediately while valid knowledge does so directly. Thus valid knowledge is the direct means knowing, while perception, inference and verbal testimony are secondary. When compared to Shankra, Madhava too, like Ramanuja, leans heavily on Puranas and connected literature, to support his doctrine. According to him seven senses are instrumental in acquiring knowledge, including Manas (internal organ) and Sakshin (the pure self as viewer of things). God and the selves are sentient and this sentience is taken to be Sakshin (viewer), i.e., it can know through one of the senses, and also know directly; direct knowledge in invariably correct. Own self, pain, pleasure, time and space, are known directly; all else is known through one or the other of the remaining senses. That self knows itself by itself was dismissed by Shankra as a contradiction. In his view if we say that pain, pleasure, time, space, are known by the self directly, then we reduce the internal organ to a mere aid in the process of knowing. It ceases to have its own specific role of making the self know, as given in other doctrines, like Nyaya-Vaisheshika; it becomes just an aid in the recollection process.

Sansara, or transmigration, is beginning less ignorance, Avidya, which is specific to each individual; Avidya is considered a substance. It obscures the true nature of God, and of the person himself. Release is secured by overcoming Avidya. Correct self knowledge is obtained by study of scriptures, but this knowledge is only mediate, and becomes direct when final release is attained, through God's grace. True knowledge of God is more essential than of the self, and this also is attained through the study of scriptures, and then conversion of this knowledge into personal experience by meditation. The best effort can bring bliss only in keeping with the intrinsic worth of each self, distinction between selves persists even in Moksha. Bliss of the released souls is finite, while that of God is infinite; bliss realized in Moksha cannot be experienced in mundane life.

Final release comes through Bhagti, the love for God, and this brings God's grace which is what brings release. For this there has to be detachment, performance of duties as enjoined in Bhagvad Gita (Karma Yoga), study of scriptures under the guidance of a Guru, and reflection on what has been learnt, and finally meditation. Duties of the station of life have to be performed till the very end, including the rites as prescribed in the scriptures; these are obligatory. Jeevanmukti, liberation during the current life itself is rejected.

6

The Non-Vedic Systems

In the preceding pages we have had a brief glimpse of the Systems of Philosophy which accept the authority of the Veda, the Astika Darshanas as they are called, or the Vedic Schools, also called the orthodox or traditional systems. In the following pages are covered the heterodox systems, the ones which do not accept the authority of the Veda; also called the Avaidika schools or Nastika Darshanas. There are three such systems, viz., Charvaka, Jainism and Buddhism.

Charvaka

The main work of this system which was compiled in the Brahaspati Sutra around 600 BC, has been lost. Therefore, not much is known about this system, particularly about its earlier stages. The systems is also referred to as Lokayata, i.e., belief in the existence only of this world; that there is nothing beyond. It accepts only perception as the one means to valid knowledge (Parmana), and rejects inference and verbal testimony, for there is a lack of finality in reasoned conclusions as the reasoning in such cases depends on some inductive truth which is not demonstrable. But observation like 'North Star' will appear at night in the north in the northern hemisphere' is valid. As perception is the only form of valid knowledge, physical matter in its movements and modifications is the only reality, and everything in the universe, including thought, feeling, mind can be explained in terms of physical laws. The elements recognized are earth, fire, water and air; space, the fifth element of the Upanishads, is not recognized.

Ajita (nick name Kesa Kambli—hair blanket) was about the first historically recognized person who preached this materialist doctrine. He said good deeds and charity achieved nothing in the end, that the body dissolved into primary elements at death and there after Karmas had no meaning. Lokyata school from which brutally practical theories of Maghadan statecraft developed, borrowed from the teachings of Ajita. Charvaka view is that consciousness is a material and transitory modification of the four elements and will disappear after some time when these elements have ceased to be together. The intelligence which is found embodied in the forms produced from the combination of the elements, is produced the same way as the green colour of the leaves or the red colour of a flower. Soul is only the body qualified by intelligence ; it has no existence apart from the body. Postulates of religion, God, freedom, morality are mere illusions. Nature is indifferent to good or evil, and history does not bear witness to Divine Providence. Pain and pleasure are central facts of life, while vice and virtue are not absolute values but only social norms laid down by the society for its convenience. Therefore, while life is yours, live it fully and joyously. Chastity and such like traits, which are praised by religion too, are mooted by misguided or cunning or weak and dishonest people; the latter under the cover of such ideas only further their own interests. It is not logical to regard something as perceived unless it is actually perceived, otherwise it would be an undue assumption. It is not possible to understand the relation of cause and effect. Knowledge is not different from the object of knowledge as both are forms of existence and have no other form; in fact they are one and the same. Only fools imagine that the spirit is different from body, that they would reap the reward of actions in some future state. They assume existence of something that does not exist. Only sustenance and love are the objects of human existence. Death is blessedness. If victims slain in sacrifice ascend to heaven, why are parents not slain for this purpose? Some materialists do agree to recognize the internal organ as soul, so long as it is accepted that it has no existence after the body has perished. Besides there is a tacit acceptance of the law, Dharma and the principal 'as you sow so shall you reap,' for the duration of life on earth.

Jainism

The system too was a revolt against Brahmanism and the cult of animal sacrifice. It does not recognise any supreme God. It was established during the later Vedic period, during the time of the Brahmanas. Its author was Vardhmana (599-527 BC), who is referred to as Mahavira (the great hero) by his followers. The followers believe he was not the author but only the 24th prophet guide (Tirathankara: Tiratha is religious order and Ankara, the organiser who lays down the doctrine, discipline, order and other aspects of the organisation); they claim the doctrine is much older and already had 23 Tirathankaras before Vardhman Mahavira. Mahavira followed four rules ascribed to his predecessor Parashava which laid down: (a) possess no property, (b) take no property from others, (c) take no life, and (d) be truthful. He added celibacy. However, notwithstanding the earlier Tarathankaras, the exposition of the essential doctrine and laying down the structure of the religious order was done only by Mahavira. He was from a princely family of Kundagram, in the Vaishali republic of North Bihar and lived as a householder till the age of thirty. Then he left his home in search of the truth, and after nearly 13 years of study and meditation he achieved illumination and became a Jina—the spiritual conque; his followers founded Jainism based on his teachings. The religion has two sects of believers (a) Svetambaras who dress in white robes, and (b) Digambaras, who go about naked; it is their belief that any ownership, even of a lion cloth, is in the way of enlightenment.

They believe that universe comprises two types of substances, viz., the soul and the non-soul. The soul bound by body is Jiva or an embodied soul. A free or not bound soul is Paramatma, or the perfect soul. That which transforms a soul into a perfect soul is Dharma or religion. Spirit and matter (Jiva and Ajiva) have eternal, independent existence; neither the inanimate is born out of the animate, nor vice versa. There are infinite number of souls and each has independent existence. But the souls and the matter possess a number of common characteristics; these are conducive to their interaction. The animate, because of the exertion of its inherent force, consumes the inanimate, including Karmas, and gets associated with it. This is bondage, and this matures into attachment and/or aversion which causes the performance of good or evil deeds and that causes the influx of Karmas (Asrava) which further strengthens the bondage. And so the process goes on. This is Sansara, the mundane existence in the cycle of rebirths, and the soul caught in this process experiences mental and physical suffering caused by rebirths, disease, old age and death. Besides, bondage, i.e., lack of unfettered freedom, is the cause of suffering. The sum total of the fundamental elements in the universe is constant; not even a single particle can ever be added or removed.

Knowledge (or sentience) is the essence of Jiva, but this is restricted because of the limitations of the internal organ and the body. Once the mortal sheaths of the body and the internal organ have been cast away for good, the soul is free and in this state it is omniscient and has full and comprehensive knowledge of all things through direct intuition; during this stage the knowledge could come only through intuition as all the physical attachments capable of providing knowledge directly, parish with the body. This is the state of Kevalaya, and the knowledge acquired is Keval-Gyan. In this state the spirit is omniscient.

The soul goes through transmigration, and the cause of this are the Karmas, or the good and the bad deeds. Karmas are non-souls (Ajivas), which contaminate the soul and cause rebirth. The Jivas are of lower or higher order depending upon their sense organs. Grass, the lowest in the classification of living things, has only the touch as the sense organ, while a human being has all the five senses and the internal organ.

The soul is not perceptible to the senses; it is just not possible to establish its existence on logical reasoning, as logic is limited only to those items as can be perceived by the senses; only intuitive knowledge establishes the existence of soul. The soul attracts the subtle atoms of Karmas, (and thus gets contaminated) by the exertion of its own inherent force. These atoms are of previous Karmas which cause rebirth but exclude Karmas not relevant to the rebirth, like the routines performed in the simple, honest process of living. Depending upon the types of atoms accumulated by the soul it takes form in the next birth, between a human being to some other lower form of life like, maybe, vegetation. The bondage between Karmas and the soul is beginning less, i.e., at no time is the soul not bound by the Karmas. But the aim of the religion is to secure the release. The righteous and sinful deeds are not mere social occurrences; they are not governed by systems of the society. They are products of man's natural instincts, caused to be born with him by his Karmas. The state of liberation (Nirvana) is not the end of the existence of the soul. It is only a change in its state; having been freed from the Karma atoms it does not transmigrate and stays changeless.

Ajivas are devoid of consciousness. There are five kinds of Ajivas, being matter, time, space, the medium of motion and the medium of rest. Matter is of many types and is made up of atoms. When atoms combine in different proportions we get things that give the common experience by way of colour, taste, touch and smell. Sound also is an attribute of matter but only in its composite and not in its atomic form. Atoms are identical, but they produce a variety of objects with various combinations, the objects being earth, water, air and fire. All atoms, or aggregates of them, have souls; the universe is infested with life.

Time and space pervade everywhere. All things are situated in time and all changes take place in it. The universe is finite in substance and space, i.e., both things have a beginning and an end. But it is infinite as far as time and the modification of substance are concerned, i.e., it is for ever changing, and it time dimension is in finite.

As stated earlier, the soul attracts matter and this results in the influx of Karma, and bondage is caused. This bondage causes attachment and aversion, and that further strengthens bondage, perpetrating suffering. This is repetitive and strengthens bondage continuously. This is Sansara, living through unending cycles of births and deaths. Dharma is what strikes at the roots of suffering. Therefore the first step is the study of dharma. Once the right knowledge has been gained, detachment is developed and there is freedom and bandhas (shackles) of fresh Karmas cease, and simultaneously the past Karmas are shed off. This is the road to liberation, Moksha. Complete liquidation of Bandhas leads to complete freedom. Time, individual disposition, universal laws, also influence the capacity to act in addition to Karmas, which are the most powerful factor. Karmas are born from the doings of the person himself and he has to bear the consequences. He can get rid of the effects of Karmas only after they have been separated from the soul after developing complete detachment.

Mahavira, however, did not accept Karma as the supreme power, for that would amount to accepting Karma as God, the Creator or the controller; it would have substituted Karma for God; he did not accept God. He accepted the power of Karma in a limited sense only, for, as he taught, Karmas could be liquidated by spiritual exertion. He accepted that Karmas influenced man, but spiritual exertion, in the capability of man, had power over Karmas. There is, thus, a tussle going on all the time between the past Karmas, i.e., fate or destiny and the power of man in the form of physical, mental and spiritual exertion. Sometimes it is the Karma, and sometimes it is the spiritual, physical and mental exertion which has the upper hand. But it is Karma which is the instrumental cause of man's condition, his pains and pleasures, and not the efficient cause. It is possible to fight against an instrumental cause by adopting suitable counter measures. Pain and pleasure are felt within the person, in his psyche, and it is in there that changes have to be made. Thus, a person's inside has to be strong, spiritually, to withstand the onslaught of Karma and negate its effects. That is where asceticism comes in; it may take even the form of self-mortification. Mere softening of external conditions in the form of good deeds or pursuing noble activities, will, no doubt, help, to a great extent actually, but this cannot entirely free the person of the effects of Karma. For that counter Karmic activity is called for. Mahavira, thus, has not put forth a pessimistic doctrine, as is sometimes believed. He has, in fact, given a clarion call to humanity to not to lose heart, as a person has it within himself to surmount any opposition, from fate or whatever else, with his innate capability for spiritual exertion, Purushartha, which includes mental and physical exertion, including hard ascetic discipline and self-mortification.

Before complete detachment is achieved, a person has to undergo certain disciplines, like getting to know and experience reality, developing faith in truth, inculcating spiritual uprightness and washing off the accumulated Karmas through right austerities. Amongst the important rules of discipline are: (i) equality for all living beings, including human beings (egalitarianism), animals and plant life, (ii) non-killing of any living being, or causing pain, or enslaving, (iii) not imposing one-self on anyone. The religion emphasises complete non-violence, mental and physical, and enjoins to be fearless, and free of hatred and flattery, and not be bothered by failure or success. Truth is supreme and the essence of the universe. The followers are advised to shed anger, and not be covetous or be thieves, and control desires and keep the needs to the minimum, and be celibate, and not be attached to sound, beauty, fragrance, taste and touch, and observe the discipline of walking, speaking, collecting food and eating it and keeping clean pollution free environments. All these and tough austerities, were required to be followed by monks and nuns. The religion accepts equality of women and men and advises them to renounce their household life and accept the discipline of the ascetic. Compared to the ascetic the regimen for the householder is lighter. Truth and non-violence are prescribed for him. He is, in any case, not to be incontinent, or covetous, or a thief, and should practice looking inwards into himself, and renounce whatever is not essential for his living, and lead a simple life free of ostentations, and practice detachment and be free of superstitions, and be fearless. All this is Dharma, designed to rid the soul of the Karmas of the past and prevent the generation of new Karmas, and thus bring liberation and Kaivalya, i.e., make the spirit omniscient and restored to its pristine radiance and purity. To achieve this, world has to be renounced, and there has to be asceticism; the life of the householder has to be given up.

It has been stated earlier that religion stresses non-violence and equality, and co-existence. It discourages dogmatism and/or fundamentalism in any form and stresses that there generally are many angles to a viewpoint, and that the requirement is to understand them and make co-existence easier. This is the doctrine of Anekantavada (synthesis), i.e., there is more than one justification for a certain action, activity, situation, proposition, and it is possible to understand the different viewpoints, and avoid being dogmatic or fundamentalist. Such an approach would lead to synthesis of different viewpoints and remove uncalled for tensions between individuals or different section of the society.

Vardhman Mahavira laid great stress on the need to look inwards, for he preached that he who did not would not realise the self. Such a person's knowledge was acquired either through verbal testimony or through the sense organs and the mind. To practice religion knowledge of the self was important, otherwise the person would not secure freedom from attachment, aversion and delusion, and therefore, would not achieve emancipation, or reach the stage of Moksha or Nirvana; the very first step for nirvana was self-knowledge. Mahavira said, learn the truth yourself and develop your own spiritual vision and do not depend only upon what I say. He did not encourage dogmatism and wanted a person to develop his own judgement and be convinced that the course he had adopted was in fact the right one.

Buddhism

Sixth century BC was a period of religious and intellectual activity in Asia. This is the time of Confucius and perhaps of Lao-Tzu in China, Zoroaster in Iran, the greatest of the Hebrew prophets, Deutero-Issiah in the Middle East and Pythagoras in Greece. This was also the period of Greek's Golden Age when their thinkers were looking for a single principal to explain the material world. In India it was the time of the Buddha and Vardhman Mahavira. In fact, with the silent revolt that the philosophy of the Upanishads had started against the ritualistic Brahmanical ritualism, many new teachers had sprung up, Buddha and Mahavira being just two amongst them, and not the most renowned ones either. Gautama, also called Siddhartha by his followers, is the founder of Buddhism. He belonged to the Sakya tribe (for this reason he is also called Sakya-Muni) who spoke Aryan language, and claimed to be Aryans, though they had no priestly class (Brahmans) or Varanas; i.e., class distinction on the basis of the profession or colour of the skin was not there. They lived around Kapilvastu, 150 odd Kilometre north-east of Varanasi and 50 odd

KM south of the Himalayan Range. They lived mainly on agriculture and breeding cattle. And were ruled by King Parsenajeet of the Koasala Empire; he was emperor during the early days of the Buddha; during this time only the emperor had the power of life and death over his subjects. The chief of the tribe was probably elected by rotation. Buddha's father Shuddodana, the chief of the tribe, had two wives, both sisters, daughters of neighbouring Koli chief (Kolis had the kol tree as their totem; this tribe claimed Buddha's ashes). Both the ladies, the wives of the king, were childless, till in her 45 year, Maya the elder sister, gave birth to Gautama in a grove of the Sala trees, after a bath in the sacred tank (Pushkara, the artificial lotus pond) in the midst of the grove. Sala tree was sacred to mother goddess Lumbini and was the totem tree of the Sakyas. But Gautama's mother died after seven days of the birth. The goddess is still worshipped as Rukmini Devi at the same spot, though Buddha is forgotten.

There are a number of views on the date of Buddha's birth, but the commonly accepted date is 563 BC. He lived for about 80 years and died in the year 483 BC.

Young Gautama was trained in the martial arts as a Kshatriya prince, which included the handling of weapons and state craft. At the age of sixteen he was married to a Sakyan princess, Yashodhra, and time they got a son, Rahula. Early in life Gautama was troubled by the human vanity and the sorrow of disease, old age and death. He left his home, wife and son at the age of 29 and set out in search of the answers to the riddle of life. He was joined by five others and together they spent six years seeking guidance of scholars and teachers of eminence. But he was not satisfied. In time his companions left him and he decided to do his own study and reflection on the basis of whatever he had learnt and experienced so far and decided to follow the middle course. After a lot of study, reflection, meditation and even penance he attained the knowledge of the ultimate truth, enlightenment, while reflecting and meditating, seated under a Bo-tree (Pipal) on the bank of River Neranjara, near Gaya, in Bihar; the place probably had been a humble cult spot. That was when he became the Buddha, the enlightened one. During his later years a young disciple, Ananda, who was also his cousin, looked after him, and after his end, Ananda gave out from his memory, many of his discourses. Buddha preached mostly in central Uttar Pradesh and parts of Bihar and Nepal, and converted a lot of followers, including Yakshas, a powerful non-Aryan tribe, and befriended Bimbisar, the Magadhan king and a host of other noted people of his time. Brahmans were his leading disciples; Sangha, the Buddhist order owes its growth, early philosophy and organisation to them. Towards the last days of his life, Chunda, a blacksmith, served him a special dish of mushrooms, and that brought a relapse of an earlier attack of dysentery, leading to the master's final illness. The end came while he was resting between two Sala trees in a grove at Kushinagara, a place in the city-state of the Mallas, on way to Rajgir from Sevatthi. His birth, enlightenment and Parinirvana (the end) have been given to have happened on the same day of a week and month.

Buddhism had a wide acceptance and spread to all corners of Asia. In South-East Asia, China, Japan, Korea, Mangolia, Manchuria, it is the faith of the majority of the people to this day. Its spread to South and West Asia was almost immediate. The writings ascribed to a ascetic Mediterranean community, first found in 1747 AD, the Dead Sea Scrolls (dated to 250 BC to about 70 AD) containing Hebrew and Aramaic scriptural texts and liturgical system of public worship, appear to be of Buddhist origin. The practice of living in a monastery located on a cemetery is Buddhist; the teacher of righteousness, as mentioned in the scrolls, is the precise title of the Buddha.

There is a prevalent belief in the east that Christianity took off from Buddhism, and some of Christ's miracles, such as walking on water, were earlier ascribed to the Buddha. The legend of Barlaam and Josaphat is a direct adaptation of Buddha's life story. In the life story of Jesus Christ little information is available for the period when he was 12 to the time when he was 30. One view is that he spent the whole or part of this period in the Buddhist monastery of Himis, located on the river Indus, some 25 odd kilometres north-west of Leh, in Ladakh, India. It is claimed that documents in Buddhist and Pali languages, which at time, it is claimed, were in the possession of this monastery, told of the days that Jesus spent, and where he was not only a very welcome student but also a teacher. His Sermon on the Mount has a strong Buddhist flavour. In fact, it is also believed that the 'Promised Land' of Moses was not Palestine but Kashmir, that out of the 12 tribes that set out of Egypt under Moses, one did not make it to the promised land; Semitic Kashmiris are believed to be the descendents of this tribe. The remaining 11 tribes were in fact lost in the desert and had perforce to settle in the Palestinian wasteland; no one could call a desert a promised land. According to this view Jesus did not die on the cross, that after his wounds had been treated he was well again, but he was a man hunted by his enemies, he had to flee, along with his mother, to any hospitable land which could give him shelter. His journey of flight to Kashmir was long and arduous. On the way Mary the mother, died and was buried at a place called Mai Mari Ka Asthan (the resting place of Mother Mary), in a place where a town came up later with the name of Murree (named after her), some 50 km north-west of Islamabad in Pakistan. Jesus, the account narrates, lived for many years, greatly respected, and was buried at Rauza Bal, in Khaniyar, a locality of Srinagar in Kashmir. The tomb standing there is stated to be of prophet Yuz Asaf, according to the account that was the name Jesus had taken to conceal his identity during his flight to the Valley.

It will, thus, be seen that Buddhism had a widespread in Asia (including West Asia) and there is a lot of similarity in the Buddhist and Christian teachings, which suggests that the latter possibly borrowed extensively from the former, and for that the two streams of thought must have flowed side by side during the early days of the development of Christianity. At this time the Hindu Orthodox Systems had been established, and Jainism had laid a lot of emphasis on severe penance, essentially for those who had adopted renunciation and asceticism. Abstinence, control of breath and body posture were emphasized, leading to Yoga doctrine. Charvaka followers, on the other hand, said there was nothing like the soul, or the effect of the deeds after death. Makkhali Goshala was teaching that not effected by the Karmas, the soul went through a number of preordained birth cycles as a part of the system of creation, and, therefore it was right to make the best of the life while one lived. Buddhism followed the middle course.

The doctrine got a fillip when around 210 years after the Parinirvana, i.e., Buddha's passing away, Asoka the great, the great Magadhan king (ruled between 274-232 BC), lent his support to it; he sent emissaries to different countries with Buddha's message. He sent his own son Mahindra (Mahinda) and daughter Sanghamitra, to Lanka, modern Sri Lanka with a sapling from the Bodhi Tree at Gaya (the tree under which the Buddha had achieved enlightenment) and they with their zeal and enthusiasm, converted the whole of the island to the Buddhist faith. The religion reached China by the first century AD, Korea, the fourth and Japan the sixth century AD.

The doctrine denied self or a continuous subject of thought, or soul, or Atma. It denies God working in the manifold phenomenon of the universe. It denies any real matter. But it believes in gods. The doctrine believes that the entire cosmos is filled with infinite trains of consciousness, but these are not souls having their own identity or existence. Each train is, in fact, a succession of moments of consciousness, each moment a direct resultant of the preceding moments. At a point of time a train gets infected by Karma, and no sooner that happens, ego is born, and that brings ignorance and then engulfment by Maya. At this stage conformations come into being, i.e., potentialities of love and hate and such like weaknesses of the spirit which are resultants of acts committed in past lives and which shape and direct the acts to be committed in the future (Sanskaras). Stage now set for the birth of the sentient being. The first to appear is the consciousness, which is followed by name and form, or the development of a finite world of particulars. Then the sense organs develop and these provide the capability of contact with the apparent world, resulting in the experience of sensation, the growth of desires and attraction and attachment to individual life and finite existence, all in that order. The existence finally passes through birth, disease, sorrow and death. At the last stage the Karmas leave the material body to ride another train of consciousness.

The Buddhists believe that there is no real existence of a sentient being. What we see is only a phenomenal personality, which comes into being through the combination of name and form (Nama and Roopa). Name includes all the four subjective phenomenon of thought, viz., (a) feelings, (b) conformations (Sanskaras), which, in fact, are potentialities of love and hate and similar emotions born from the deeds of past lives and which have bearing on the deeds of the future, (c) general notions like the concept of a definite world of particulars, and (d) definite consciousness. These constitute four Skandhas (aggregations), (Khandhas in Pali). Fifth Khandha is 'form', born out of the four elements of the physical world, i.e., earth, water, fire, and air. The force that binds the five Khandhas into an individual or personality is Karma. Karma here includes mental, physical or oral deeds, though involuntary or inadvertent acts are not Karma. But the Karmas are not imposed. A person has the freedom to act in spite of the past Karmas, and, thus, has the potential for Naishkarmya, freedom from Karma. And this leads to Aerhatship and thence to Nirvana. To get to this last stage spiritual discipline has to be practiced, and there has to be contemplation, and cultivation of the four noble virtues, which being universal love, compassion, sympathetic joy and equanimity. At death all the five Khandas perish. Only Karmas remain which ride on another train of consciousness and assemble another set of Khandas, and a new life comes into being. Karmas are the link that preserves the identity of a being through all the countless changes that it undergoes during its journey through Sansara, the chain of rebirths. It is the Karmas that determine the type of being to be reborn. This is the doctrine of Pratitya-Samutpada, the doctrine explains how individual existence and consciousness evolve in the cosmic process. What has been given here is but one of its interpretations; there are others, equally plausible, by other authorities.

The goal of the monastic order is Nirvana, while that for the lay devotee or the householder it is rebirth in a higher heaven. To achieve the goal the person has to comprehend the four noble truths, and follow the noble eight-fold path of the fourth noble truth. The four noble truths are:

(a) Life is evil (leading to persistent suffering).

(b) Ignorance is the source of evil (suffering). Ignorance (Avidya) is about the true nature of a being, that it is phenomenal, in a state of flux, constituted by the force of Karmas by uniting the five Khandhas, which perish at death. The Karmas, however, survive, and they force another set of Khandhas to start another life; only in Nirvana the process ceases.

(c) The evil (suffering) can be overcome. After the coming into being of name and form, there is the evolution of the sense organs which establish contact with the apparent world and there are feelings and sensations, leading to desires, and attractions for and attachment to individual life. This is the finite existence, which goes through disease, sorrow and death, and thence to rebirth; rebirth can also be caused by unfulfilled cravings so that these may be satisfied during the next lives. But the main reason for rebirth is Karma.

(d) Evil (suffering) is overcome by following the noble eightfold path. It is the middle course between the two extremes viz., self-mortification as preached by Jainism and some other schools following similar philosophy and self-indulgence as advocated by the Yogcharā school and its variants—advocating indulgence as the so-called Karmas have no meaning. The steps to be followed have been logically thought out and the seeker progresses in stages without encountering contradictions and repletions. The steps are:

  (i) The right views. Cleanse the mind of all superstitions, animism, primitive rites and consider animal sacrifice as sin. Regard all human beings as equal and depend upon your own power of reasoning rather any divine miracle. Buddha disapproved violence in any form, including animal sacrifice, or wars. He placed forbearance above bravery where killing or cruelty was involved while defending a principal, or ones country. He stressed virtue and wisdom. He preached Dharma for welfare and happiness of human beings. He did not advocate any system of prayers and emphasized the purity of thinking, speaking, and action. He emphasised that every man was his own saviour and no outside power could do anything for deliverance from rebirths.

(ii) Right mental resolve, after developing the right vie,

(iii) Right speech,

(iv) Right action after having trained in the first three,

(v) Right livelihood, on the basis of right action,

(vi) Right effort, for own mental and moral elevation,

(vii) Right mindfulness; attention to weaknesses of own body and mind,

(viii) Right concentration, by fixing the mind on a single object; without no progress is possible.

All this would mean avoidance of all sins, and only acquisition of merit, and maintaining the purification of the mind. This is the essence of the middle path.

Buddha did not get embroiled in the philosophy concerning the deepest mysteries of life; he did not encourage his followers to waste time pondering over such issues as they were irrelevant to the goal, which was attaining of Nirvana; for lay followers it was rebirth in a higher heaven. Buddha said Nirvana could be achieved by love and faith as well, and that all issues could not be resolved by reasoning alone. Critical approach no doubt was important but it had its limitation and beyond that it was only the teacher who could show the way. He is believed to have said that in this world there were so many things which were accessible to ordinary intelligence, but their existence could not be denied for that reason. He was silent on the origin of Karma and the state or the condition in Nirvana and when pressed he is believed to have said that it was not possible to know anything about Nirvana. He is believed to have said that in this state there is neither the element of extension nor of cohesion or heat or motion (the four elements of nature), nor sphere of space, nor sphere of infinity of consciousness, nor sphere of nothingness, nor of perception or of non-perception, neither of this world or of the world beyond, neither of sun or of moon. There is neither coming nor going, neither staying or of passing away, or of moving or arising. This indeed is the end of suffering.

Is Nirvana eternal existence or eternal annihilation? One view is that it is not the annihilation of the self but of the self-hood. But Buddhists recognise no self as such, as in the Hindu doctrines. For them it is just a train of consciousness in flux getting caught in Karma which force the five Khandas and generate life, a being. Nothing finite exists in itself; Every living being is a collection of Khandas, temporarily united, or, we can say, everything is phenomenal. All data of finite experience is subjective phenomenon corresponding to no objective reality. The truth is that Nirvana is both eternal existence and eternal annihilation. In this state the train of consciousness has finally been delivered of the Karma and is freed and joins the overall content of consciousness, like space contained in a vessel becomes one with the infinite space after the vessel has been broken. In this state it is eternal existence. But it is eternal annihilation as well because space in the vessel has lost for ever its existence. The Buddha called the abode of Nirvana as void, *Shunya*. It is that which is selfless and can be realized only by those who have utterly ended craving and have entered solitude based on the sphere of neither perception nor non-perception, and have then moved to the state of concentration of mind wherein awareness and feelings ease. This is the condition when the seeker is completely free and enters the utterly purified and incomparably high void. Otherwise there are voids at every stage, like solitude of the forest means void of human beings only the solitude of the forest remaining, and the void of the forest means only that of the earth remaining, and that of the earth means only that of the infinite space remaining, and so on till the highest void has been attained. In real terms, however, it is difficult to distinguish between Void and Brahma, for the distinguishing characteristic of each is the absence of any characteristic at all. Each is other than non-Being. In each case *neti neti* (not this, not this) formula had been used in the description attempt.

It cannot, however, be said with certainty that everything attributed to the Buddha did in fact come from him, or had his approval. With time Buddhism broke off into branches and there was a lot of intermixture of ideas and to and fro movement of views, with the result that some material which had not originated from the Buddha got treated as if it had. Otherwise the Buddha's attitude was positive and agnostic. His aim was to remedy the world's sorrow by teaching his followers to escape from the stranglehold of the Karmas, and thus *Sansara* (wandering through rebirths). He emphasized that a person is the controller of Karmas and has the ability to achieve Nirvana. But such a cut and dried formula did not go well with some of his followers, for while it was accepted by the intellectuals it did not satisfy the emotional needs of common followers. In the main stream Hinduism Vaishnav *Bhakti* was extensively practiced in those days and in its midst Buddhism was having problems in satisfying the needs of its followers. They needed a deity who could serve as the father figure, an all powerful, omnipotent, omniscient god whom they could visualize in an image familiar to them, i.e., human image, and whom they could worship with love and devotion to satisfy a powerful emotional urge, and to whom they could turn for relief and succour, and for the pursuit of the final goal. The religious activity was essentially pursued to secure personal release from the cycle of rebirths. But this in time came to be considered a selfish pursuit. Once a person had acquired that degree of moral and religious excellence, he ought to be working not only for his own emancipation but also of other fellow beings. In addition a person wanted to believe that the faith he followed originated from a mysterious, divine source and not from the thought of a mere human being. All this and the positive course on which Buddha had set his followers, led to the evolution of Mahayana Buddhism.

According to one Buddhist account of how the creation came into being (there could be different accounts in the books of different

Buddhist schools), any view regarding the train of consciousness, or the universe being eternal would be wrong. After a lapse of many *yugas*, ages, the system of the universe comes to an end and the spirits live in a zone of radiance and rapture. Then the universe begins to develop again. The plane of God is empty in the beginning, till some being, because his term in the zone of radiance has come to an end, or his merit has been exhausted, drops from that plane on the God plane, and lives there made of mind and feeding on rapture. Many ages pass and this being feels lonesome and desires company and in course of time other beings also drop on this plane, having finished their, lives or exhausted their merit, and are reborn, made of mind and feeding on rapture. The first being who has had the longest life and is endowed with maximum power and beauty, now thinks he was the creator of the beings who came after him, and believes he is God. Other beings too recognise him as God Almighty. Then a being drops from the God-plane and is born a man. And when he is lonely or is otherwise disheartened, or needs to visualise a potent father figure, he can think up to the God-plane only. That is how soul and the universe are partly eternal and partly non-eternal.

In order to formalize the teachings of the Buddha into a religion and maintain their originality and authenticity, the first council of the leading monks was held at Rajagriha (modern Rajgir) immediately after his *Parinirvana* (the final release). In this Ananda, who had attained *Arhatship* on the eve of this council, played a significant role.

The second council was held at Vaisali after a century of the *Parinirvana*, essentially to look into the legitimacy of some of the practices followed by some sections of monks, particularly those of the *Vijji* country, like accepting gold or silver as alms, drinking butter milk after meals or taking intoxicants, and such like matters.

The third council was held at *Patliputra* (modern Patna) under the aegis of the great Magadhan Emperor Ashoka, around 236 years after the *Parinirvana*. It was summoned by a learned monk Tissa Moggaliputta, again to rid the brotherhood of heresy; it was under the influence of this monk that the Emperor had accepted Buddhism. It was possibly not a general council but a meeting of a particular school of the Order.

The fourth council was held under Kanishka around 100 AD; numismatic evidence suggests that the king converted to Buddhism from some Iranian religion. The aim of this council too was to remove anomalies and contradictions in the Buddhist scriptures. It was held either at Jalandhar or Kashmir. The king ruled a vast country extending to Afghanistan, including the Punjab, Sindh and Kashmir. Southern Buddhists do not recognise this council and there is no mention of it in the Sinhalese chronicles. Also there is no evidence that Mahayana Buddhism was represented. This branch, i.e., Mahayana Buddhism, came into prominence only after Nagarjuna, and that happened much after the time of this council. But by this time Buddhist schism was complete. One notable feature of this council was the adoption of Sanskrit as the language for the Buddhist literature. Councils were also held from time to time, in different countries to which Buddhism spread, essentially to ensure that Buddha's teachings did not get coloured or corrupted by the local cults or lore.

The two main branches into which Buddhism split are Mahayana, the Great Vehicle, and the Hinayana, the Little Vehicle—called Theravada by its followers, for they felt to call it Little Vehicle was rather presumptuous and pompous on the part of the followers giving the classifications. Theravada is the popular religion followed in Sri Lanka, Burma and Thailand. Further south-east, along the coast and in the north, the religion is Mahayana. Buddhism spread along the coast of South-East Asia, and the silk route through Central Asia. In China it flourished alongside the ethical systems of Kung-Futzu or Confucius (551-479 BC) and Lao-tzu's mystical religion of the Tao. Tao means 'the way', the way of the universe. The requirement is to be in harmony with the Tao by practising quietude. While Confuciusism and Taoism were religions followed by the rich and the well-to-do people, Buddhism was the religion of the common folk.

In the older thought Buddha, though risen above the status of gods on account of his enlightenment, was like another person passed away from the world like any other person, gone for ever, no longer capable to influence physically; his teachings could at best serve as guide. His Nirvana was no different from any other person's who might achieve it in normal course, and could not bring about Nirvana for his followers. A monk had to have the will power to achieve it, and he had to be in the monastic order for this purpose. Thus in the older order Buddha was essentially a Guru who had shown the way. The school followed the old view that everything existed as a series of continuous changes, over a period of time, till at the end of this time it is no longer there. When an idea constituting a particular self disappears with that self, it leaves behind its mark, and thus the self of the next moment is informed of the happenings of the past, and thereby a continuity is maintained. That is why the moral responsibility for an act is considered to be of the individual who performs the act.

Mahayana believed that Buddha had trained gurus who helped the brotherhood to improve their lives and finally attain *Nirvana*. A concept of Bodhisattava was formulated, that is, a person endowed with wisdom who had gone past the stage of *Arhatship* and was ready to enter Nirvana, but had held back for the good of others, to help them to achieve the goal of Nirvana. Buddha now became the god of the first order. Below him there were countless Buddhas with domains run by Bodhisattavas. With time Buddha receded into the background and Buddha 'Amitabha', he of the infinite light, came to be worshipped, and all Buddhas became active dispensers of grace. The heaven of Amitabha is 'Sukhavati' (the place of well being, the happy place, fairy land tenanted by divine population in perfect bliss. Amitabha's chief administrator is Avalokiteshvara—a Bodhisattava, who has taken a vow not to enter nirvana till he has rescued the whole world. The ideal in Mahayana system is to strive for the nirvana of the fellow beings. Their Buddhas are associated with Taras—saviour ladies, and sexual opposites—typifying their consorts' energy of grace.

According to Mahayana, the train of consciousness, or self, is but a stream of ideas. Being and thought are, thus, one. Everything that is conceived or can be conceived by the mind, is only subjective imagination existing by virtue of Karma. There is no permanent treaty except void; this is a reality too vast, a truth before which thought is stilled. It is not possible to define it except as *Neti, Neti* (not this, not this). Otherwise everything is in emptiness, and is of it, with no beginning and no end. The five *Khandas* are empty. Form is empty and emptiness form. Perception, name, conception, knowledge are all empty. The doctrine, thus, recognises two spheres of reality, viz., the absolute reality which is the void, corresponding to Hindu Brahma, and the relative truth which is everything perceived by the senses and is in the sphere where doctrines and myths are worked out. This latter is the truth in a mutual relationship of things, as it obtains at the mundane level. Being and thought, as stated above, are one according to this school of Buddhism. In the objects of thought there dwells no reality except the thought that conceives it. The highest being is the 'Void' and understanding of this is the highest truth, the enlightenment (*Bodhi*) or the perfect wisdom (*prajnaparamita*), which is the peculiar possession of a Buddha. This knowledge is actually realized by a Buddha in the ecstasy of his *Nirvana*, where he dwells forever in the utter stillness of infinite thought. This enlightenment in *Nirvana*, actual or potential (potential in the case of *Bodhi-Sattavas* who hold back their entry to *Nirvana* for the well being of other human beings), together with the 'void' which is its object and, therefore, is identical with it, is the *Dharma-Kaya*, the body of the law'.

The need for history and myth are satisfied by the Mahayana by introducing two more concepts, viz., *Sambhog-kaya* or Body of enjoyment, and *Nirmana-Kaya* or the body of magical form. Every Buddha has a domain of his own, *Buddhakshetra*, a universe under the law preached by him, the magnificence of which is determined by the nobility of deeds of the ruling Buddha he was a Bodhis-Sattava. He is revealed to the attendant Bodhi-Sattavas in absolute spiritual radiance; the latter also appear in similarly transfigured bodies. This beatific form is *Sambhog-Kaya*. This is reward for the virtue and suffering that the Buddhas and Bodhi-Sattavas undergo while performing deeds for the well-being of earthly creatures. Finally the Buddha enters the ultimate Nirvana, and the Stupa or the monument sanctuary, appears in recognition:

Buddha now rests in perfect stillness. However, this transfiguration is essentially illusory, for once a Buddha has passed into Nirvana or the Void, he is identified with the Body of Law, which has no finitude. But the merit of his good deeds lives on in the finite world, and that works for the well-being and happiness other beings, creating *Sambhog-Kaya* in the holy Bodhi-Sattavas, i.e., their Buddha reveals itself in beatific form for their joy.

The 'Body of Magical Form' (*Nirman-Kaya*) explains the appearance of Buddhas and Bodhi-Sattavas in the world of mortals. In fact as the concept goes, they never really appear, they are mere illusions which they in their Body of Enjoyment create in compassion in order to help and instruct the beings of the world. Just as Bodhi-Sattavas get visions of their transfigured forms in heaven so also the people of the earth get visions of the Buddhas and Bodhi-Sattavas teaching the Law. To the Buddhists the object of subject of thought are really one, so that the *Dharma-Kaya* represents both the infinite and the understanding of the infinite. Likewise *Nirman-Kaya* is also the universal intellect, and when under the influence of the *Sanskaras* or 'conformations' resulting from former births, it conceives its objects as universe of finite forms. Thus universal intellect gets the individual mind to believe that they dwell in finite worlds under the dispensations of the Buddhas. This seeming individuality and finitude is the illusion of the lower orders of the the creatures from which the laws of the Buddha alone can uplift them to the union with the absolute. In Mahayana also Nirvana is achieved only after envelopment of consciousness caused by Karma has been eliminated. The soul of man, the train of consciousness, reflects faintly the divine glory. In the stillness of transcendental unity of joy, love and peace, all spirits are one.

According to *Yogchara School*, here is only self, conceived as a stream of ideas. Reality is reduced to thought. There is inseparable connection between knowledge and object. Object is a form of knowledge and is distinguished from other objects by the mind on the basis of former impressions collected during previous experiences. The diversity in the objects is also caused by the nature of the impressions from previous experiences. The main problem with this doctrine is that it abolishes distinction between truth and illusion and considers all experience as dream. In real life dream is false when compared with waking experience. But if the waking experience itself is false, then how is the falsity established; by comparing with what? By rejecting all external objects, even people get rejected and the inevitable conclusion would be that there is only one reality, the self, and the rest is all a figment of the mind.

Madhyamika school, a forerunner of the Mahayana, denies any reality, of the external objects as well as the self, the argument is that both physical and the mental phenomena have so many complications and contradictions that they cannot be accepted as real. While general Buddhist view is that everything has a cause of origination, Madhyamikas do not accept this and call the notion of causation as a delusion; conclusion is that the universe itself is a delision. Nagarjuna, the greatest exponent of this school, says, "there is neither being nor cessation of it, there is neither bondage nor escape from it. "This is the doctrine of 'void' (Shunya-vada). But the doctrine accepts that delusion is only from the ultimate point of view. In the day to day activity there is reality between subject and the object. But although we know feel and act in the course of our daily activity the ultimate significance of this amounts to nothing. The ultimate reality for the Madhyamikas is Shunya, which amounts to nothing because it in comprehensible. It is defined neither as 'is' nor 'is not'. It is beyond conception, very much like the Hindu or the Jain view. Thus absolute consciousness is accepted, though undefinable, in addition to particular egos.

Both Hinayana and the Mahayana accept the doctrine of momentariness, i.e., nothing lasts longer than a mere instant: there is a constant and continuous change in everything. All things, therefore, are impermanent; reality is a flow; it is not static. However, as opposed to Hinayana, where the goal is freedom of the train of consciousness from the hold of the Karmas and then merge with the infinite consciousness and thus, be freed from the cycle of *Sansara*, in Mahayana it is to merge with the absolute, which is the 'void'. *Zen Buddhism* asks its followers to look into the mind to find Buddhahood and emphasizes meditation for attaining spiritual enlightenment. According to it intuition rather than reasoning, is what is important for attaining the goal, which is salvation, and which is possible only through self-enlightenment. It believes that all human beings have already been enlightened, i.e., every spirit has the potential for self-enlightenment: every one is born a Buddha; he has only to strive to uncover this reality.

Blacksmith Chunda's mushroom preparation brought the final illness of the Buddha. But he told Ananda to tell Chunda he had done him as great a favour as had been done by the lady Sujata before his reaching the supreme wisdom, for Chunda's cooking would be the cause of his Nirvana, like Sujata's offering had preceded his attaining enlightenment. But he had instructed that Chunda's preparation be buried. To his monks he said: "I have nothing more to tell you, except that all that is composed is liable to decay. Strive for salvation energetically!"

He said: 'Nirvana is a territory in which there is no earth, no water, no light, no air, no sky, no directions, no time, no consciousness, no emptiness. There is nothing like even the moon or the sun, the planets or stars, this world or the other world, birth or death—nothing. In this territory there is the end of sorrow, and there is the final truth and eternity. It is not possible to define Nirvana, for it cannot be imagined, and is beyond all ideas and logic. It is desirable to keep silent about the revelation of this greatest truth."

7

The Religion

Hinduism is one of the oldest religions of the world, It is essentially a growth and not a construction, in that it is not based on the sayings or teachings if any single person, messiah or prophet. It is an accumulation of religious thoughts over the ages like 'the frail Bark of each passing epoch, put together by the hand of the past, in order make over its experiences and thoughts to the future.' This religion has provided religious and emotional satisfaction to its followers who have steadfastly respected its injunctions in preference to the alternatives that other religions or creeds offered. 'It is possible, for instance, to reconstruct the contribution of the people of the Nile, but these people irretrievably relaxed their hold upon their past and broke the continuity and brought to a halt a process which should made a significant contribution to the development of civilization and learning. The qualities of stubbornness, the dogged loyalty, the conservatism, are the criteria of a strong national sentiment. And in India these have been steadily maintained since the beginning of history.'

Hinduism is a synthesis deriving its constituents from a hundred different directions. It has within its ambit diverse practices like earth worship, sun worship, nature worship, sky worship, mother and father worship, prayers for the dead, worship of certain trees and plants and animals: all these and more have been synthesized in the broad structure of Hinduism. The ideas originated from people who arrived in this subcontinent from the times immemorial, and from time to time religious leaders have synthesized these thoughts into a rational whole, in the belief that they have provided emotional and psychic satisfaction to their followers. The religion is, thus, a collage of ideas which germinated on its soil or which were brought by the people who immigrated into this land. And they followed those ideas, even when they were in conflict with some of them already being followed here. For example, the practice of ancestor worship goes directly against the concept of transmigration of soul based on the Karmas. Ancestor worship visualises ancestors enjoying alongside the gods in the *Pitri Loka* (the region of the ancestors) the power and comforts as are available to the latter, i.e., after death the soul just uplifts and gets into the joyous and peaceful environs of the *Pitri Loka* and stays there till its turn once again to accept another birth; but that happens after a long gap. Another example could be the myth behind the purificatory baths during certain auspicious times at certain locations, to secure a place in heaven (*Swarga Loka*), this also goes against the grain of the Karma philosophy. The mythological legend, as given in the Vaishnav aspect of the religion is that under the instructions of the creator Vishnu, the gods (referred to as *Suras*) and the *Asuras*, the malevolent beings were engaged to extract ambrosia by churning the ocean of milk (*amrita manthan*), using mountain Mandara as the churning rod, and the king of serpents, Vasuki, as the rope for this purpose. After a long toil the ambrosia surfaced, butter like, but a god Dhanwantari, fearing that *Asuras* might take a forcible possession of this beverage of immortality, picked up the vessel in which it was contained, and bolted. He was chased by the *Asuras* and the situation was saved in favour of gods by Vishnu himself, by assuming the form of a pretty damsel and thus distracting the pursuers, and gaining time for Dhanwantari for delivery of the ambrosia to the gods. But during the chase some ambrosia got spilt at some spots on the earth, and the belief is that if a person takes a bath in the tanks and streams where ambrosia fell, (Ujjain in central India, Hardwar and Allahabad in Uttar Pradesh) he is rid of the effects of Karmas and ascends to heaven after death. However, the Karma theory visualises nothing of this sort; for them it is as you sow so shall you reap, and the process of rebirth shall continue unabated, without reprieve, no matter how many times one bathed and where.

Believers, however, are free to follow any concept which provides them solace and contributes to their spiritual well being. There are differences in different thoughts and practices, but no serious disputes. The concept of the Supreme God itself varies in different situations. He beyond human comprehension, but at the mundane level. He is worshipped in the human form, as Rama or Krishna, or Vishnu or Shiva, or in the form of Mother Goddess, Durga. Then there are gods and goddesses of smaller denominations, a pantheon, in whom people have faith and to whom they take their mental and psychic woes to draw solace and comfort which make the process of living bearable and easier for them. It would be wrong to compare different methods of worship, for worship is a very personalized and individual affair.

Negritos and Proto Australoids believed in animism and the power of the spirits, and worshipped, in addition certain trees and plants (tribal totems), and stones and rocks which they believed were endowed with special powers, and the sun and the moon and so on. They also had zoomorphic deities (also tribal totems), including the serpent deities. Tortoise, given as the incarnation of Vishnu, for He, after assuming its form as tortoise went under the ocean of milk to support the Mandara Mountain when the ocean was being churned for ambrosia. Monkey god Hanuman has been given as the son of the Aryan god of wind, while the elephant headed Ganesha is the son of another partly Aryan god Shiva. All this synthesis has happened with time and this brought unity and harmony amongst the people and a fairly uniform religion and philosophy. The essential of this belief are as under:

(a) The creation, after it has come into being, expands and, with time, ascends to its zenith and then, after it has run the course, collapses unto itself, on the basis of Dharma, the Law. Then, after the interval during which it has been out of action, has, so to say, been sleeping, it again stirs and comes into being. This interval when it is out of action is the same as that when it is in action.

(b) The essence of the soul is freedom and bliss, but because of an inherent attraction between the spirit and the matter, it gets trapped by the latter. Then ego develops and that brings ignorance which causes negative deeds which, in turn, bring about birth and rebirth, and suffering. To be freed of the rebirth cycle ignorance has to be banished, and reality has to be understood and good and expiating deeds performed.

(c) Everything in the universe, spirit or matter, is in a state flux, changing continuously and eternally; peace, rest, bliss are the prerogatives only of the free and blissful souls.

(d) All organic matter has life, or the capability to generate or sustain it. From simple grass to the complex human being, life is endowed with varying sense organs, minimal in the lower form—grass has only touch—and increasing gradually, to the maximum in the human being. What form of life a spirit will take will depend upon the deeds, Karmas. Karma is what supports *Sansara*, the unending of the spirit.

(e) Even though the power of the creator is beyond definition and human understanding; He is *Nirguna Brahma*, i.e., Brahma without attributes. But there is no objection to worshipping this power in a form that is comprehensible to the individual intelligence and understanding, i.e., as *Sa Guna Brahma*, i.e., *Brahma with attributes*, so long as it does not violate the tenets of Dharma.

Dravidians worshipped Rudra, later day Shiva, and the Mother Goddess. Originally Rudra and Shiva were independent of each other, worshipped by different people of different creeds, although some authorities have placed the origin of both the deities in the period of Proto-Australoids. The idea probably has its basis in the practice of tilling the ground with a wooden pole. It is plausible that the root of Hinduism is in the religion of the Proto Australoids, duly modified by the people who arrived later, each making own contribution to the Australoid concepts. The literature where the relevant legends of the time are contained are the *Puranas, the Ramayana and the Mahabharata* and other literature. The legends contained in them bear evidence of Australoid influence, for any people who came after them, including Dravidians, the Aryans and others, were all in distinct minority when compared to the Australoid Group. No group could overwhelm them with their religious thoughts or culture. This point has to be kept in view when studying the performance of the Indians in the subsequent history. The overwhelming presence of the Australoids has affected the whole of South and South-East Asia. They spread a culture which abhored violence, lacking in aggressiveness, and were easily subjugated by the aggressive invaders. The result was that they have been at the receiving end throughout the history. In fact anthropologists have come to the conclusion, at least some of them who have considered the problem with a lot of thought and considered it in detail, that way back during the movement of the human beings from the African continent, some peculiar genetic mutation, of however mild degree, brought forth this specimen of humanity: he lacks not only in physical prowess, strength, brain power, but in all organizational activity and is pretty confused in chalking out the future for himself. He, no doubt, gave Buddhism and Jainism to the world. Gandhi ended the curse of slavery using non-violence as the weapon against aggressive conquerors. But that cannot obliterate the fact that throughout history, thanks to the Austric Australoid philosophy, these people have suffered only slavery.

The first recorded religion is that of the Aryans, and their work of surpassing interest is the *Rig Veda*, a work of such a lofty dimension as has not been produced anywhere during such an early stage in the development of a civilization. The gods of their pantheon are *Devas*, emanating light, splendours beings associated with natural phenomena, like the all encompassing sky, the sun in its utter brilliance, the omnipotent thunder cloud, the divinely beautiful dawn, the roaring storm. For this pantheon no formal temple is visualised, though the gods have been personalized and they receive sacrifice and listen to prayers and hymns and dwell in a region of light, beyond the sun and the stars, living in immortal joy.

Indra is the most powerful and the greatest of all gods. He is believed to nourish and sustain his devotees by bringing rain for the crops. He is armed with thunder bolts and flanked by Maruts and wild winds, and with his weapons he smites *Ahi,* the malevolent god who tries to keep the lakes and rivers dry, and the land thirsting for water, so as to spread misery so that the human race and the beautiful creation might perish. In later times Indra came to be associated with omnipotence, and became the great war god of conquering Aryans. From this stage the concept of an almighty Creator who supports his creation in His benevolence, was just a step ahead.

Next in importance is god *Agni,* Fire, the high priest of gods and men, who accepts the offering to the gods and takes them heavenwards, and purifies the hearts of men, and their dwellings, and the air they breathe, and thus bestows upon them the gift of health and prosperity. Alongside him is *Soma,* partly intoxicating juice of a plant used for oblations, deified as god sought for wish fulfillment. He is considered effective and potent, and many hymns have been written in his praise, particularly in the *Sam Veda.* Then there are the *Surya,* the Sun (*Savar, Pushan, Vishnu,* are only different forms of this god). *Ushas,* is dawn, fair and blushing maidens, and *Ashvins,* the sons of the mare, are the light bearers of morning sky. *Rudra,* the Roarer is the god associated with storms, while *Vayu* is wind. The ancient divinities which fell in the background are (*Zeus*) and *Prithvi,* Heaven and Earth. *Yama* the first mortal to discover the path followed by the righteous after their death, to join their ancestors and gods, is honoured as a god. With time he came to be regarded as the arbiter of the deeds of the dead performed when they lived, and decided whether a spirit was to go to hell or heaven. He is also believed to dispatch his assistants to snuff out the life after it has lived its duration and bring the spirit to his region where both heaven and hell are located. In this concept heaven has all the beauty, joy and plenty, and is the reward for valour in battle, for generous gifts to the priestly class, and for austerity and other deeds of merit, and upholding Dharma, while hell has scorching heat, misery and suffering

Another group of gods are the *Adityas*, the seven sons of *Aditi*, Eternity. We do not know the names of all of them, except for *Varuna, Mitra, Aryaman, Bhaga*. Nor do we know of the source of their origination. They are the highest of the divinities, particularly *Varuna* and *Mitra*. And we conceived as the power behind other gods, rulers who have set the path for others to follow. In the Rig Veda, *Varuna* is the noblest of all the gods. He was the centre of the theistic movement of the Indo-Iranian age, and represents the loftiest thoughts connected with the divinity of that time. Originally conceived as 'the all embracing heavens, he soon acquired the status of the creator, and the sustainer of the Universe, and that is how he has been praised in the hymns contained in a section of Rig Veda. He is omniscient, the protector, the compassionate helper, the holy one from whom *Rta* the cosmic order, emanates and who rewards the righteous and sternly punishes those who violate *Dharma*. There hymns which seek his pardon, and forgiveness for violating his laws: 'whether we have sinned consciously or otherwise', or for whichever of thy laws, known or unknown, we have broken. At one stage he is close to the concept of God as visualized in Christianity or Islam, and many a scholar has felt distressed at the fading away of this to the status of the mere god of water, a second rate Neptune, overtaken first by Indra, the great war god, and later by the impersonal Brahma (the one beyond good and evil, immanent in all things and all beings of the universe; he is in fact the Universe), and still later by Vishnu and Shiva. As for the idea of rebirth, only in the tenth book of the Rig Veda are there two passages which vaguely suggest the idea. This clearly was not the belief of the Aryans; it developed in India towards the end of the Rig Vedic period, apparently after their intermixing with other racial groups.

The Rig Vedic Aryans were polytheistic, but with time all the attributes of the gods of the pantheon got transferred to one deity, and monotheism came into being. Then non-dualism, and even monoism came to be followed. But that was many centuries later, during the Upanishadic age. Otherwise, the original religion was based on sacrifice and chanting of the Vedic hymns. The family gathered in the open, along with the priest, around the altar comprising a shallow trench cut according to rules and filled with sacrificial grass. Closeby burnt three sacrificial fires where the priest chanted the incantations and made the offerings of butter, milk and grains. The animal were sacrifices over a shallow trench, to the chantings of hymns, and prayers were made to the gods beseeching them to accept the sacrifice and grant the wishes of the householder.

The religion of sacrifice reached its zenith during the period of the *Brahmanas*, and that attracted the adverse attention of some renowned thinkers and scholars, a majority of them from the *Kshatriya* class. Alongside, the ideas and thoughts of the earlier people exerted their influence. The Aryans under such influence modified their ideas about animal sacrifice, and, with time, got converted to the idea of the Dravidian *Pooja*, offering prayers with grains and flowers for the sacrificial items. Dravidian prayer brought in the worship of Shiva and the Mother Goddess. Aryans had devised four stages for the life of an individual, each stage of 25 years; they called each of them an *Ashram*, and the four Ashrams were Brahmacharya, the first 25 years during which a person abstained and studied, including the scriptures, and other arts and crafts, and acquired knowledge in different disciplines. Then was the Grahistha Ashrama, period of next 25 years, upto the age of 50 years, when the person lived as a householder and raised a family and brought forth children and trained and educated them according to the injunctions and traditions of the community and society. Then came the *Van Prastha* Ashram upto the age of 75 years, when the person passed the benefits of his experiences to the community, and where possible educated them in the ways of the world and arts and sciences. And finally it was the *Sanyas* Ashrama when he gave up the ways of the world and turned a recluse spending his time in prayers and generally preparing for his departure from this world. During this period he was generally on his own, all by himself.

Upanishadic phase of the religion of the Aryans came into being mostly through the work of the forest dwellers who had come in extensive contact with the followers of the old faiths. These thoughts had been recorded in *Aranayakas*; which had put forth views which were a near complete break from the religion of animal sacrifice. The Upanishads, in most cases, are either contained in specific *Aranayakas* or they form their supplements; only some of them are independent works. Aranayakas are appended to *Brahmanas*, and have the same style of language and content, and have given the opinion that sacrifice as detailed in the Vedic texts has only allegorical meaning and is not meant to be physically executed; they have expressed views on the meaning of the *Sanhita* text. A number of ideas are contained in the Upanishadic texts since each one of them is based on an *Aranayaka* or even otherwise, had a different author or commentator. These documents are like theses. They are research works on the ontological and the eschatological aspects of the creation of the universe. Some of them are of a rather poor religious or philosophical merit, while some contain lofty thoughts which have influenced the religious philosophy not only in India but even else where. They have emphasised one God. *Aitareya* Upanishad stresses on one *Atman* who is everything, i.e., Brahma, Indra, all the gods, the five elements, things born out of an egg or womb, all organic life, static or moving and so on. This is complete non-duality, *Advaita* as we have seen in the Systems of Philosophy, and to get complete understanding of it one has to practice austerity, self-control including negations of all passions.

As the flowing rivers disappear in the ocean

Quitting name and form,

So the knower, being liberated from name and form,

Goes unto the heavenly person, higher than the high.

And then,

He, verily, who knows that supreme Brahma

Becomes the very Brahma, and crosses over sorrow and sink,

Liberated from the knots of the heart, he becomes immortal.

When Sakalya, the disciple, asked Yajnavakaya, the great Upanishadic master and teacher as to how many gods there were in the pantheon, the latter gave the conventional number 33 major gods and 306 *Devas* or the lesser deities. But when pressed he reduced the number successively to six, three and finally one, and he called this the *Prana*, or the life force—the breath of life.

The Upanishad's time was the age of intellectual and spiritual fervour, and it is certain that the entire literature of this time has not been passed down to posterity. *Kena Upanishad*, one of the shorter works, expounds the doctrine of prevenience of Brahma, who, though in scrutable, precedes and conditions all that there is. The power behind every activity of nature and of man is Brahma, and after this truth has been realized man becomes immortal.

The *Katha Upanishad*, a highly acclaimed work, describes the divine reality as invisible, all pervading but hidden, and only intense spiritual effort, and no kind of reasoning, including philosophical, can bring the mystical experience which might give an idea—only an idea—of this great reality. The secret to immortality lies in the purification of the heart, in meditation, in realising the identity of the self within and Brahma without. For immortality is union with God. The *Prasna Upanishad* is concerned with the psychological aspects of the human personality; dividing it into 16 parts. It also has a hymn in praise of the life force. The human being is composed of such elements as vital breath, deeds, thoughts and senses deriving their being from the self. They have come out of the self, and unto the self they ultimately disappear, like a river disappearing in the sea. *Mundaka Upanishad* condemns animal sacrifice and castigates it as the profession of ignorant people. It believes that the knowledge of the divine reality can be had only through proper instruction and self discipline. Action alone is not enough, as all actions of men are merely phases of universal process of creation. A seeker has to distinguish between knowledge and wisdom. The former concerns things, acts and relations, but the latter is of Brahma alone. Beyond everything He abides for ever. The wisdom lies in becoming one with Him. *The Mandukya*, a small Upanishad, has expressed revolutionary views. It says life is divided between waking, dreaming and dreamless sleep. But transcending these is the fourth state of super conscious vision. The philosophy has been explained in terms of Ishwara, which is God with attributes, i.e., God as visualised by a normal human being. Dreamless sleep is considered as ignorance, and within this exist the states of waking and dreaming. Ishwara, would be Brahma associated with *Maya,* which is universal ignorance, and while man is associated with individual ignorance. Thus, while Ishwara controls ignorance, man is controlled by it. It states that the divine reality itself is unperceived, and unrelated to experience, unknowable, unthinkable, unnameable, not definable, the one in which everything else has ceased. These thoughts made a major contribution to the later nihilistic doctrines of monastic Buddhism.

The *Taittirya Upanishad* expresses the view that Brahma realisation leads to pure bliss, the quality of which is unthinkable by the mind and unutterable in speech. Man, it says, in his ignorance, identifies himself with the material sheaths which are wrapped around his true self. Transcending these he becomes one with Brahma, who is pure bliss. Another Upanishad, *Chandogya,* a rather long work, is of the view that the entire universe is just the highest self, even though broken into numerous entities endowed with name and form. Brahma is all, it says. From Brahma come appearances, sensations, desires, deeds. But all these are only name and form. To know Brahma one has to experience the identity between Him and the self, or the Brahma dwelling within the lotus of the heart. Only by so doing can there be escape from sorrow and death, and only thus can a being merge with the subtle essence beyond all knowledge.

Brihadranyaka Upanishad, essentially an Aranayaka and a rather long treatise, notable for its stress on the devotion to the Essential Self, explains that duality is an illusion, that devotion to the Self is not an 'I-Thou relationship', but an identification which is the quality of pure bliss. It also stresses the need to love all beings, and says that all being can experience this bliss because the Great Self is the final cause of them all. Most *Bhagti* movements in this country have their foundations in this literature. Even Buddha's essential teachings have emanated from this Upanishad.

These works are research papers wherein the authors (seers and masters) have noted down their mystic experiences and their considered findings as to the nature of the ultimate reality. No doubt there are differences in views and perceptions. Some works describe Brahma as the lord of the universe, and operator of systems that run it, while some postulate, in addition, Brahma as the inner essence of man. No work has, however, explained in detail how the multifaceted universe has emerged out of the single great self, or how its reality can be considered to be spiritual or based in the consciousness attribute of Brahma. This, one surmises, is where intuition comes in, or is realized by mystical experience. *Isha Upanishad*, a work of extreme brevity, most profound but difficult to understand, is emphatic about the need to surrender everything to the Great Self, whom it calls *Isha*. Life in the world and the life as a spiritual being, it postulates, are not compatible. Work or action does not come in the way of knowledge about God, *Isha* but when performed without attachment to reward, becomes a means to it. Renunciation implies renunciation of ego, selfishness, and not of the activity of life. The aim of all activity, as also of renunciation, is to know the self within and Brahma without and to realise that to two are the same. The self is Brahma, and Brahma is all.

Filled with Brahma are the things we see,

Filled with Brahma are the things we see not,

From out of Brahma floweth all that is:

From Brahma all; yet he is the same.

What the Upanishads have put forth is—and it is a discovery of the Upanishadic seers—that there is no difference in the identity of the highest reality and that of the innermost self of man, that the entire universe is Brahma, including everything around us, that our thoughts, being and experience originate in Him, and in spite of the apparent diversity, there is only one Ultimate Reality, and the entire microcosm and the macrocosm unite in that Reality.

As stated, the religion of the Indo-Aryans was of sacrifice. By the time of the, Sama and the Yajur Vedas, and the Brahmanas, the cult of sacrifice had so dominated that even the gods had receded to a position of secondary importance. The incantations contained in these books were considered to be potent enough to bend the gods to grant the wishes. Some minor deities of the Rig Veda had either altogether ceased to be venerated or had diminished in status. *Prajapati*, the lord of the created beings has been visualized in the Brahmanas as the creator and the preserver of the universe; there are numerous invocations addressed to him. He is believed to have created the universe by practising severe austerities and indulging in self torture and mortification. But there are other legends too, about creation. In some Prajapati is a created being, and the creation is caused by primeval waters, or Brahma or the force or energy which is indefinable. Desire is the germ of existence, the motive power of all creation.

The Shaivas

Prajapati is not the god of the people, *Rudra* is, as can be surmised from the incantations addressed to him in the Yajur Veda *Sanhita* and the important Brahmanas of that time, like the *Aitareya, Kaushitaki* and the *Satpatha*. This *Rudra*, though a god mentioned in the Rig Veda, is, in fact, a deity of much older times. He is a god of the non-Aryans, who outnumbered the Aryans. He is deity of the masses. On the Indus Valley seals there is an etching of an ascetic, having his member erect, and wearing a head-gear carrying horns, his arms covered with bangles. He is surrounded by wild animals and is seated in the meditation posture, *Pashupati* (lord and protector of the cattle). The erect member is typical of another very old form of this god, Lakulisha. Horns were a symbol of divinity in Egypt and the ancient Near East, while in India they have been used as emblems, as in the early Pallava sculptures, for the figures are shown as attendants on Shiva. On another seal the same god—or so it appears—is again shown as wearing horns. His matted hair are failing on his back, and he is shown between the branches of a tree, and a priest with a bull with a human face, is kneeling before him, and in the foreground seven votaries wearing conical head-dresses seem to be performing a ritual dance. *Rudra* as *Bhupati* (lord of the malevolent, evil spirits) is a dreaded god, he appears at the sacrifice in black dress and claims the sacrificial victim. Dravidians refined this concept and called him 'Shiva', the Auspicious One, or *Mahadeva* (the great god. The details of the philosophy of Shaivism as given in the *Shvetahvatara Upanishad* reflects the transition of the concept from the time of the *Atharva Veda*. *Shiva Purana*, in its sixty ninth chapter gives more than a thousand names to this god, each meant to signify an attribute of his. He is the lord of the universe, the creator, the destroyer who assimilates the entire creation unto himself when it is time for it. He is the very time, who from the moment of creation, while sustaining it on time basis, is causing its movement towards the final annihilation.

The phallic symbol of Shiva, the 'Linga', is of Proto-Australoid origin. We know they had upright conical stones as objects of veneration. The idea seems to have originated from the digging stick used by them as plough. The digging implement became the symbol of fertility, the male aspect, and what it dug into, the female aspect, in the activity of reproduction. The Dravidians symbolized the Linga as the consciousness component of the Creative power, the Supreme Self, and what it dug into, the material aspect of the creation, *Prakriti*, that which is the other component of the process of creation, but which draws its action potential only from the Supreme Self, the ocean of consciousness. By itself *Prakriti* is inert. It has the potential but that is activated only in the presence of the Supreme Self. Together the two are the constituents of God: the consciousness element the Linga, and the material element, the *Prakriti, Yoni*, the source of origination.

The story is told of a wonderous Pillar, a fiery column without beginning or end, source or summit. The gods puzzled over the mystery for a long time, and finally prayed to the Supreme God to grant them wisdom to understand the meaning of the effulgent shaft. Then Shaiva, *Lingodbhava* (in the shape of Linga), emerged out of it, and the gods were filled with awe and veneration at what they saw, and bowed and acknowledged that Shiva indeed was the infinite, the greatest of all. The great column was, in fact, the center of the universe, as also the Creator of the universe, *the Nirguna Brahma*. The shape of the Linga, it may be noted, together with the lower portion into which it is embedded, *yoni*, is like the silhouette of a person in deep meditation, the torso representing the Linga portion, while the lower cross-legged seated portion, *the yoni*. It represents the Creator in profound contemplation, in the process of creating, sustaining and annihilating the universe.

The universe, the Shaivas believe is the product of *Maya* (illusion) and is to be the scene of countless births, and of actions, both good and evil. Just as an earthen pot has clay for the material cause, the potter's wheel for the instrumental cause and the potter himself for the first or the efficient cause, the universe has Maya for the material cause, the potency of Shiva (*Shakti*)—*mythologically* Shakti is the consort of a deity, and Shiva's Shakti is *Parvati*—and the efficient cause is Shiva himself

The *Linga Purana* explains the objects of life, being *Dharma, Artha, Kaama* and *Moksha* that is follow the rules and laws of religion, generate wealth through business, trade and industry, and enjoy in good measure the pleasures of life—all these within the laws of Dharma—; and work for liberation from the cycle of rebirths. The Purana claims that its author is none other than the great Shiva himself. At no stage in this Purana has Linga been connected with sex, or has been referred to in phallic overtones; nor has this been done in any other work of the Shaivas. Some western writers and Christian missionaries, Abbe Dubois amongst them, have likened the symbol to the Priapus of the Romans and the phallus of the Egyptians. This likening is incorrect. In the remote past, some thousands of years ago, symbols might have represented the human generative organs, likening the process of creation at the cosmic level to the way the animal kingdom multiplies. But now the concept does not exist. The creator is a power of two polarities, one constituting matter, and the other consciousness. Linga is consciousness, while the source of creation, *Yoni*, is matter; in the process of explanation the Linga has been given the male polarity while the Yoni the female polarity, the latter, however, activates only at the command of consciousness. The two function in harmony. The symbol as a whole represents the creator, in creation, in harmony and complete ecstasy.

Another representation of Shiva as creator, sustainer and the annihilator is Shiva in the dancing mode, enacting the

Tandava, his dance of action, of creation and annihilation. In this his creation emerges out of a ring of fire, and under his right foot lies the demon *Muyulaga Kali*, the demon of ignorance, disorder and chaos, and in one of his left hands, out of the total four, is the torch of knowledge which alone provides liberation from the cycle of births. The left foot raised in the dance posture signifies the orderliness of the creation process, while a hand drum in one of his right hands is time, and the other hand is raised in blessing, exhorting his believers to be fearless and be above all false knowledge, including superstition. One of his left hands pointing to the rhythmic left foot, tells that the creation is governed by Dharma, the Law. It tells them that life is not a simple game, but a delicate act where each movement has to be carefully balanced so that Dharma is not violated. Shiva is the soul of all, and his dance is the creation, preservation and the annihilation process. The dance is ceaseless and eternal. It has been variously interpreted by different scholars. It represents Shiva as the source of all movement within the universe, the ceaseless movement causing the five acts of creation, preservation, annihilation, embodiment and release. The place of dance, Tillai or Chidambram, is in fact the human heart, and the release is secured once the knowledge of the reality has been gained. Some opinions suggest that the dance is enacted in a cremation ground and Shiva is the terrible and the destroyer. For some others the burning ground is the heart of the devotee, waste and desolate, where the self and its deeds get burnt including all else except the dancer himself.

In the iconography of the Shaivas, Shiva is also shown as *Ardhnarishvara*, the right half male and the left female, both together forming one whole, suggesting male and female polarity in the one, like in a seed, and that manifested universe emerges out of this seed, that is, the two polarities are not different entities, but attributes of one Being. The icon also signifies desire, the simultaneous experience of longing and union—the left female side merging softly and unobtrusively with the right male side. Desire along with fervour, is the germ that initiates the activity of creation.

Shiva is the reality, *sat* (being), hidden behind the folds of appearance cast by that attribute of His which creates the phenomenal universe. He is visualized in the posture of deep meditation, sustaining among others, the dance of phenomenal creation.

Thus the concept of Shiva started as god *Lakulisa* of the Proto-Australoids, and was in vogue for a couple of thousand years; he is the god of fertility, the great impregnator, the creator, the sustainer, in total harmony, for ever in ecstasy and deep meditation. He is benevolent but also the annihilator. His devotees worship him as the auspicious one, the supporter of good, the destroy of evil, the great redeemer who takes care of his followers, gives them abundant crops and protects their cattle, *Pashupati*, whose ride is a bull and weapon a trident.

In the Rig Veda there are few early hymns devoted to god Rudra, literally 'the howler'. He commands the destructive constituents of nature, like floods, storms, lightning. His abode is in the mountains, and he is rough and terrifying and has to be worshipped for protection against his malevolence. Soon enough, however, this god merged with Shiva, who is the auspicious one, and not the malevolent, terrifying one. In the later portions of the Veda and in the *Svetasvatara Upanishad* he is the lord of the universe, the god whose one concern is the well-being of his creation. He is Time, justice, fire, water, the sun, the destroyer, the creator. He is riding a white bull as god of justice. When the god and the non-gods together churned the ocean of milk for the nectar of immortality, the first thing to surface was the deadly poison, and it was Shiva who swallowed this poison to render the nectar pure. In the process his throat turned blue. For this he is called *Neelkantha*, the one with the blue throat. Though the Shaivas and the Vaishnavas duly air the superiority of their respective deities, there is little difference in the concept and the philosophy of either.

Shiva's hair has a light reddish tinge, like the hair of Proto Australoids, and these are thickly matted and gathered over the head in a bun, like the hair of an ascetic. He has four arms, looking after the four directions in which the universe is spread, and seated in the meditation posture. He has three eyes, the third one in the center of the forehead, all three together taking care of the three divisions of time, viz., the past, present and the future. He holds a trident in one of his hands, and this, according to some, shows him as the master of all waters. Some believe that the trident signifies his being the creator and the sustainer of the universe and also the one who eventually folds it up. The hand drum shows his being the creator and annihilator of time as also its regulator at the astronomical level. There is a crescent on the bun of hair on his head to denote the measurement time by the phases of the moon, the serpent around the neck is for the measurement time by years. Sometimes he is shown with necklace of human skulls to depict lapse and re-emergence of ages and the extinction and succession of generation of life. Sometimes he is shown totally covered with serpents to denote immortality. His followers believe him to be the lord of the universe, its creator, sustainer and destroyer. He is the time, the conqueror of life and death, the cause of life and being, the dispenser of the tears of the mortals. He is the great god, Mahadeva, the creator, Sadashiva, lord of the universe, Jagesvara, and eternally in meditation, Yogeshvara, supporter of the moon, Somnatha, Chandrashekhra, and of the milky way, the universe, Gangadhara, the divine dancer, Natraja, the conqueror of evil, Tripurantaka, and of death, Mrityunjaya, the terrible, Bhairava, the destroyer, Mahakala, the lord of the demons, Bhutanatha. In the final version, however, 'Shiva is all and all is Shiva, All that is seen, heard or perceived is but a manifestation of the great God; in everything and everything is in him.

The *Shiva Upa-Purana*, essentially a Shaiva manual and not a Purana in the real sense, written in the form of a discourse to ascetics and Rishis, covers the rules for the Linga worship and the prayers to addressed to Shiva during the different times of the day, month, year, and the places and things sanctioned by Him, i.e., when, where or with what items of worship could the prayers be made for maximum effect. It talks about the birth of Vishnu and Brahma, the creation and the division of the universe, and the creation of all things from the Linga, and has the details of the flower offerings to the Linga, the methods of practising Yoga and rule of observances in honour of Shiva. It glorifies Varanasi and some other places where the god can be worshipped with effect. The second part of the manual is almost wholly devoted to Shiva stories.

With the devotional mode of worship gaining popularity during a few centuries before Christ, Shiva is God with attributes and is worshipped in the human male form. The matter of the universe is termed His Shakti, power, energy, and is inseparable from Him, and is the source of all energy when activated by Him. In the common parlance this energy is represented as His spouse, the Great Goddess, Mahadevi, Maheshvari, the glorious Gauri, emitting fire from her mouth, Jawalamukhi, with eyes laden with love, Kamakshi, the great beauty Mahalakshmi, the daughter of the mountains, Parvati, devoted wife, Sati, Virgin, Kumari, Durga, Mother Uma, Ambika, the great force Mahashakti and also the terrible Bhairavi, the destroyer, Kali, Chamunda, goddess of epidemics, Sitala and so on. Apart from the other epithets, Shiva also has one calling him a loving husband Kalyansundra. While the Immanence of Shiva is eternal, unperishable, his Shaktis appear only during a period of creation and merge with him at the time of dissolution. The Shaktis represent the attributes of the great energy that creates.

With time triad of Brahma, Vishnu, and Shiva came to be recognized as different aspects of the creator: Brahma as the creator aspect, Vishnu the sustenance and Shiva the annihilation aspect.

As Joseph Campbell writes in his book. *The Myths to Live By*, mythologies and their deities are projections of the psyche, like the stuff the dreams are made up of, and because all human beings have evolved from a common background, the stuff they dream about, or put in their mythologies, is strikingly similar throughout the world. The essentials of most religious thoughts and philosophies are based on these mythologies. The Linga of the Proto-Australoids, the *Skambha*, the great fiery pillar without the beginning or the end, of the Shaivas, the minarets of the structure of a mosque, the dome of Christian Church are all embellishments of the basic original thought, viz,, the male symbol of fertility. The concepts of 'Father, Son and the Holy Spirit', and

'Shiva, Ganesha, and the Cosmic Energy', are strikingly similar. In the beginning the human being felt it were the elements, the floods, quakes, droughts and similar natural phenomena, which were his worst enemies, and he also noted that the hardship he had to endure had little to do with his personal performance or conduct. He, therefore, took these forces to be all powerful deities and in order to escape their malevolence he did whatever he thought he ought to do to escape their negativity. There is, thus, a certain commonness in the pattern of primitive religions. Worship of the motherhood of God came first. It continues in most religions, in one form or another to this day. Then came the worship of fertility. Human being learnt to worship the forces he thought were there to harm him. His keen observation showed him that most of the time things did not perish for good; there was only a change of form. The trees shed their leaves which partly turned into dist and partly the food for other vegetation. The elements grind the mighty hills and get soil. The conclusion was that the material content in the world, and the universe, was for ever constant.

If the material content for ever remained constant, so did the spiritual content, the content of consciousness. He realised that although his personal effort had a lot to do with his success or failure, it did not account for everything that his effort brought. That is where the idea of religion came in, idea that there were powers superior to him, in heavens or other worlds, which controlled his destiny. Some times he felt that his behaviour, even his physical actions, like kind of genuflexions he did, or the way he raised his hands in prayers, or skywards, or the like of things he did, like telling lies etc., had a direct impact on the kind of fate he met with. Not being able to solve the mystery of life he resorted to magic etc. to secure his safety and the safety of his progeny. He found life to be harsh, a losing struggle. He turned to gods for help, recited prayers, incantations, sacrificed, killed, indulged in sexual rituals, and came to the conclusion that like in the visible world each action precipitates certain results, in the hereafter too this must hold good. Thus was born the theory of Karma. It presumes that nothing ever perishes, matter or spirit. At the time of death the material element in the body goes back to the materials of the world, while the spiritual merges with the overall consciousness. But the deeds of a being, which also do not perish, influence the spirit, and force it to pick up the matter again and, thus, push it into yet another birth. What form emerges in the next birth, depends upon the quality of the deeds. No species, other than the human beings, have much of a volitional capability in this regard, and the soul goes through this stage of the journey, mechanically. It is only after it has assumed the human form, it acquires the capacity to fight the deeds and be freed of their hold and attain liberation and merge in the vast sea of consciousness, which the abode of unbounded bliss. Thus, it is the law, the Dharma, which precipitates the effect depending upon the effect generating activity. Any activity against the Dharma would be troublesome. Man's intuition guided him to this conclusion.

Dharma regulates the universe. But who regulates Dharma? The conclusion is that Dharma is an attribute of the Creator, that the universe is only a manifestation of His, for He is consciousness, and matter, and time and dharma and anything else that mind can think of, and also all else which is beyond the comprehension of the frail and limited human experience.

Broadly the Hindu philosophy has done away with God. The universe and its functioning is a system operating under prescribed laws at the physical, spiritual, intellectual and any number of other levels. To attain peace, health and happiness it is necessary to understand the system and then work in unison with it. It is a harsh, unforgiving system, for above all it does not accommodate weakness. The meek might inherit the kingdom of God, but the weak shall never do it. With the popularity of the devotional worship, however, God was ascribed attributes which the weak were made to believe, were beneficial to them, to their distress, pain, misery. But the main philosophical thought of Hinduism, like that of Buddhism, or Jainism, supported the system view-point.

At the other end of the spectrum are the atheists, not in small numbers, who believe the universe is only a physical system. But people with theistic beliefs contribute to *Sa Guna* Brahma, God with attributes, a personal God who is the Creator and the

Ruler of the universe. Along side there is a pantheon of smaller gods, like Hanuman in northern parts of India and Ganesha in the Central Indian areas. The approach is that of the four activities prescribed for an individual, viz., *Dharma Artha, Kaama* and *Moksha,* (righteousness, generation of wealth, enjoying the legitimate pleasures of life and seeking freedom from the birth cycle), the blessings of lesser deities are good enough and beneficial enough for success in the case of the first three group of activities. But for *Moksha,* liberation from the birth cycle, grace of God has to be secured through wholehearted devotion to Him. With higher understanding the pantheon vanishes out of sight and all that remains is the personal God, the ruler of the universe. In the final stage, however, it is only the Nirguna Brahma, the one without attributes, That which is all there is in creation, which is the creation itself, the one who cannot be divided, everything is but a manifestation of His.

Thus, Shiva Iconography has a glorious aspect and also a frightening one. The latter based directly on the religion of the Proto-Australoids, shows him with his Shakti, Parvati, both black and naked, in ascetic guise, smeared with funeral ashes, their matted secured in buns over their heads, the snakes and a necklace of human heads serving as ornaments, drinking blood out of skulls, munching flesh and dancing on corpses to the sound of drums, in drunken ecstasy, in the company of demons and witches, around a fire in lonely cremation ground. The iconography is based on the myths around Shiva, on his being the glorious God, the Lord of the universe, in his being in his abode on Mount Kailasha, in the company of adoring gods, deities and saints, his spouse Parvati seated next to him, while in the depth of the mountain the demon king Ravana is held in captivity (possibly to emphasize the inferiority of demoniacal deities). In this mode Shiva is showering blessings on his devotees, granting their wishes and showing them the way to eternal liberation.

Once when Shiva had been in meditation for too long a time, and his spouse had been missing and pining for him, Kaama, the god of love, felt sympathy for the spouse and felt he ought to awaken desire in him so that he (Shiva) might satisfy the desires of the great goddess, and with this end in view he spread desire around and that awakened Shiva from his meditation, but the disturbance so enraged the god that he opened his third eye and burnt Kaama to cinders. This evoked a strong protest from Ratti, Kaama's spouse, and she took Kaama's body to Shiva and told him that what Kaama had done was for the good of Shiva's spouse so that she might not pine for him (Shiva) and thus be in misery, and requested him to restore his life and his position amongst gods. Other gods also joined Ratti. But Shiva refused to relent and after a lot of cajoling agreed that Kaama would be alive for the duration of each spring, when he shall, in keeping with his role as the god of love, turn the world beautiful and load it with desire. This brought joy amongst the gods.

The devotees, however, also worship Shiva for his fear infusing mode also, for they regard this as an attribute of the transcendental god head, like light and darkness, life and death, for Shiva or Bhairava or Bhutanatha, Gauri or Kali are the same. Even the great goddess is no more than an aspect of the great god, who is male and female *Ardhanarishvara,* and who ultimately is neither one nor the other. He is Nirguna Brahma, one who is beyond comprehension and beyond definition.

The Mother Goddess

The religion of the Mother Goddess is as old and as wide spread as the human race. The first observation of man was his birth from the womb of a woman, his mother. He imagined to creator in the image of a woman. The mother not only brought him into the world. But even sustained him during his critical young years. It would be wrong to believe that belief in the motherhood of God is peculiar to any one country or area. This came to man as naturally as his ability and capability to hunt for food. The most ancient and primitive people of the world believed in the motherhood of god. Indus people had terracotta or faience figurines of standing, semi-nude female forms, wearing a girdle or a band around the loins, and elaborate head-dress and jewellery. Such figurines have been found in many countries in western Asia. In India they have been used as village or family goddesses. Such deities in primitive times, in some primitive areas even now, are regarded as village deities, the all powerful Mother, goddess, protecting the family and showering blessings.

One Harappa seal shows a nude female turned upside down, legs spread, and a plant coming out of her vagina. The reverse side of this seal has a man in the process of beheading a woman with a sickle: this apparently is a sacrifice to the goddess of fertility. The concept of the fatherhood of God came much later; the acceptance Mother Goddess came first. The former got in when the system property ownership came into being. Man being the stronger of the two sexes, became the owner of the property, and everything else that depended on it. The property generated wealth, shelter, food, cattle: all the means of survival, leisure, development of arts, crafts, sciences, and scientific outlook. He made laws that put him above the women; he made his position totally unassailable. He was the hero of strife and war. He was a great killer of other human beings, the fellow human beings, and would not tolerate systems designed by others that differed from his. Nature had designed him to be an egoist, which trait often took him to the heights of achievement, but also sank him to the depths of degradation, intolerance, and reduced him to the level of a killer machine, a despot, tyrant, developing into a kind of a monster who ceaselessly worked for his own selfish interests, a kind of an ogre who was forever out to swallow whatever bolstered his ego, status, position. He was a dangerous species, one who laid waste the God's creation.

Some dispassionately thinking people saw through this and pleaded with him of the futility of this behaviour pattern, and preached good things, bringing in religion, but even religion, which wise men preached to cool him off from his intolerance hardly made any difference. The different viewpoints instead became the arguments for intolerance. And so the fight, killing, plunder goes on. The other trait which played havoc with his efforts for comfort and tranquility, was his passion to possess. He strove hard to possess, while men of religion told him possessions only brought misery and suffering, he did not understand the logic behind this kind of preaching. The conclusion is that perhaps the creator of human beings is a violent self indulging for, and his progeny, the human species, has been created by Him just for strife, just to provide him amusement, he, the human being, is the variety in the segments of His creation.

Would any species be happy in zone of no-strife? Perhaps not. He would then be growing up in a zone of total vacuum, a situation devoid of vitality, freshness, energy, love, hate, and so on. For us earthlings, because of the way we have been created by the Great Being, and the way we vanish out of existence, the life of strife would be the most rewarding. To be different would be like a species from a different environment for ever choking for fresh air.

There is no evidence of the Linga-Yoni worship during the Indus culture. They seem to have confined themselves to the worship of *Lakulisa*, possibly the deity of the primitive people, though clearly this god appears to have been adopted by the others as well. The cult of this deity appears to have been developed by some sect, possibly the *Siddhas*. This sect have placed great emphasis on celibacy. They were possibly anterior in time to the onset of Indus culture, and could have been a off-shoot of the Proto-Australoids. Amongst South Indian Proto-Australoids, Siddha tradition is practised even to this day. Siddhas, the perfect ones, renounce the world, practise celibacy and meditative mode of worship, live away from human habitations, and avoid being covetous, concupiscent or indulge in love or hatred, or participate in worldly activities. They observe austerities in their worship, even to the extent of self-mortification. They initiated a system of medicine which is particularly popular in South India. In North India the followers of this system are called the Sadhus, although the term now applies to any hermit. Their one belief is that human mind and body have latent energy which, when harnessed, can endow extraordinary powers to the seeker. They believe that through the control of breath and concentration of thought in the meditative posture an individual attains powers, including the capability to survive without food, or harshness of weather even without clothes or proper shelter, and attain mental bliss and freedom from sensual desires or pain of hurt, infirmity or grief, and attain true knowledge about his being, and the universe, acquire the capability to walk on air or water or be anywhere without physically travelling, take to repose at any time or place.

The sect believes that each person carries within him a psychic force, *Kundalini* (the nearest equivalent modern expression would be *Libido*) which in normal course lies coiled up like a serpent at the bottom of the spinal column, and when activated or awakened, this force can achieve all that has been mentioned above, and more. The awakening is achieved by practising *Kundalini* Yoga, which has to be practiced under the guidance of a Guru. This Yoga is a combination of ordinary Yoga practices, breath control exercises and meditation. During the awakening process the seat of the energy rises gradually from the bottom of the spine to the level of the lower abdomen, the abdomen proper, heart, throat and finally to the cerebrum. The explanation is that an ordinary person is a being of the senses, engrossed entirely in the process of eating, secreting, and pro-creation, like any other species: thus he is born, and performing the same functions he passes out of this world. With the awakening of the *Kundalini* he becomes aware of the pattern and purpose of creation, the aspect of the universal nature of the consciousness, and as he rises higher, above the abdominal stage, he enters the level of intellect, and finally that of wisdom, which is the same as Brahma realisation. The stage is now set for his final release. During the meditative practices the seeker collects what are called *Siddhis*, which bestow upon him the powers to achieve what has been-stated-above (he is now in—a position—to perform miracles), but he is advised not to get distracted by the power of the rising. *Kundalini* and stay on course till the end of the journey, at which stage all his organs and faculties integrate into a complete whole, resulting in spiritual joy, *Ananda*.

It is, however, not to be believed that the entire doctrine (these people have put forth mutually supporting ideas in the fields of religion, medicine, astrology, astronomy), is of the pre-Indus time. Indeed the ideas kept flowing into it (the followers being totally freed from all worldly problems and given entirely to thinking about the phenomena of divinity and creation, sustenance, death, and they did this for a long time, till almost the end of the Vedic era. *Siddhas* contributed to the basic Hindu thought and philosophy. Most religious ideas which originated in this country have been influenced by the teachings of the *Siddhas*; like

Buddhism, Jainism, Sikhism. Indeed even the original religion of the Aryans was almost wiped out. The followers this belief are sprinkled throughout the length and the breadth of the country. A vast majority of them wear simple saffron clothes and are respected by the people for their knowledge of the esoteric aspects of the religion. They live in seclusion, some wearing no clothes at a through out the year, (they are called the Nagas, the nude ones) during heat, rain or cold away from sources of temptation, studying religion, the Vedas. They keep their bodies smeared with ash secured from burning wood, and cinders. They appear in public, including the nude ones, once in a while, on the occasions of religious baths, when they have priority over everyone and for all rites. Seeing them naked is considered auspicious by the believers. Properly clothed most of them spend time in leisure, in discussions, and smoking *Marijuna* or *Hashish*. They do not communicate with laity and do not indulge in preaching, or express their views on any aspect of religion. For food they have to either depend on charity or begging. Their influence on the social and political aspects of the lives of the people is minimal. They have influenced religious leaders from time to time, but most of the time they are not aggressively active in any political, social or religious activity of the society. In fact their approach is that of a total lack of interest in any worldly thing. They have the aim of achieving *Moksha* in life, and have been given a regimen to follow, and they have been trained to work directly to achieve their aim.

Durga is the Mother Goddess (she goes by many other names as well, as has been explained earlier). Her complete subjugation of powerful male opponent is illustrated in the legends. The name Durga is derived from a mighty demon king whom she had to killed to deliver the humanity of his oppression. She was brave and was, an active warrior when it came to the defence of her devotees, of the good and orderly, of *dharma*. The other powerful opponent was the demon *Mahishasura*, who was oppressing humanity just to destroy Dharma. It came to the stage when the demon expressed a resolve to ravish the beautiful goddess. A fight ensued and the legend has it that the demon was initially successful and the goddess had to retreat to the cave at a place now called Vaishno Devi, after her. With remarkable sanguinity; legend puts forth, the goddess got the better of the demon and slew him. Much is made of this religious tale, and in North India, during the auspicious days of the Navratras her victory over the demon is celebrated with much fan fare. In Eastern India she is the Great Goddess who visits the earth for ten days and showers her beneficence. The occasion is celebrated as Durga Puja, worship of Durga.

In the Shaiva beliefs Durga is the consort of Shiva, and at the end of her visit to the earth she goes back to him. But the noteworthy feature is that the worship is directed towards the Great Goddess as Mother and not as the spouse of the male god Shiva; it has nothing to do with Shiva.

An important legend in this lore, as contained in the Vayu Purana is that of Daksha, a celebrated Prajapati born from the thumb of Brahma. Prajapati is the lord of the creatures, the primordial God, father of gods and all things. He is the one to whom all sacrifices and prayers are addressed in the Brahmanas. One of his daughters, Sati, was married to Shiva. Both Shiva and Sati were not invited by Daksha to an important sacrifice that he had organized, for he considered Shiva to be a mendicant and uncouth, not good enough to qualify to be an invitee for the occasion. Daughter Sati was distressed and against the advice of Shiva decided to attend the function anyway. During the function Daksha and his sons poured insults and contempt on Shiva, calling him a beggarly person, keeping company of demons and snakes, and this so incensed Sati that she flung herself into the sacrificial fire and burnt herself to death. Shiva was displeased with Daksha, and sent Vir Bhadra of one thousand arms, created out of a lock of his hair, to completely disrupt the sacrifice. This the latter did, but the perishing of Sati saddened Shiva so much that he closely clasped her body and flew about the heavens to get over the grief. With time, the limbs of the goddess dropped off bit by bit, and the places where they dropped have become sacred to the worshippers of Mother Goddess. Pilgrims visit the places to seek her blessings. Here again the Great Mother has identity independent of Shiva, and is worshipped as such, and not as the spouse of Shiva. In some accounts Daksha gets killed by Vir Bhadra, and only after entreaties of Brahma and Vishnu is he revived by Shiva, but with the head of a ram for his own head could not be found at the site of the sacrifice. In the Puranic accounts apart from the vanquishing of Daksha a number of other Vedic gods get mauled in this episode. May be by the time this account was formulated the Dravidian group of races were in the process of gaining ascendancy, the account appears to be an interpolation by the Dravidian group of races.

The definition of 'Sati' is derived from this episode and implies a widow's consent to be bound with the corpse of her husband, once that has happened she is regarded as having perished as his wife. She does not have to be physically burnt with the corpse.

Alongside the belief in the motherhood of God, animism i.e., belief in natural phenomena and things animate or inanimate possessing individual souls, also flourished, and that made gods out of phenomena like winds, fire, stones, trees, animals, and brought in zoomorphic deities like monkey god Hanuman or elephant headed Ganesha, or Nagas, or Yakshas. With the fatherhood of God, these deities were visualized in male form. As property oriented patriarchal societies developed and fatherhood of God came to be widely accepted. The motherhood concept was followed mostly in the eastern and the north-eastern and the western and the north-western parts of the country; while Shiva worship became common in the Himalayan foothills and south India (under extensive Dravidian influence), although to a lesser or greater degree he has a following throughout the country. In fact most Hindu temples to day provide facilities for the worship of God in all the major recognized forms.

The Shaktas

The followers of this branch of religion worship *Shakti*, the power that creates the universe, for Shakti and Shiva are two poles of the creation; Shiva being the immanence, wisdom or consciousness, the dominant and the all pervading principle, the Shakti is the active principle, the power of creation, and the Shaktas believe that when the prayers to the Great Goddess are addressed with a certain methodology, the path for the realisation of the ultimate goal, which is to secure liberation from the cycle of rebirths, *Sansara,* becomes shorter and the chances of achievement more certain. The original idea is perhaps of the pre-Indus Valley times, and may have been contribution of the *Siddhas*, but in its final form it does not appear to be older than 800-1000 years. In this style of worship the emphasis is on recitation of specified incantations and the worship of the goddess sacrificing grains, flowers, grass etc., arranged in a specifies manner on the sanctified altar, on geometrically drawn triangles and circles. These are made with flour or powdered colour, mostly red or saffron worship is called Puja and distinctly different from the worship with fire and sacrifice which was the practice followed by the Aryans. This style of worship is known as *Tantric.*

During the later stages of the Vedic religion the Tantric method of worship had not only been accepted but was given a higher place by some authorities. The system, however, is not to be confused with worship of Mother Goddess. In fact it is not the ordinary type of worship. It is based on magic formulas and some specified activity, under the guidance of a preceptor, all designed to speed up the process of union with Shiva, for Shiva is the seat of bliss; he is that level to which nothing can be added, and wherefrom nothing can be deducted; it has externality, constance, a no-agitation situation. This creates a vastness of unbounded peace, a being in total bliss; it is the ultimate goal in the process of liberation.

This worship is a complex process, and time consuming, and is not something that one might take on alongside other mundane occupations, or during the time one might have after attending to normal chores. The details of the prescribed methods are contained in the books called the *Tantras*. The system is based on the belief that Shiva and Shakti are in fact one whole, that the active aspect is Shakti and the path to union with Shiva, or Brahma, the Immanence, where the store house of bliss is, through Shakti, the active principle.

The core literature has sometimes been written in esoteric language, called the *Sandhbhasha*, and the rituals to be performed are often written out using erotic expressions. The approach is not fundamentalistic; the individual is free to select a course that he considers to be the most suitable for his background and temperament. Before an individual gets to the higher stages of worship, he has to know the scriptures and other religious literature, including the Ramayana, the Mahabharata, the Vedas and the important Upanishads. In this worship pilgrimages or circumambulations are not as important as meditation and Yoga. The person prays to his favourite goddess with ardency, devotion and sincerity under the guidance of his preceptor, maintaining his system toned up practicing Yoga. This gives a lasting purity to his body and mind and all base and unclean thoughts get banished. The next stage is meditation when he awakens the *Kundalini* energy, and finally after a lot of rituals, prayer, recitation of incantations, yoga and meditation, he reaches the goal.

The *Kundalini* energy that rises from the base of the spine is visualised as female, while the brain center where to it rises is identified with Shiva, the Absolute Wisdom. This union of the male and the female principles is often described in esoteric and erotic language.

Apart from the emphasis on following the details of rituals, Tantras lay stress on the need to follow spiritual discipline, *Sadhna*. Its aim is to eliminate the distinction between the phenomenal and the absolute world in the mind of the disciple; this is achieved through constant contemplation till he sees the whole as one reality. This thought is basic to the monoistic doctrine as well. The person practicing *tantras* experiences his own being, including his mind and intellect, to be non-substantial, and that leads to the realization that Brahma is all. 'I am Brahma *Aham Brahm Amsi*, for his own non-substantiality in fact resides within the substantiality of the ultimate Creator. There is hardly any difference between Tantric and non-Tantric philosophy except that the Tantrics are talking about actual experience. Their's is a psycho-experimental interpretation of the non-Tantric view of the phenomenal and the absolute worlds. To know the truth the Tantric experiments and while doing so he is not rigidly following the conventional moral or social norms. They claim the course they follow is dangerous and radical, but along it lies the short cut to liberation. 'It the ego stuff is the product of the mind, the thought process, *Manas*, when it is experiencing the materialized world. But when the *Manas* turns its attention away from the world perceived through senses and ponders over the primordial cause of its own being, and that of the universal source of all consciousness, it becomes aware of its own transient status, and realises that beyond the transience lies the wholly substantive Brahma. This revelation is not secured through analytical thought or logical reasoning. It is achieved by bringing the mind, *Manas*, to complete rest and relinquishing all thought-activities. The process takes the person through a series of rising dimensions of spiritual awareness which, though it cannot be described, is experienced with the hitherto undeveloped organs of intuitive consciousness into which *Manas* is transformed after it has turned away from the activities of the outer senses, and the discriminatory activity of the intellect. At the final level it is the experience of infinity and the merging of the phenomenal and the absolute worlds. It is the experience of the union of the two poles and of the oneness of Brahma/Shiva and His creation.

This is achieved through meditation, by closing the mind to the thoughts provoked by the senses, and the analytical activity of the intellect and also, as Anagrika Govinda says, "by reversing the direction of the inner vision from the manifold to the unified, limited to the unlimited, intellectual to the intuitive, till all else is banished and it is only infinity". Success in the meditative process is achieved with *Mantra*, incantation, mystical utterance. A *Mantra* is not a hymn or a realm. It has been variously defined, but in essence it is a composition of certain letters and words, purposely arranged to produce a sequence of sounds designed to bestow magical or spiritual powers on the reciter. For this, the words have to be intoned in a prescribed manner. The words need not necessarily have meanings in the ordinary sense; to a lay listener some of them may be just gibber. But to an adept or the aspirant, these are pronouncements containing an experience content of the realm of the gods and mystical powers. The *Mantra* is given by a Guru to his disciple, in secrecy, during a specified ritual. Otherwise, mere reciting a collection of words, which may be given as *Mantra*, has little meaning. In the non-tantric religion, however, the *Mantra* by itself has the necessary potency.

The essential purpose of the *Mantra* is to secure the support of the good and the malevolent gods for a fruitful, happy life, including the life of family, or the clan; to seek things of life which are not easily available or not available at all, or as in the Tantra system) to identify with the object of prayer, like *Aham Brahm Amsi* (I am Brahma). A *mantra* has two portions, one, where the word have meaning, and together they make a pithy statement designed to give its purpose, and two, where the syllables make no sense (these are called *Bija*, Seed), e.g., word 'OM' which is part of most *mantras*, has no meaning whatsoever. Their origin, it is believed, is through some super sensory perception during a meditation! It is revealed in a flash as a complete unit, and this is considered to be the most powerful portion of a *Mantra*. There are differing views, however, on the potency of the *bijas*. Materialists of the *Charvaka School* term them as meaningless gibber. Most traditionalists do not accept the claim of their efficacy. Tantras, however, say *bijas* produce vibrations within the psyche which lift the *manas* to the level of intuitive consciousness. This is said to be particularly true of the *mantras* which are used for meditation, the ones which are given by a Guru, and also those which are used in rituals, like purifying a place of all evil influences, like before starting meditation. There are *Mantras* which are believed to have been revealed by Shiva himself; these have been compiled in a book called *Mantra Shastra*. These *mantras* fall in two categories: *Hadi and Kadi Mantras*. The former are used where the aim is union with Shiva, while the latter are used for mundane purposes.

Mantra then is the means to get the mind detached from the senses or the wanderings of the intellect. It is through Yoga that the mind acquires the discipline and the capability to concentrate only on *Mantra* and banish all other thoughts or feelings and eventually reach a state of deep meditation. There are four categories of yoga:

(a) *Mantra Yoga* aims to secure the concentration of thought by repeating mentally the Mantra and fixing the thought upon it, holding it there and not letting it go astray.

(b) *Hatha Yoga*, comprising a number of physical exercises which condition the body and make it healthy and fit so that the mind can concentrate and not be bothered by physical frailties. The exercises comprise body postures in different positions: lying, sitting, kneeling, standing, and breathing exercises which are believed to awaken the dormant *Kundalini*, and improve the deep meditation capability.

(c) *Laya Yoga*, the third stage when the mind can be fully and deeply engaged in meditation, when the seeker's *prana*, the vital breath, the breath of life or the life force holding the body together, merges with the cosmic consciousness and he acquires the power to direct this life force to any part of the body—this body, in fact, is a miniature universe. This is the stage when he has acquired full knowledge of the total creation and has developed the power to have his desires fulfilled, if so required; this is the essence of *shakti sadhna*; when life force is fully controlled. The individual is now a *shakti sadhak* one who has attained *shakti*, power, in the form of *siddhis*.

(d) The final stage is termed as the Raj Yoga, the ultimate stage wherein the seeker or the Sadhaka concentrates the mind through the control of the vital breath and gets into a state of trance, *samadhi*, and loses his own identity in cosmic consciousness, in the process experiencing indescribable peace and bliss. He is now free from the cycle of rebirth and has merged with the Great Shiva. The ecstasy of this state can be assessed from the story of Shiva who when disturbed in this state by the god of ecstatic love, was so incensed that he opened his third eye and reduced the poor god to ashes. This is the stage beyond which there is nothing to seek.

Initiation, Diksha, of an adept is done by a Guru with giving him a Mantra. This is done in secrecy. The Guru himself should have been initiated in his time, and he should have gone through the Sadhna, the spiritual discipline, and should have secured results. He should be a learned man of some repute, and should possess spiritual maturity and should have the experience and maturity to guide his disciple. Before a person receives *diksha* he must have the urge for spiritual experience. This would make him visit renowned teachers, and finally select for himself the one from whom he would accept the initiation. He then visits this person, listens to his discourses, gets known to him, and then states his purpose, and if the Guru feels the person would measure up to his expectations, he would agree to be his Guru. There are any number of accounts where the seekers have steadfastly sought the Gurus of their choice, even when the latter have shown reluctance. But if the Guru is convinced that the man is genuine, he gives his consent, but not before he compares his horoscope with that of the seeker to see whether their relationship would be fruitful. He then makes an assessment of the spiritual qualifications of the person and decides upon the *mantra* to be given to him, and then, on the basis of the astrological calculations, decides on the time, place and the manner of conducting the initiation; the place for this purpose is generally the Guru's residence, though it could also be a cowpen, a mango tree, temple, garden, river bank, foot of a mountain, or the bank of the Ganges: such places greatly enhance the chances of success. Then the disciple departs but only after he has paid the Guru's fee, *Dakshina* and touched his feet in humility and respect and has circumambulated him three times and accepted the *Prasad*, a small amount of eatable—some fruit or sweet—from a plate that has been touched by the Guru. He then meditates upon the *Mantra*. It is the belief of the *Tantrics* that without initiation no amount of worship has any merit.

Meditation on the *Mantra* brings results because by resting the mind on it all thoughts are progressively stilled. The mind then is like a clean slate which would have the capability to sense or experience divinity. Then the words of the *Mantra* have certain sound-vibrations which are in harmony with the deity being sought for, and those attract him. For this reason the words of the *Mantra* have to depend upon the deity and the purpose of seeking him.

The *Mantra* also establishes a direct link between the Guru and the disciple and secures the support of the former in attaining the goal. Through its medium the Guru inspires him, keeps his spiritual urge alive and does not let him lose faith in his capability or in the efficacy of the *Mantra*. It also inspires confidence in the power and the beneficence of the Guru. *Mantra* is the vehicle that takes the adept to his goal.

The Vedanta system postulates that the ultimate reality is indivisible, non-dual. But in essence it concedes the existence of two aspects within this non-duality, viz., the spiritual aspect comprising wisdom, experience of the supreme reality and the joy and bliss flowing there from, and the non-spiritual aspect comprising compassion, and the method adopted to reach spiritual enlightenment, energy and the like; the former may be termed as the static aspects and latter the dynamic. In the scheme of things the static aspect has been classified as the male principle while the dynamic the female principle. How exactly this allocation has been arrived at, it is not possible to state with any degree of certainty, it could be purely intuitive, though in the creation of life more important and crucial role is played by the female, though without the male life cannot evolve. In fact the oldest system of Indian philosophy, the Sankhya as outlined by Kapila (circa 8th century BC), postulates that the universe consists of two principles, viz., inert nature, *Prakriti*, (the later day female principle) and consciousness, *Purusha*. The universe evolves through *Prakriti*; consciousness has no role in this, it being only a spectator. But *Prakriti* in the absence of *Purusha*. In other words *Purusha* energises the dynamic principle, and then let it perform unhindered. Consciousness but only an indulgent on-looker, although the Sankhya system visualizes two distinct principles in the creation process, the later day Vedic religion combines the two as two poles of the same whole.

Shakta religion is about this dual aspect of the source of creation. It recognizes that the approach to the final experience is through the dynamic aspect and advises the seeker to latch on to it, as it were, till it transports him to the region of the psyche, beyond the level of senses and the intellect, and he experiences the merging of the two into one whole, and enjoys bliss and beatitude, and secures liberation from the cycle of births. In their iconography Shaktas have the male principle, Shiva being trampled upon by the female principle, Kali. This emphasizes the predominance of the female principle in the creation process. Shiva without Shakti is a corpse, is the belief of the Shaktas. The male principle though all pervading lies dormant, wrapped up in layers of *Prakriti*. It is also interpreted as the balance being drawn by the system between dharma and materialism. In the Kali trampling Shiva, she is believed to be in great rage, out to demolish any and everything that has violated *Dharma*. The only method of restraining her in her dance of death was for Shiva to lie down in her way and offer himself to be trampled over, and he does this, and she arrests her movements realising she had violated the wishes of the creator (who does not want his creation to be demolished), and she breaks into a kind smile, and her right hand rises in assurance of protection to the creation, exhorting them to be fearless; while lower right hand rises in a gesture of blessing. Earlier she was destructive and that is shown by the raised sword in the upper left hand and the severed head of a demon in the lower left hand. Shiva's entreaties for mercy even for the sinful, are conceded; the sinners have, no doubt, to mend their ways in the hereafter. Some suggest that Shiva, *Mahakaal*, rolling under her feet suggests the annihilation of time and space, (which what *Mahakaal* is) which ultimately get assimilated into her, before she gets assimilated into the infinite sea of consciousness.

Of the Hindu religious literature, Tantras are the most liberal and cosmopolitan in their approach. They laid down only the broad course, but they do not bind the seeker to any fundamentalistic approach or rituals. They have given full liberty to the individual to strike his own course. In fact the belief is that no two persons can follow similar courses while moving to the final destination. There will be differences depending on the physical constitution and the mental and the psychical make up. Once the initiation has been done it for the individual to decide how to tackle the problems confronted during the *sadhna*. It is accepted that religious urge is a common emotion of all mankind, and thus no one not even a Shudra or a woman may be denied the privilege of receiving the *Mantra*, or seeking the benediction of Shiva, or following a course which might open to his/her view the nature of the ultimate reality. Thus, there has to be no distinction between individuals. This led to different interpretations of the Tantric injunctions, and practices which ranged between completely orthodox, laying stress on celibacy and strict regimen for food and other habits, and total unorthodox which disregarded the accepted religious norms and advocated seeking union with the infinite even through sensual practices.

A lot of Tantric instruction is in esoteric, erotic, language, commonly termed as *Sandh Bhasha*. Of this Eliade, as quoted by Agehananda Bharti, says "... Tantric texts are frequently couched in intentional language—a secret obscure language with double meanings, wherein a particular state of consciousness is expressed in erotic terminology." The purpose, the author feels, is to camouflage the doctrine against the non-initiates and to project the *yogi* in a situation which is indispensable for his spiritual training. Another view is that as a devotee progresses towards the goal of experiencing the divinity of Shiva, a stage is reached when mind and the senses are totally purified and his prayer becomes contemplation and the mind is illumined, and he soars beyond the time and space limits, at the intuitive level. He is part of the Great Shiva, a witness to all, having an experience that would never be able to describe in the language in the normal use. He borrows the language of carnal love. It is like the work of an abstract painter who depicts dimensions of additional emotions through his abstract work, this cannot be achieved through conventional painting. Yet another view is that this is a way of representing the experiences of meditation in the form of easily comprehensible outer events. There is, thus, no question of attaching any sexuality to the yoga practices of the Tantras. The underlying object of the instructions or the details of experience, is to guide the seeker to a stage where he comprehends *shakti*, intuitively, and experiences it and moves even higher in spiritual realization, till he experiences the merging of Shakti and Shiva.

This Sandh Bhasha could even be a code language designed to repel a casual seeker, create, may be, in his mind a sense of abhorrence, and dissuade him from taking this course when his inner self is not thirsting for it. For instance term Bodhi Chitta in normal writing would mean Bodhi mind, or illumined mind, but in the intentional language, Sandh Bhasha, its meaning is believed to be semen virile. Lama Anagarika Govinda quotes a passage from one of the treatises: "all women should be enjoyed by the Sadhaka in order to experience the *Mahamudra*. Clearly this passage cannot be taken literally. It obviously is referring to that higher form of love which is not restricted to a single object. Another passage in the same genre translates: Sadhaka who has sexual intercourse with his mother, his sister, his daughter and his sister's daughter will easily succeed in his effort to secure the ultimate goal". Here again literal meaning is not intended to be followed, the instruction is conveying in esoteric language something remarkably relevant to the *sadhna*.

But there is another angle to this mode of worship. After the adept has gone through the preliminary stages of the discipline and acquired the basic capability to concentrate his mind on aspects beyond the realm of the senses and intellect, he has, preferably, to proceed further by having a female alongside him during the worship ritual. He is then equipped to unite with Shiva, immanence, the eternal wisdom, the sea of consciousness, through the medium of female polarity, the Shakti. For to secure complete experience he has to have his Shakti, like Shiva has His. During the ritual if the female sits on his left side, the ritual called left handed and when she is on his right side it is right handed. The main difference is that in the former case the items as prescribed for the ritual are actually used while in the latter case only substitutes are used.

Some followers of the left handed mode of worship emphasise that sexual contact is essential for obtaining the complete experience. The other ingredients, apart from sexual contact (*Mithuna*), prescribed for this practice are *Madya* (wine), *Matsya* (fish), *Mansa* (meat) and *Mudra*, hand movements as in a dance, but also kidney beans or parched grain. All these put together are called *Panch Makaars*, the five M's or the five essentials. Barren women and sexually impotent men are forbidden from such rituals.

At the face of it, the idea appears to be to consume high protein diet and build assured sexual potency before going for the sexual contact. No doubt elaborate ritual accompanies the consumption of the ingredients and, as the *Tantrics* say in defence of their practice that if the idea was just to have illicit sex there are many ways to do so without much fuss and noise. After taking the first four essential ingredients with due elaborate rituals the adept is ready to go in for the fifth, *mithuna*, the sexual contact. His *Shakti* is invited at this stage and the adept bathes her and dresses her in red garments and there is a lot of ritual and reciting of *Mantras* and describing this or that *Mandala*, but in essence process goes through a brief courtship, the fore play, and finally the fornication at the culmination of which the yogi releases his semen virile into his Shakti as an act of sacrifice and, thus, experiences the merging of the dynamic phenomenal aspect with the eternal wisdom. The ritual is gone through in the presence of the Guru and where applicable, his wife, if they are available; they do not have to be witnesses to the final act. In the absence of the Guru the function is presided over by the senior *sadhaka* of the group.

The ritual is gone through in single pairs or in *Chakras*, circles, in which case a number of pairs participate simultaneously, each male of the pair equivalent of Shiva and his female partner Shakti. In the right handed practices the five M's are not actually used. Either substitutes are taken, like milk for Madya or wine, or the ingredients are just in the mind while reciting the designated *Mantras* and performing the meditation. The left handed practice is, thus, considered dangerous, fit only for the most accomplished. The basic yardstick to decide whether the adept is mature enough and well versed in the *Mantra Yoga* and meditation, and has the capability to focus the mind on the object of worship and succeeded in unfolding the *Kundalini* and has the capability to merge with the cosmic wisdom when means become available, is his *bhavatraya*, disposition. There are three types in dispositions: Pashu Bhava (animal disposition), Vir Bhava (heroic disposition) and Divya Bhava (divine disposition). This last one is the highest in the order, but animal disposition is not to be considered as negative. The very fact that the Sadhaka has qualified to be considered in this light, shows he is on the road to progress, though he may yet have some way to cover and might not be suited for the Panch Makaar Sadhna, or spiritual, disciplines. Generally green disciples or Brahmans were put in this category, Brahmans because they were thoroughly opposed to the left handed practices, also referred to as *Vamchara*, and called them diabolical and unethical, taught by people of lose morals. In normal usage *Vamchara* means unrestricted fornication.

The disciple's progress from the lower to the higher disposition depends upon his ability and the intensity of his desire to seek the knowledge. The general indicators in this process are hatred, fear, backbiting, doubt, shame, feeling of family or racial superiority, or a lack of capability to break from the established tradition. Bound by these characteristics the person would still be striving on the road to progress, but freed the ranks with the very Sadashiva, the highest phenomenal aspect of God Shiva.

Once the person has reached the Vir Bhava stage, he has acquired the capability to control his senses and has been freed from the chaotic wanderings of his mind and has stepped into the region of intuition. At this stage he has uncoiled the *Kundalini* and direct it for union with eternal wisdom. He is now fit for the *Panch Makaar Sadhna*, and after a series of successful spiritual rituals he attains Divya Bhava, the divine disposition. According to Bamakeshwar Tantra, Pashu Bhava dominates a person till he attains the age of sixteen, and thereafter till the age of fifty it is Vir Bhava, and after that it is Divya Bhava. At the ultimate level the three Bhavas unite to produce a state of the mind called Kaluchara. At this stage man becomes godlike and is liberated. He is *Jeevan Mukta*, for he has attained *Jeevan Mukti*.

The essential doctrine and the practical teachings of the Buddhists and the left handed Hindu Tantras are quite similar, in both cases sexual contact is essential to the Sadhna. However, while the Buddhists allocate the male principle to the active aspect, i.e., energy, compassion, *upaya* (method), and the female principle to the static aspect, i.e., wisdom, realisation, beatitude, the Hindu Tantra, have done just the reverse. But in spite of the subtle, differences in the concepts of male and female principles, the practices followed in either case do not differ much. While some authorities, like Lama Anagrika Govinda, state that sexuality as such plays no part in the Tibetan mode of the Sadhna, others like Agehananda Bharti say that Tantric practices, particularly of the Vajrayana School, show only a few differences from the left handed Hindu Tantric system.

It is fairly certain that both the religious practices have bad some common source. Possibly Tibetan brand of Buddhism could have had its source in the Taoism of southern China, or in the pre-Buddhist Bon religion of Tibet, Bon Buddhism had its origin in Mongolia. On scrutiny, however, these hypotheses do not hold, and it seems the source was in India itself. On the basis of the evidence of the Harappan seals we know that apart from the Mother worship, the Indus Valley people were well acquainted with the ideas of Pashupati, Yoga, and asceticism. During the peak of their culture the Proto-Australoids had already organized themselves in village communities, and their priests, who probably were Siddhas, possibly performed the same kind of functions as the Shamans. There possibly were no temples as such, but these shamans, or the Siddhas, with time, seem to have developed a cult that gave a lot of importance to the male semen, and the female's capability to get fertilized. Both, i.e., the male semen and the female's capability to bear a child, were considered by them to be divine, important aspects of the Great Power that precipitated the Creation.

The mother was goddess Kali, a pitch black female demon who needed the basic substances of the created world in sacrifice for propitiation, and this included blood in the form of animal or human sacrifice, including a host of other items found in nature, like water, grains, flowers, fruit. With time there appeared Bijas, the portions of Mantras that make no literal sense. These possibly did come to the Shamans psychically, and they did use them in genuine faith in their efficacy. With the arrival of the Dravidians, things changed. Human or animal sacrifice was condemned. The religion of Shiva became more sophisticated and, with time, it embraced even the concept of Mother Goddess. This possibly led to the embellishment of the Linga-Yoni concept. But the original religion of the Australoids stayed, for these people were in majority, particularly in the rural centers where the impact of education was minimal and the religion code was framed mostly by Shamans. This state of affairs lasted, to a large or small extent till the middle of the 20th century, and even today it is fairly widespread in the rural countryside, though in the urban centres it has got mixed with other variations of Hinduism. The gods of the Australoids were visualised as some kind of despotic criminals who could be propitiated for the success of commission of any crime, provided right Mantras were recited along side right rituals. The practice of *thuggee*, loot, arson, plunder were preceded by rituals and sacrifice, even sex rites and human sacrifice, basically to Kali, the demon goddess, her blood thirsty tongue for ever hanging out to devour the victims. The shamans claimed they could precipitate success in any activity with their *bijas* and rituals.

On the other hand the Siddhas, who had generally retired to the seclusion of the forests, pondered over the issues pertaining to the methods of uniting with the ultimate reality, and came to the conclusion that *panch makaar sadhna* did cut down the time to reach the final goal. After having set the Sadhaka on the broad course, he was left to himself. It was emphasised that the narrow track to the final destination had to be discovered by the Sadhaka himself. When the Sadhna, it was claimed, was progressing along the right lines, the experience of reaching the goal was exhilarating.

Shakta concept accepts the Sankhya view that *Prakriti* or *Shakti* is the cause of the creation, and allots it the dynamic principle, but adds that ultimately it dissolves into Shiva, Purusha, Brahma, whose constituent part it is, and re-emerges at the time of the next cycle of creation. Yoga of Patanjli, which is considered a part of the Sankhya system, dwells on the rising power of Hatha Yoga, from the physical level to the higher intellectual and spiritual levels, or higher levels of awareness and consciousness, which make a person realize the reality of *Purusha* and *Prakriti*, and experience the ultimate bliss and peace. But no male or female polarity has been allotted to either of them, for *Prakriti* is not female nor *Purusha* male. They are the agencies of creation; *Prakriti* creates, and it does so in the presence of *Purusha*; put together they are just two attributes of energy. But Shaktas, while broadly accepting this, have visualized *Prakriti* as the dynamic principle and the female aspect, and *Purusha* the quiescent principle and the male aspect. The division has, apparently, been done on the basis of some kind of intuitive wisdom; the *tantric* literature does not give any reason. Having allocated the polarity, the Shaktas say that awakening of *Kundalini* puts the female energy at higher levels of consciousness, and makes it climb to the still higher ones of wisdom, till it, the physical energy, Shakti, completely loses itself and merges with this wisdom, as would happen at the time of dissolution. That is the state of liberation, absolute bliss. The short cut to this state, according to them, is through the *Panch Makaar Sadhna.*

Sometime around the beginning of the Christian era, when reading and writing had become more extensive, these ideas were reduced to writing, and these had extensive circulation by the early centuries of the current millennium; the assimilation was a slow but a sure process. The ideas were particularly popular amongst the people of Australoid extraction.

It is difficult to say whether the persons who followed these ideas did eventually realize the Para Shiva, the Creator, under the Monoistic philosophy, but drugs like cannabis, marijuana or hashish do produce euphoria quite similar to the experience during the awakening of the *Kundalini.* A lot of Sadhaka take just that and convince themselves they are on the road to progress. From around the twelfth or thirteenth centuries the Shakta philosophy started asserting and openly ridiculed the Vedic rituals, strongly denouncing the caste system that the latter supported and its injunctions forbidding the lower classes and the women from reading or practising the Vedas. This revolt was no doubt in keeping with their teachings, but their concepts had too many generalities which gave too much freedom to an individual and contained loopholes which led to outright exploitation. The followers never had it so easy—securing liberation from the birth cycle and forever live in peace and ecstasy by committing unrestricted fornication! The religion told them they would possess the Sukhas (comforts) of both the worlds. Came people joined by the droves and all varieties of gurus and godmen sprang up, who too hadn't had it so good, for they enjoyed position and status that in earlier years had not even been dreamt of by people in their vocations. Men ranging from water carriers, road sweepers and the like, to officials and dignitaries, and even kings and maharajas, were amongst the seekers. Fornication was the rage of the time. A rot set in. The vitality of the Hindu nation oozed out in the form of the *panch makaars* at the altar of the great goddess. The Muslim invaders had no serious problem in subjugating the areas where such religion existed, and later years just a handful of the British soldiers enslaved the whole country with an organization which was no more than a trading company, and which had no more military strength than local guards protecting premises of the factories operated by it. The East India Company, which came to be called Company Bahadur, the Hon'ble Company, had not arrived in India for conquest. It fell to their lot because of the degenerated rotting Indians. The opportunity was too good to be missed, for it was clear that would enrich the Company Bahadur, its officials, and even the British Crown. The religion of dissolution of the Austro Australoids was without spunk, vitality and self respect—this was the kind of culture of the Australoids and from this cultural pattern they have not got out even to this day. They are a species whose social, moral, intellectual and genetic fibre makes them a unique specimen of the non-performing humanity on this earth.

Today, extensive Vedic and modern Western education has struck at the roots of this religion of carnality, which is what it sunk into in spite of the arguments to the contrary of its supporters. But this is only a part of the Sakta religion. In the other part of the right handed rites, with its practice of Yoga and meditation, it is perfectly in line with the mainstream Hindu thought.

The Vaishnavas

The branches of Hinduism which have so far been covered had their foundation in the faiths prevalent in this country before the arrival of the Aryans. The Vaishnava Branch developed during the Vedic period, although it has borrowed ideas from the earlier cultures. It is the most popular and the most practised branch of

Hinduism. The concept has its base in the sun worship. In the Vedic hymns he is the lord of light and life. He is the Creator and beyond him there is nothing. He is the supreme God. This kind of thinking erased, almost completely, the Aryan pantheon of gods, including Mitra, Varuna, Indra, Agni, Vayu, and greatly contributed to the theistic dualism as preached by Ramanuja and Madhava, Monotheism came into being on the divine authority of the Veda. Brahma who in the earlier Vedic literature, signified the supreme God, by the time of the Brahmanas was being referred to as Prajapati, the lord of the creatures. Prayer verses and formulas were composed which were designed to give power to person, to get the gods to fulfill desires and wishes. Later, however, *Trayi Vidya*, i.e., the knowledge of the verses and formulas contained in the Veda, assumed importance. The Atharva Veda was excluded, for the learned Brahmans did accept it as of divine origin: it is essentially a collection of magic formulas and rites of the Proto-Australoids. Trayi, it was believed, was created the first, for it was the word of God, *Shabda*, breathed by the self existent to the inspired seers, who gave it, for the good of mankind, by word of mouth, from teacher to pupil, in unbroken sequence, over untold generations. Thus word was the first, in importance comparable to God Himself, for it was his breath, and it communicated what the creation was all about. The thought, thus, contemplated that which was the cause of the Trayi, and then of all creation, i.e., Vishnu. This is the time of the Brahmanas and Aranyakas.

Vishnu by this time was the all important deity to whom a important sacrifices were addressed. Another parallel concept is that of Narayana, which means 'that whose dwelling is far in the deep,' or that 'where everything eventually rests'. Like Vishnu, the origin of Narayana can also be traced to the Rig Veda. The relationship between Vishnu and Narayana concepts was established in the *Taitirilya Aranyaka*. In course of time, however both concepts almost coincided: Narayana is in everything and everything is in Narayana. There is little change in other gods of the pantheon. *Shesh Naga*, the lord of the serpent deities of the Proto-Australoids, is elevated to a position around Vishnu himself. In the creation legend Vishnu as absolute consciousness, rests in eternal peace, tranquility, bliss, upon the coiled body of Shesh Naga floating upon the sea of cosmic waters.

Another important part of the Vaishnava faith is the teachings of Shri Krishna, who is reputed to be a great reformer and philosopher, operating in the area of the Yamuna basin of north-west India, sometime before the advent of Buddhism and Jainism. He called the supreme God Bhagvata, i.e., the adorable, glorious, and venerable Lord. The term can also be used for holy persons. His followers were called the Bhagvatas. The literature about this faith is contained in Bhagvatam, while the essence of the teachings is contained in Bhagavad Gita, the song of the Supreme God. In later years Shri Krishna was deified as an *Avatara*, an incarnation of Vishnu and his teachings as contained in the Bhagavad Gita form a very important part of the Vaishnava literature, and faith.

The essential details of this faith are contained in the Vishnu Purana. The total work is divided into six lengthy books. The first of these is essentially ontological, covering details of primary and secondary creation, *Sarga and Pratisarga*. It generally follows the Sankhya system of philosophy and explains how during the *Sarga* stage the universe proceeds from *Prakriti*, the eternal crude matter and chaos, and how during the *Pratisarga* stage the form of things are developed from the elementary substances previously evolved, or how they reappear after their temporary destruction at the end of a Kalpa. The crude eternal substance is hewn into shape and form by Rta and Dharma, giving rise to phenomenal universe which lasts for one Kalpa which is one day of Brahma, equal to 4.32 billion years. Likewise one night of Brahma, when he rests, is also equal to the same number of years. Life of Brahma is 100 years, each of 360 days and 360 nights. After 100 years another Brahma takes over, the process of creation and annihilation is, thus, interminable. Both types of creations are periodical. The termination of Sarga takes place at the end of the life of Brahma, when everything gets annihilated including the gods, and the elements merge with the primary matter, *Prakriti*, besides which only the spiritual being, Vishnu, exists. The termination of Pratisarga, however, takes place at the end of every

Kalpa, and affects only the forms of lower creatures and lower worlds, leaving intact the substance of the universe and the sages and the gods. The detailed description of time over which these events take place is included in this first book. A lot of detail contained in this book has been lost but its cosmogony is known to be of great antiquity. While essentially based on the Sankhya system of philosophy, the Purana postulates that it is *Maya* that creates the illusion that *prakriti,* the energy that manipulates matter is thoroughly independent except that it creates in the presence of *Purusha* in the absence of which it is totally inert, which means that material creation, even when it takes place in the presence of *Purusha,* is non-eternal, constantly changing. All its forms are like passing shadows. Actually the Vaishnava concept differs somewhat from the Sankhya system and accepts the Vedanta system of non-dualism, *Advaita,* for it is repeatedly stated in the Purana that Vishnu is all embracing, that he is the Purusha, the spirit or consciousness, and *pradhana,* the crude matter, *vyakta* the visible form, and *Kaala,* time, while Vishnu, Purusha, is eternal and without attributes and is central to the creation process, the other three elements together constitute His Maya, the non-entity, which is what causes the Creation. At the time of dissolution Maya along with its constituents merges with Vishnu. He is both male and female like in the concept of *ardhanarishtvara* Shiva, which emphasizes the transcendental nature of God, and shows that in Him he has all the characteristics of all the pairs of the opposites. He is in everything that is created through his Maya, and everything thus created has its source in him. In the creation legend Vishnu, the ocean of consciousness, reclines in eternal peace on the coiled body of *Shesha Naga,* and out of his naval is born Brahma, destined to be the creator of the universe. Vishnu, the eternal being, thus, is the material and the efficient cause of the creation but he does not perform the deed as such, for that would be agitation, a continuous process of changing form, a continuous state of non-eternality. The job is done Brahma, born out of him, for a duration of 100 cosmic years, after which another Brahma takes over, while the previous one goes back into the sea of consciousness, thus merging with creator. For Vishnu is beyond Prakriti, Maya, and he is beyond Brahma, Purusha. He is far away in the deep, the final resting place, the abode of eternal peace and bliss.

The supreme God performs three functions, namely creation, preservation of whatever has been created and final annihilation. On the of the Rig Vedic hymn a view has been taken that these functions are performed respectively by Brahma, Vishnu and Shiva. But both the Shaivas and the Vaishnavas do not contribute to this concept. For them their respective god is supreme and is the creator, preserver and also the destroyer. Vaishnavas believe in non-dualism at the *nirguna* (without attributes) level, but at the *saguna* (with attributes) level it becomes theistic as will be seen from the expositions of Madhava. At this level, where God has attributes. He becomes a personal God, the ruler of the universe, and intense love for and devotion to Him are advocated to secure deliverance from the birth cycle.

According to the first book of Vishnu Purana the human race originated from the-will-engendered sons of Brahma. For this purpose the Brahma has two facets, namely male and female. Daughters are also begotten who are married to the Prajapatis, and there are seven sages in the line, and they have wives and the human race originates. The first pair are Manu Swayambhuva, the son of the self born or uncreated, and his wife Satarupa. Basically the entire mythology concerning the origin of the human race is allegorical, woven around the point that it all started from a single pair, that *rishis* and other learned men were historical personages who authored the 'system of social, moral, and religious obligations' and studied the heavens and developed the science of astronomy. The first book also has stories like that of Prahlada or Dhruva, which, seem to have been borrowed from other sources, like the pre-Aryan folklore. It also describe the earth as having been under the rule of kings, and people who introduced agriculture and civilization.

The second book continues with the prominent people, and the kings of the first *Manwanra*, one of the prominent amongst whom was Bharata of the Bharata clan, after whom India has chosen to give itself the name of Bharata Varsha, the land of the

Bharatas. Manvantra is a period during which one Manu takes care of the affairs of the universe. The book also gives the geographical description of the subcontinent, particularly its northern part, and also planetary details, and details of concerning astronomy. It contained a lot of mythology. The third book deals with the Vedas and other sacred literature and also sages like Vyasa, and the duties of the castes, and obligations during different stages of life, the Laws of Manu, and so on. The work is of a time earlier than most of the other Puranas, and for this reason contains no sectarian prejudices.

The fourth book is about the ancient, history, and has a comprehensive list of dynasties and persons and events. From a historical point of view it is an important work. It may not be possible from the details given to work out exactly when an event took place, or an important person appeared in that distant past, but it is possible to have a good idea of their antiquity. The likely date, for example, for the Mahabharata war from the Puranic detail, would work out to around 1500 BC and for the first regal dynasty in northern India to around 2700 BC. This would put the age of stable monarchies, following one another in continuous succession, very comparable with monarchies anywhere in the world.

The fifth book is exclusively devoted to the life of Krishna, from his birth till he destroys, as a boy cowherd, the evil king Kansa. Krishna has been mentioned in the Veda only once, and in the Mahabharata where he plays an important role, his divinity has only been alluded to. In none of the works he has been described as god incarnate; he is mostly shown as a youngster, playing naughty pranks as given in the Purana. There is thus a possibility that this part of the Purana about child Krishna is of a later date, and about a person different from Krishna of the Mahabharata or Dwarka. Similar stories about Krishna appearing in Brahma and Bhagavata, Purana and Hari Vansha, are definitely of a comparatively later date.

The sixth book is about dissolution, in the minor and major cataclysmic aspects: end of all things by fire and water, *pralaya*, and then of rebirth. It also covers the metaphysical annihilation of the universe by the withdrawal of the spiritual component from-the physical existence.

Ramayana

Ramayana, or the adventure of Rama is another important epic of the Vaishnavas. It is the story of Rama of the line of Manu Vaivasvata, (c. 3100 BC), whose son Ikshavaku of the solar dynasty was the first king of Ayodhya, and according to the Puranas this line came all the way down to king Sagara and then to Bhagiratha, Raghu, and Dashratha, and then to Rama, around 1950 BC. Historicity of Rama is well founded on the basis of the Puranic accounts. He was a great king, just and very concerned about the well being of his subjects. He vanquished the pre-Aryan tribes, including aboriginals and established a rule of law with the consequent flourishing of trade and commerce which brought happiness amongst his subjects. Even today the term 'Ram Rajya' the rule of Rama is synonymous with the rule that provides justice, contentment and happiness to the citizens.

In the Ramayana story, Dashratha the noble and brave king of Ayodhya, a descendent of the illustrious king Raghu (originally of the Ikshavaku line, but later it came to be called Raghuvansh, or Raghu's dynasty) had four sons from his three queens. The eldest Ram was born to Kaushalya, the eldest wife, and Lakshman and Shatrughana were born to Sumitra, the second wife, and Kaikeyi the youngest had Bharata. The brothers were attached to each other, Lakshman and Rama particularly so that whatever task was assigned to Rama, Lakshmana always accompanied him. Their first assignment was against aggressive pre-Aryan tribes at the behest of sage Vishwamitra, for these tribes were against the Aryans systems and opposed them at every step. While chasing them in hills and forests, Vishwamitra and the two princes arrived at Mithila where Rama won in a contest of strength, Sita, the daughter of the king Janaka. The legend has it that Sita (means furrow) was, in fact, daughter of Mother Earth and found by Janaka in a furrow during a tilling. The condition laid down for wedding Sita was the stringing of a bow of Shiva, held in the charge of Janaka. Of all the princes present from different nations, only Rama could accomplish the feat, and at the time of his wedding other princes of Ayodhya were married off to other princesses of Mithila. Thus, it was a huge marriage procession which departed from Mithila for Ayodhya, to the delight of the people of Mithila as well as of Ayodhya: Dashratha and his sons were held in high esteem by the people of both the territories. At this stage Rama and his brothers were in late adolescence.

Once Kaikeyi, who was the most charming of the three queens and the favourite of the king, had accompanied her husband to a battle, and there at a critical stage she had rendered to him service of such signal importance as had turned the fate of the battle in his favour. The king was very happy with her and offered to fulfill any one wish of hers. The queen, however, said whatever she had done was out of her love and regard for him. But the king insisted she asked for a favour and after a lot of persuasion from him she eventually agreed but said she was not disposed to ask for anything just then but would do so in the future at an appropriate time.

After the return of the Princes from Mithila, Dashratha decided to appoint Rama as the crown prince. This did not suit the part of the palace who had put their bets on Bharata, Kaikeyi's son. So they poisoned the mind of Kaikeyi; the leader of this conspiring group was Kaikeyi's personal maid, who eventually managed to catch the ear of he mistress and persuade her to get the king to redeem his promise he had made her in return for her service at a critical time in a battle. A crisis situation developed within the Palace. Kaikeyi demanded that her son Bharat be appointed the Crown Prince and Rama be banished from Ayodhya for a period of fourteen years. This plunged Dashratha into deep shock. But Rama said he had nothing against the demand of his step-mother and would gladly accept banishment and let Bharata be the ruler. Both Bharata and Lakshmana were at Mithila having fun at the house of their maternal grandfather and were not aware of the developments. Rama, however, decided to act quickly and leave on banishment, and before Bharat and Shatrughana could even be informed of the developments, he and Lakshmana and his newly wedded wife Sita were already out on an arduous journey, away from their home and hearth, heading for the forests of central India.

Bharata and Shatrughana were informed of the developments and they returned post haste and when Bharata learnt of what his mother had done he was filled with remorse and went after Rama to persuade him to return, but the latter declined, for he said, the pledge of their father had to be redeemed Dashratha was so smitten with grief that he had died before Bharata's return. Rama along with younger brother Lakshmana and wife Sita spent the first thirteen years of the exile in the Vindhyas and Central India. Many other people of Aryan extraction, including colonizers, traders, workmen and Brahmans, had preceded him; renowned sage Agastya had been touring the Vindhyas and areas of Central India and had established a working relationship with the inhabitants and there was trade and commercial activity, and inter-racial marriages, and Brahmans were putting across the essentials of the Aryan religion, culture and beliefs. A lot of positive interaction was in progress between the pre-Aryans and the Aryans. Rama helped to consolidate the gains.

At the beginning of the fourteenth year in exile, Rama along with brother Lakshmana and wife Sita moved to the area of Panchvaṭi in the central Deccan plateau. This area right down to south, towards the Island now called Sri Lanka (it was then called just Lanka) was under the influence of the powerful Lankan king Ravana. Aryans were generally hostile towards him as he resisted any Aryan territorial expansion bid; there was, thus, a conflict of interests Rama as the symbol of Aryan expansion and colonialism, came in conflict with Ravana. The Aryans were winning over the tribes in those areas and Ravana was disturbed, and he dispatched two of his brothers for an on the spot study of the situation and, if possible, to check the hostile infiltration. According to the story, Ravana's sister Swaroop Nakha also went along with the brothers. The Lankans now increased their hostile activity, more so against the Aryans pursuing their religious activity, and the Aryan friendly local population. The oppressed people approached Rama for help, and Rama told brother Lakshmana to look into the matter. A number of Ravana's soldiers from the outposts got killed in the conflict that followed. Ravana's sister Swaroop Nakha tried to seduce Lakshmana into submission and so offended the latter that he chopped off her nose (it was mended by plastic surgery by Susruta, the renowned plastic surgeon of the time), and that angered her both brothers, the commanders of the force, and in the fight that followed, both of them got killed. When the news of the disaster reached Ravana he was enraged, and arrived at the site to take stock of the situation. Through a clever stratagem he managed to abduct Sita from her cottage when both Rama and Lakshmana were away, and carried her all the way to Lanka and imprisoned her there, hoping that some day she would agree to be one of his queens. Rama marched on Lanka, having mustered some allies enroute—most important of the allies were the followers of the monkey god Hanumana. Ravana was a rich king but Rama crossed the cape from a place called Rameshwaram on the gulf of Mannar in the present times, and attacked, and burnt Lanka and killed Ravana and his kinsmen and rescued Sita and after proclaiming Bhabikshana, Ravana's estranged brother, who had deserted for he had considered Sita's detention as immoral and had urged for her immediate release, the king of Lanka, he along with Brother Lakshmana and wife Sita left for Ayodhya. The limit of the exile period was already due to expire and Rama and his party which included Hanumana, are supposed to have flown back in a flying vehicle. People of Ayodhya were happy to receive him and organized a festival of light; the return is celebrated to this day when every year on this day people light oil lamps and candles to commemorate the event.

There is a later addition entitled 'Uttarakhand' which is about the banishment of Sita. Rama banished her because he learnt that his subjects were not happy to accept, her as their Queen after she had been forced to spend almost one year in Lanka king's captivity, he could have used her any way he liked. Sita was pregnant then, and one version goes that Ramà had told Lakshmana to take her to a dense forest and there put her to death, for he saw no further good in her staying alive. But Lakshmana just took her to the dense forests above what is now called Rishikesh, beyond Hardwar, on the bank of the Ganges and after explaining his compulsions to Sita abandoned her. The place was closeby to the hermitage of a renowned non-Aryan sage Valmiki, and he gave her shelter, and Sita, soon gave birth to twin sons who, under the tutorship of Valmiki grew up to be fine, brave youths, particularly adept in martial arts, and while still in adolescence, they roundly thrashed Rama's soldiers who were guarding the horse which had been let lose as a challenge for Ashvamedha Yagna; normally a great king who wanted to assert his authority let out a horse in the open so that any one who decided to challenge him took the horse in captivity and that served as the challenge against the king who let out the horse in the first instance. If the king got the horse through challenges, he won the title of a great king, *Chakravartin* and there were celebrations in his honour and the neighbouring kingdoms paid obeisance and accepted his supremacy. But if there was a failure, then the ambitious king had to suffer humiliation, and, may be, even lose his kingdom at the hands of the challenger.

After the horse had been captured by the two youths Rama's generals tried force to take the horse, but failed. Even Hanuman and Lakshmana failed and were taken by the brothers. Then Rama himself arrived at the scene, but the boys challenged him as well, and Rama learnt that the young men were in fact his own sons and he felt pleased and took the two to Ayodhya. The court requested Rama to terminate Sita's exile and invite her to Ayodhya and be the queen. And she came, when the whole court and prominent citizens had assembled to receive her, the resplendent goddess, and stood in their midst her mind in anguish at the thought of having been once banished by her own people, and her supplicant arms rose, and unable to bear the agony of the fickle human mind, in a voice loaded with agony, she prayed to Mother Earth, whose daughter she was, to take her back into her fold, for she could no longer bear the torment she was experiencing. The earth then parted and out of it emerged a beautiful throne, seated upon which was the Mother Earth in full resplendence, her arms extended in invitation towards Sita, and Sita just went into them, and then within every one's view, including the all powerful Rama, the throne descended and the earth closed over it. This was the moment of sadness and retribution for every one for having laid a foul suspicion, blame, on a woman who was chaste and pure as the Mother Earth herself.

The story of Rama was apparently a popular folklore even before Valmiki compiled his version of it in verse form. In some versions of the folklore Rama is reluctant to accept his wife after she had been in Ravana's custody for one year or so, and this inspite of her protestations. This caused Sita's banishment. In some Rama instructs Lakshmana to take her to a dense forest and there put her to death; the problem had arisen because his subjects were not prepared to accept her as their queen after she had been in Ravana's custody. Lakshmana, however, out of respect for the queen and taking into account the fact of her pregnancy, does not carry out the order and to convince Rama showed him a sword smeared with the blood of some animal. For some people this was a rather harsh ending to an otherwise great and heroic saga. Valmiki got over the banishment problem by bringing in the fire ordeal, when to prove her fidelity and purity she walks through a burning fire and comes out unscathed. But apparently so strong were the views related to the fidelity factor that inspite of the fire ordeal brought in by Valmiki the banishment chapter stayed; it was not compiled by Valmiki. Feminists all through the ages have been unhappy with the banishment chapter, *Uttarakhand*. Additionally some views of Rama have been criticized by scholars; they have criticised his views on Shudras and the untouchables, although these appear to be later interpolations. He has thus been classified as God incarnate only upto the time of vanquishing Ravana, the king of Lanka. Thereafter he was just the king, ruling his country in accordance with the rules and customs of the time, though he is supposed to have done that so well and justly that even to this day it has been considered to be the just rule, for it brought happiness and prosperity all around.

Rama never married again, and ruled for many years, and after he felt he had accomplished whatever he had to, he left this world. As has been said historicity of Rama is well established. He was deified for his being a just king and for his having looked after his subjects, and he brought so much prosperity, happiness and contentment to his subjects that to this day this is considered to be the ideal rule—Rama Rajya, the rule of Rama, the rule of happiness contentment and prosperity, and justice, truth, nobility and plenty, a rule where the needs, desires of the people got fulfilled. This was Rama's example for posterity. He caused the spread of the Aryan religion and culture throughout the subcontinent, and that happened because he was a valiant king, and supported all progressive moves, moves which not only brought modernity but also laid the foundations of a uniform culture and religion. He was the epitome of nobility, generosity and bravery. He was great king, kind and just. And for all this he was deified.

All this happened around 1950 BC. But once deified he ceased to be a personage of history and is respected as a deified being, God incarnate, having attributes of God. When he is worshipped, the devotee is not worshipping the Rama of history. He is instead worshipping God whom he calls Rama. Therefore any comment on the basis of some historical detail, corroborated or otherwise on the life and deeds of Rama would be totally out of place. It would be against the idea behind *Avatara*. This being has divine spark and assumes the brightness of the ultimate reality itself and activates the forces of good, annihilating evil and restoring Dharma. It is this divine spark which is worshipped, and not necessarily the human being possessing it.

The idea of incarnation of God or *Avatara*, in the human form, to put mankind on the Dharma course and eliminate that which threatens the growth of the human society, is one of the basic beliefs of the Vaishnava faith. Although both Rama and Krishna are considered to be incarnations, the two strains of religion which so accept them, viz., the Vaishnavas and the Bhagvatas, are much older than this idea. It is completely absent from the old Upanishads, though it is present in the popular religion from about the second century B.C. In the Vedic literature too there is no mention of Rama and Krishna as divine beings. In fact Rama is never mentioned at all and Krishna is mentioned but once and that too as Krishna Devkiputra, a mere man, a Vedic student. In Bouquet's view the Avatara concept found its way into India from Iran. The Buddhists too, he suggests, borrowed some important concepts from there. Bodhisattava Amitabha apparently resembles significantly a divinity of the Zoroastrian faith.

Ramayana is a work of about 24,000 verses arranged in 500 cantos. The original work is by sage Valmiki and corresponds with the books II-IV of the present Ramayana. There is no reference to Buddhism in this work and there is no mention of the Upanishadic philosophy. This gives the latest date of its writing or being composed around 600 BC. The earliest could be much earlier. In Valmiki's epic Rama is a brave noble prince and not God incarnate. There is no suggestion that people so-considered him, or that he knew that he was such a divinity. On the other hand Krishna knew all along he was the *Avatara* and acted as such. This difference has to be kept in mind when going through the two epics. The despair and grief that Rama went through when confronted with difficult situations did not have to be experienced by Krishna, the latter just straightened out the problems with a view to establishing the supremacy of Dharma. Ramayana is not history or biography as C. Rajagopalachari has said. It is part of the Hindu mythology. To understand Hindu Dharma one has to study the Ramayana and understand the different characters who form part of it. Mythology is an essential part of a religion, like philosophy or ritual, and to get a proper grasp of it, a sound understanding of all the three is essential.

A brief Ramayana is also contained in the Buddhist *Jatakas* or birth stories. But the rendering of distinction and religious significance is the work of Tulsi Das, the sixteenth century poet. It is the image of Rama as contained in this work which is recognised as the incarnation of Vishnu and not the image as contained in the *Jatakas* or any other account. *Valmiki's* Ramayana has enough mythology to place his Rama in the category of *Avatara*. Tulsi Das Ramayana is based on this. Once Rama has been recognized as an *Avatara* comment on him on the basis of some detail as might be contained in the *Jatakas* or another contemporary literature make little sense. Even to consider *Jatakas* as history would be naive, incorrect. These are just stories with little historical relevance. Rama is God incarnate with attributes as detailed by poet Tulsid as. Any comment in a historical perspective, which may or may not be based on facts, is not relevant.

Ramayana has been translated into all the major Indian languages, and read by the devout not merely as a work of fine literature, but a sacred text which bestows religious merit and uplifts mentally and spiritually. Shankra, the *Advaita* exponent has said that to secure freedom from the stranglehold of Karmas one should have Rama in one's and meditate upon him. The date of Rama as c. 1950 is based on traditional accounts contained in the Puranas and not on corroborated historical facts, which do not always back the traditional accounts. Although Rama is not mentioned in the Vedas, some earlier or later kings have been, and it is with reference to them that the Rama period has been worked out. One important landmark in traditional history is the *Dasharajana* war, or the battle of the ten kings, which finally brought victory to Sudasa, a king of the *Panchalas* or five tribes, in pitched battle on the bank of River Ravi (Parushni) against a confederacy of ten kings who ruled the area from the present day Punjab to Afghanistan in the north-west. The ten kings had got together to check Sudasa's territorial ambitions. This battle was fought not much after the Rama period, and around 400 years later was fought the Mahabharata war. Thus if Dasharajana was 1800 BC, Mahabharata would be 1400 BC. But by some other accounts Mahabharata could be as late as 1000 BC; then the time for different events would change accordingly. Dasharajana has been mentioned in the Rig Veda too, but we know that by the time of this Veda, the Aryans had not gone much beyond the line of the *Saryu* river (Ayodhya) in the east and the Vindhyas in the south. But by the time of the Rama period the Aryans seem to have traversed most of the Peninsula. Therefore, if Dasharajana was soon after the Rama period, and if that was the period of the Rig Veda, and if Rama preceded Mahabharata, as he did, then there is error in assuming 1950 as the Rama period. The confusion is caused by the assumption that during the Rama period the Aryans had territory under their control which exceeded that they had during the Mahabharata period. The assumption is incorrect as even casual contact of the Aryans as they have been written out in documents of that age, have been taken to mean Aryan conquests. Mahabharata is set in the northern Indo-Gangetic plane, whereas Ramayana covers territory extending southwards from Ayodhya. To assume the extent of Aryan expansion on the basis of the territory covered in these epics alone would be incorrect. There have to be other corroborative incidents and geographical details. Panini (c. sixth century BC Sanskrit grammarian), mentions Deccan in his book *Ashtadhyayi*, but not the south. But Katyayana (fourth century BC) in his commentary on Panini, has covered most of south India. Conclusion could be that the Aryans came in contact with the people of the south in the fourth century BC.

On the other hand it is not necessary that people to people contact has to find place in an academic work like the grammar of Panini. The Aryans may have been in the south during the Rama period, right from c. 1950 BC or even earlier, but after the Rama-Ravana war there presence was marginal and they made no contribution of historical significance in the region during that period, or even the period following, as might merit mention in history, or inclusion in the Puranic lore or the Epics. It is well known that in the south the Aryans met a civilization which was already well developed and rather insular to their culture and religion of sacrifice. That the south resolutely followed its culture is clearly seen today in the extent of the spread of the Dravidian culture in South India.

India is a land of many people, races, clans, groups, communities. They arrived primarily from the west, over a long period, and brought with the new social, religious, cultural customs and practices. With time there was synthesis of these practices and customs, and today the Indian archetype is fairly distinguishable. Nevertheless, the diversity is there. After every couple of hundred kilometres there is a perceptible change in the culture pattern, religious concepts, social behaviour and values, language and dialect, customs, dress, even the physiognomy of the people. In spite of the togetherness of millenniums and a certain uniformity in some aspects of the day to day life, the differences persist; each group tries to maintain its identity. During the second millennium AD, an age marked for the decline of Hindu religion, culture, or social values, a lot of literature authored or edited by second rate, sometimes even bigoted, thinkers got churned out and many negative social and religious practices, new or based on some past custom or tradition, received the approval of communities, which not only took pride in following them but considered them vital for their identity. A section of Kshatriyas, for example, particularly of the landlord or the ruler classes, followed the custom of *Sati* where under a widow was burnt alive on the pyre of her deceased husband. Originally this custom was followed by the warrior classes of Hun or Sythian extraction, like the Rajputs of Rajasthan. Generally they fought their battles to the finish, and if they faced defeat they preferred to die fighting rather than bear the ignominy of being taken prisoners, and their women immolated themselves and became *Satis* and did not wait to be distributed as war prizes amongst the enemy soldiers or serve as hand maidens the houses of their captors. Sometimes a widow immolated herself with her deceased husband even when it was not war, but there was no pressure on her to do this. But with time the practice of a woman immolating herself became a custom even when the man had not died in battle, and more often she was compelled, often just thrown in the burning fire of the pyre of her deceased husband.

At the other end of the scale was the custom of *Nyoga* (Levirate) followed by some communities in northern India. Under this the widow had the option to pick a man, generally a brother of the deceased husband or his other close relative, to be her second husband. The practice was generally followed to enable the widow to get a child (particularly a mate), and generally be content sexually rather than be a sex deprived being and create problems in the society. Such like practices, including child marriages, killing of the newly born girls, temple prostitutes, assigning a lower status to the woman, were being followed by groups of different people. Some are still there to a lesser or greater degree, though a number of them have got discarded with time.

Apart from the four main branches of religion as described in this chapter, viz., Shaivas, Shaktas, the worshippers of Mother Goddess and the Vaishnavas, there are many others followed by different sections of people, having their own gods or deities, or who worship unconventionally like worshipping trees, or stones or some specified spots on the ground, or their Gurus (like the followers of Gorakh Nath), or some deceased head of their clan, or graves of some *Sufi saints* or religious men, or just a grave of anyone. But number of such people is small.

Then there are those who feel compelled to preach the sameness in every religious thought, the inherent goodness in all religious thinking, the need for every one to be good towards people of other faiths. The number of such people is not large, but some have made a name, like the followers of Ramakrishna Paramhansa.

8

The Caste System

The most complex phenomenon of the practiced Hinduism is its caste system. Caste comprises endogamous group of people, speaking a common language and having common social customs and religious beliefs or practices; this last aspect only at the micro level, such as having own priests for ceremonies like marriages. Where a caste group is large it has a number of small groups which are sub-castes. In such a situation, endogamy is the norm only within the sub-caste. Even mutual social intercourse and common or community feeding or drinking, or smoking, is permitted within the members of the sub-caste only. The sub-caste has an identity of its own, and has a graded position within the caste structure, which structure has a graded position within the overall Hindu hierarchy. The sub-caste is an important constituent of the Hindu society and generally has its own system of management of its internal affairs; some, particularly the lower castes, have *panchayats*, a body generally of five elected representatives to whom all controversial matters are referred for resolution. In his book *Caste and Class in India*; G.S. Ghurye has observed that to get a sociologically correct idea of the caste system, it is the sub-caste which needs to be recognized as the basic or fundamental unit upon which the system rests.

Caste or sub-caste is not a racial group and exclusivity between caste and sub-castes is not necessarily on account of racial loyalties or prejudices. It is true that racial factor made significant contributions but there are other factors too, some easily identifiable, others obscure and perplexing. The population diversity has made its own contribution to the evolution of the caste system. But why and how this diversity has divided the population into rigidly compartmentalised sections is not clear. Why, for example, there is such a lot of stress on endogamy. Even in the same racial group people of different castes, when staying in close proximity, should be emotionally, culturally and economically, closer to each other, as compared to those of their caste staying in different faraway areas. Yet, when it comes to marriage, it is the caste and not the race that will decide the issue.

In the caste system there are at least two hundred groups which can be and are called castes, with distinct caste names. The number of sub-castes which are endogamous, is around two thousand. The birth of a person in any of these not only decides how and where he or she would marry but also the profession that would be followed and the social status within the society. One feature of the caste was a common priesthood. The castes sometimes lie scattered over a number of villages performing the functions of their station, like the village cobbler, the blacksmith, the carpenter. Sometimes they are in communities, like weavers. A number factors combine to decide the caste of a person, and the most important is his profession. A Brahman's function is to perform religious jobs, and promote education. A *vani*, a Banya, is a trader. He supplies consumer items to the people of the village, and also take care of the sale and purchase of the surplus agriculture produce. Kshatriyas, who have any number of castes and sub-castes within their *varna*, are the people who compose the military; kings gave them large tracts of land where they could train and maintain contingents for war. Brahman had the top position amongst the castes since he was the teacher, *guru*, preceptor, a religious guide; he helped people to establish communion with God. The Kshatriya came the next, for he was the ruler and safeguarded the integrity of the state. Vaisyas, the Vanis, came the next, and the last place went to the Shudras, who comprised the workforce, the labourers, the artisans, the people who served the other three *Varnas*. A large number of castes in the case of the Shudras went by the name of the profession they followed, like *lohar* blacksmith, *tarkhan* carpenter, and so on.

The other factor that contributed to the caste formation is tribal or ethnic identity, like, for example, Mahars, Santhals, Bhils. Then some religious movements have also caused caste formation, e.g., Bishnois, Aryas. Some castes are known by the name of the places they originated from, but these are generally sub-castes from well defined castes and the rule of endogamy does not strictly apply here. There cases where the progeny of spouses from different castes start a different caste. Here if the male belonged to a higher caste, the descendents could opt for the caste of the male after a gap of a couple of generations. Geographical isolation of different areas also contributed to the caste factor. Some tribes performed jobs which were looked down upon, like scavenging by the *choorrahs* or disposal of carcasses after skinning, by the *chamars*. Such communities were regarded as untouchables even though the *chamars* formed the backbone of the leather industry.

The system, however, was not so rigid in the earlier stages, and even today the local attitudes vary substantially. The system existed during the time of the Indus Civilisation, but could be older. There is evidence of existence of organized labour, and guilds of artisans. The working classes were segregated from people following better vocations. The untouchables, possibly, lived outside city limits. Recent excavations have shown that Indus culture was widespread in northern India and was not restricted to the Indus basin. Caste distinctions, thus, existed well before the arrival of the Rig Vedic Aryans.

The *varna* system of the Aryans was for securing apartheid and is not to be confused with the system of the castes and sub-castes. But dilutions had crept into this system as well. For example, it would not be wrong to assume that some of the great *rishis*, the seers of the early Vedic days were not the fair skinned Aryans. Krishna-Dvaipayana Vysa, almost the greatest of them all, was born to Satyavati, the daughter of a non-Aryan fisherman, from Prashara, a Brahmin, with whom she was living till she caught the eye of the local king Shantanu, and got married to him. In the caste hierarchy, a fisherman, and that too a non-Aryan, was Shudra, and yet Shantanu, the Aryan king had no qualms about marrying her, even when he knew she had borne a son to the man to whom she was not even married. Nor did the people he ruled had any objection to this wedlock. Likewise, Sumitra, one of the three queens of Dashratha, father of Rama, is stated to be a Shudra. Yet Dashratha married her and this inflicted no social disability upon her sons Lakshmana and Shatrughana when they were married to the princesses from the royal house of Mithila. But people of Ayodhya were not that unconcerned when it came to accepting Sita as their queen after her return from Ravana's captivity. They were more concerned about the chastity and character of their women rather their *varnas* or castes.

In the earlier Rig Vedic hymns there is no mention of the four *varnas*; only three, viz., Brahmans, Kshatriyas, and Vaishas, are mentioned; the first two included the priest and the warrior, and the third had the rest of the people in its ambit. Only in the Purushasukta, a later hymn about the creation emanating from the sacrifice of Prajapati, the Primeval Being, is it stated that Brahmans came from the mouth of Prajapati, the Kshatriyas from the arms, the Vaisyas from his thighs and the Shudras from his feet. This hymn has often been quoted in the later Brahmanas to support the order of precedence between the four *varnas*, thus giving the precedence a divine justification.

No sin could be greater than that of killing a Brahman. The books of religion laid down that no taxes were to be imposed on this community, that gifts have to be given to them freely on all occasions, from birth to death (the more liberal the gift greater the merit), they were not to be tried for criminal offences, and if there was compulsion to try, then the punishment had to be light. Kings and conquerors generously distributed the war booty amongst them as a reward for their prayers for victory, and this included women and land captured. The community emphasized in their literature that no sacrifice had any merit unless it had been presided over by a properly qualified priest. Otherwise Veda does not impose restrictions on priesthood. Communities could have their own priests, which was the practice during the early Vedic Age, e.g., Vishvamitra, a Kshatriya of eminence, was Sudasa's official priest.

But Brahmans were not absolved of accountability. A very strict code of conduct had been prescribed for them. They had to be well versed in the Vedas, the Adi-Vedas, Vedangas,

Dharmasutras, Smritis, and all connected literature. Not all priests, however, managed to achieve this. The minimum they had to know was the Mantras affecting their immediate vocations, e.g., the *purohita* who presided over ceremonies of births, marriages etc. had to know the relevant *mantras* and the connected literature, or the *acharya* who took care of the rituals for the dead, had to have a thorough knowledge of the rites and procedures. Though Brahman literature forbade death sentence on a Brahman, the literature relating to law and justice placed him on equal footing with the commoner. He was required to be pure of thought and deed, and do only the right things and not be involved in activity which may even remotely be sinful, and dress simply and properly, and so on. Since his activity was generally non-remunerative, his survival very much depended on whatever gifts or charity he received from his clients, which was not always enough. As the population of Brahmans increased the situation became even more difficult. Thus, barring a few of them who enjoyed the patronage of kings and courtiers or rich merchants and landed gentry, the community as a whole was poor. Their poverty in underscored by the Mahabharata story of Sudama, Krishna's Brahman boyhood friend, who in spite of his high qualifications in the Veda, had fallen on such bad days that he bad to seek Krishna's help so that his starving family might get some respite. Yet it is to the credit of this community that in spite of the hardships they stuck to their profession, and not only led religion, its culture, philosophy, and civilisation to a high mark, but also played an important role in synthesising different religious, philosophical and cultural thoughts that disparate groups of people brought with them into this country. Later when the very foundations of Hindu religion were threatened by Islam and Christianity, they were the front runners in staking their everything to hold this religion together, convincing even the most neglected Shudras that what they possessed in terms of religion and culture was the best. When Buddhism and Jainism posed threats, primarily by rejecting sacrifice, they were quick in their appraisal and readily shifted emphasis to devotional worship, *Bhagti*, no longer stressing sacrifice, and accommodating the low caste Shudras by telling them that the knowledge of the Vedas was not necessary for attaining the highest merit and freedom from the cycle of rebirths, that this could equally effectively be achieved through intense love for the deity, the *Saguna Brahma*, that there was no religious activity which could be regarded higher than pure *Bhagti* and no scriptures or elaborate knowledge of religious literature was required for this. All that was required was an intense desire.

Caste played an important role in resisting proselytizing by Christians and Muslims, for no individual could act against the wishes of the fellow members of the caste group. In agrarian environments survival outside the community was difficult. If boycotted, a person would find it hard to find work, or the wherewithal to secure the means for the survival of the family. A conversion to some other religion had to be by a whole community, even then they have to contend with the resistance from other communities. Even a part of the community seeking conversion would face problems. The castes and the sub-castes were too proud of the legacy of their forebears to even imagine that they had handed down to them in tradition and culture and religion was in any way inferior to what was preached by the aliens, or that there was anything wrong with their traditions or with whatever they had learnt. Only the dispossessed people of indigent means converted like weavers, some musicians trades, fishermen. Otherwise the castes and the sub-castes stayed pretty insular to outside influences and tenaciously held on to their age old traditions and religion.

As stated above, in the early stages the Aryan society was divided only into three *Varnas*, viz., Brahmans, Kshatriyas and the Vaishyas. The idea of the Shudras, the fourth class who served the three classes, came later and included everyone who provided manual service, like the farm hands. The term 'Arya' was used for persons of Nordic origin, fair skinned, originally emigrated to north-west India from Iran. But with time a number of pre-Aryans in the professions of soldiers, government officials, got assimilated in the Aryan society and the meaning of the term changed to imply a 'noble man'. But with the classification of the Shudras, the meaning further changed to mean a person of Brahmanic religion and possibly used Sanskrit language. The four *Varnas* now included people of the corresponding professions of the pre-Aryan people, irrespective of the colour of their skin. Additionally there appeared classes who were placed even below the Shudras, like *Chandalas*, and the untouchables. In the case of Chandalas, one parent had to be a Shudra, while the untouchables performed the lowly jobs of scavenging or handling of dead bodies of animals or human beings. Even couples where one spouse was of Shudra or Chandala caste, were put in the category of Chandalas. Such castes were definitely outside the Aryan fold.

To begin with the system was not that rigid and some mobility from the lower to higher castes possible, but with the hardening of the religion of the Brahmans, greater emphasis was laid on purity of whatever was offered in sacrifice, or to *Agni*, fire. Otherwise the merit of the sacrifice was lost; in fact there could be adverse impact. Thus, whatever was impure was forbidden, including the participation by impure beings in places or rituals which had sacred status. House was a sacred place, like the human body, and whatever was connected with them, like items of food, clothing, and other items of daily use or chores. All this required distance from low castes and untouchables.

While the Aryans classified the society into four *Varnas*, the *jati*, the caste, or the sub-caste had different connotation. Apart from the restrictions imposed by the *varna* classification, there were restrictions which came about because of the caste, like taboo and commensality. Each of the *varna* is a kind of an umbrella under which numerous *jatis* or castes/sub-castes performing jobs appropriate to the *varna* are clubbed. In northern India, for example, both Rajputs and Jats are Kshatriya *varna*, but the Rajputs consider the Jats low in the cast ranking and do not marry in their community and do not even drink water from their wells. Jats are tillers of land and their rightful place should be with Vaisyas. But they claim to have been warriors since the days of the Mahabharata. They possibly took to agriculture, trade or being artisans only to survive during the non-war periods. The artisans have been classified as Shudras, but forced by the compulsions of the no-war period, the Kshatriyas, too have to become artisans or till land for some Vaishya, for after the war period very few have their own land to till, although the rulers have generally tried to ensure they have land or other facilities to perform Kshatriya oriented jobs. Even the Brahmans have sub-castes, like the people who perform the rites appropriate only at the time of death, or those who memorize certain portions of the Veda, or those who accept alms only in the name of specified gods. All these fall into the lose system of sub-castes.

The older a tribe, the more particular it is about endogamy and commensality and maintaining its ethnic identity. In this it is influenced by concepts regarding fertility, human sacrifice in one form or another, and infanticide. It is not possible to exactly define caste or sub-caste. Their origination has been influenced by many factors, not all of which could called relevant to the forming of any one caste. According to Hutton, the description of caste which could be called as quite comprehensive, is the one given by Senart, a noted French anthropologist. He has said: "We must conceive a group which is, at least in theory, hereditary, provided with a measure of organization which is traditional and independent, with a headman and with a council, a group which meets when the need arises, more or less in full assembly, often at the time of certain festivals, and is bound together by a common occupation, and share common customs in regard to particularly to marriage, the consumption of food and drink, and pollution (brought about by eating the wrong type of food or with wrong type of people or doing things prescribed by the community's customs and tradition). Finally, it is a group which has the power to maintain its authority by means of a jurisdiction which, though not overbearing, is capable of making the power of the community effectively felt by the imposition of various penalties, the most important being permanent or temporary banishment from the group."

One factor which contributed to the stability of the system, was the inter-caste gradations. Brahmans were at the top of the ladder of the caste system. But even the subcastes carried a ranking within the caste. A variety of factors decided this, but the one important one was the type of work the sub-caste carried out, e.g., a family chaplain carried a higher ranking compared to the Brahman who performed the last rites for a deceased being. Another factor was the status of the parent's marriage. Offsprings of mixed marriages, i.e., inter-caste marriages, were placed below the offsprings of parents whose marriages had sanction of the prescribed law. Offsprings from mixed marriages gave rise to new castes or sub-castes. These are broadly classified as *Anuloma* and *Pratiloma*: in the case of the former the sons are born on women of their own mixed caste or the caste of their mothers, while in *Pratiloma* sons are born on woman of caste different from that of their fathers or mothers. *Manu Smriti* lays down that the children born to the parents of the same caste have the same status as that of their fathers, but those born from women of higher castes and men of lower castes are not considered to be of the Aryan society; Shudra's son from a Brahman wife is a *Chandala*, the lowest in the caste hierarchy. By the time of this Smriti, however, the Aryans had ceased to be a community. There had been intermixing between the Aryans, the Dravidians and the pre-Dravidian people and the Aryans as such were more like a socio-religious group based on Sanskrit language.

Another factor that influenced the formation of caste was the factor whether a society was patrilineal or matrilineal. Like the worship of the Mother Goddess, the matrilineal system widely followed amongst the pre-Aryans. Where a tribe originates from a mother the system of the caste and its taboos is strong for various psychological, psychic, sociological, shamanistic reasons. Woman bears her personality on her children more strongly than man, the father. Most matrilineal tribes moved southwards under the pressure of aggressive incursions by patrilineal tribes from the north-west, and the caste system, for this reason, is stronger in the south and matriarchy more extensive. However, the patrilineal people provided for the intermixing of the two systems. In a matrilineal house the woman enjoys the same freedom as man under the patrilineal system. But the code of Manu (of the patrilineal system) forbids the status of man to the woman. Thus when man from a patrilineal system marries a woman from a matrilineal system, he feels the need to restrict her freedom, for that way, he feels, she is better disposed to protect her fidelity; fidelity of the woman, he believes is his property. For this he devised various methods, one amongst these being the veil, *purdah*. It is for this reason that in some communities the girl is married off early, when she is a mere child, or even an infant. In this process the father is handing over his charge, in so far as her virginity, purity, character are concerned, to another patriarch, the boy's father, who when the boy is grown up sufficiently, gives her over to him, all with properly designed ceremonies. But overall, she remains the charge of the tribe, community, and, finally, the family, the husband is only a co-owner in this process. Of course, only the husband cohabits with her to impregnate her for bearing their children. The law of Manu lays down that when she is unmarried she is in the charge of her father, after marriage her husband, and after the death of her husband, if the situation arises, her sons: a woman must never be independent. These were the rules of a patrilineal society. But in the matrilineal societies of South India, there is neither the veil for the women, nor has she to be married away in childhood, although the laws regarding taboos and commensality are stringent. A love marriage is virtually out.

One reason for child marriages is the belief that a father is sinful, a criminal in the community, if he fails to marry off his daughter at the right age to an appropriate man, and for this he would assuredly land in hell. The female progeny's essential characteristic was her capability to bear children. The father had to ensure that he found a healthy man for her, in keeping in view the laws of the community and the caste system. The father of the girl would be considered blameworthy too before the community and the gods if remained barren. She grew up believing that there was nothing more unfortunate than being barren. Women sought even *Niyoga*, even illicit relationship. But for her no curse was bigger than that of staying barren. Next main factor was the male progeny, for he was the most essential requirement for the family rituals for the well being in this life as well as the hereafter. He was also essential to light the pyre of the deceased parents, which if not done, would leave the soul of the deceased in turmoil and painful agitation; such a soul would for ever be in suffering.

By the time of the later Vedic age the belief was that a woman was like a field whose function was merely to nurture the seed dropped into her, and for this reason also her status was lower, although there was also the appreciation that seed without the soil was useless. However, the onerous responsibility that befell a girl's father for finding a suitable husband, which involved gifts and dowry, and which gave the right to the husband's house to throw her out of their house whenever they so chose, the girl's father's house becomes vulnerable to undeserved disgrace for no fault of theirs. To obviate this kind of a negative situation and to keep their dignity and peace of mind, often she was done away with by her parents right after her birth. Apart from the dowry, not infrequently, she was ill treated by the in-laws. Sometimes she was turned out of the house, to the utter disgrace of her parents. Amongst the poorer castes the girl child was unpopular because she was an additional mouth to feed, unlike a boy who was a potential bread-winner. Her father's house considered her to be the trust of her future in-laws, to be handed over to them at the time of her wedding. Her vulnerability to their whims was so apparent, that they had to ensure she stayed a virgin, was well trained in handling household chores and was utterly humble and respectful towards the house of her in-laws. She was told that she would enter the house of her husband carried in a palanquin, but leave only at the time of her death, on a bier. She would bear her fate with good grace, equanimity, and not ever be rough about the atrocities she may be subjected to. This was the traditional view irrespective of whether the girl's father was a prince or a pauper. But essentially the compulsions of early marriage, or infanticide were markedly pronounced amongst the castes following the patrilineal customs. Amongst the matrilineal tribes infanticide was resorted to essentially for reasons of poverty. Otherwise the position of women amongst them was better. The situation has markedly improved in modern times, but the old customs are still there.

Some tribes have a custom to offer the hair of their heads to their deity. This practice was brought by the tribes from the countries of the Mediterranean rim and southern Europe where they made such offerings to goddesses in the belief that there was association between the hair of the head and the fertility of the soil and of the body. The practice is still observed with some modifications. In South India it is extensively practiced. In the same genre is the case of *devadasis,* women engaged in the service of the temple god. This custom is followed by a couple of castes. The women are married to the god but have children with local men. This custom too seems to have arrived from the Mediterranean rim, although there the women served the goddess and not the god. On specified occasions these women cohabit with strangers. Here too the belief is in the connection between fertility of the soil and the cohabitation between strangers in the presence of the god, and the general prosperity of the community.

Originally the agriculture was the main economic activity, but with the development of trade and industry the requirement arose for the division of labour in different trades. This tended to bind together the people following the same trade or profession into one caste. As the guilds grew they developed self-governance, giving rise to smaller groups which tended to be endogamous, possessing all the trappings of a sub-caste. In support of this Blunt suggests that a functional caste is made up of sub-castes which are endogamous, whereas non-functional castes are endogamous as a whole and not as subcastes. In fact, often endogamy within non-functional sub-castes is positively forbidden, though there are non-functional sub-castes which practise endogamy. A caste whose members follow a common vocation would be functional caste, e.g., carpenters, blacksmiths and so on, while castes like Rajputs, where members are not bound by a common vocation, Jats, or Ahirs, would be classified as non-functional.

One view is that colour of the *skin* and hereditary function caused the caste system. Senart, however, is of the view that though the colour was a contributory factor, it was not the overriding one. He traces the commensality factor to the family meal, and worship, and concludes that it was the tribe and the clan, that formed into a caste or a sub-caste. This not, however, appear to be the case, for a caste is never based on a common ancestor and, therefore, is not a clan or a tribe. He has said that the Aryan arrival in India ultimately produced two types of mixed races, one laying stress on *the purity of descent and the other on the purity of occupation. This led to the formation* of new groups and, consequently, new castes. The priestly class emphasized the purity of descent for themselves and, thus, exercised moral power over others. Colour certainly does not appear to have been the over riding factor, for the untouchable *Chamars* of north-western India who skin the dead animals and treat their hides to make good quality leather, have, in many cases near European complexion and Greek physiognomy. Possibly they were emigrants from Eastern Europe. This is also true of a number of other Shudra castes. As stated above, race and colour have made contribution, but there are other factors as well.

Hocart interprets caste in purely ritualistic terms. He says that the ruler, petty or otherwise, and the community needed men for the essential purificatory rites, like the *Dhobi* (washerman), or the *naai* (barber) and as the number of such people grew they got classified into castes. This, however, does not explain the taboo on commensality and endogamy, unless it is believed that a ritual was considered as spoilt if the person performing it was contaminated by association with people who were not entitled to perform it. This brings taboo, magic and *Mana*, the last mentioned being the personal spiritual power of the person performing the ritual. In Slater's view caste system existed in India during the pre-Aryan period, from the time when professions became hereditary and endogamy became necessary in order to preserve the trade secrets. The Aryan arrival strengthened the system and, may be on the basis of colour, led to some kind of a gradation of social precedence amongst the castes. The priest magician of the pre-Aryan times had delineated the caste structure. Mixed in this, as explained by Ghurye, was the belief of the primitive people in the power of food to transmit qualities. The idea of untouchability came from the need for ceremonial purity, possibly applied to the aboriginals in the first instance, in connection with sacrificial ritual and to theoretical impurity of certain occupations later.

Considering taboo, *mana*, commensality and magic, it would seem that the origin of caste here has been from the time of the first arrival of human beings. As the vast tracts of land were interspersed by jungles, rivers, deserts and mountains, there was geographical isolation of areas, and the means of communications were poor. The smaller groups survived on hunting and food gathering, and moved to other areas during famine and floods and other calamities. The leaders of the groups and their families formed different sub-groups, and possibly had their own magician priests. They controlled the means of production and exploited the rest of the group as their labour. Both, in time, developed their own taboos, the sense of commensality and endogamy; in much of this the isolation caused by the geographical factor played a decisive role. Into this the magician priest who guided, if not dictated, the social and political life of the community, brought in totems. The groups thus got formed, each believing in its own taboos and having its own magician priest, leading to commensality and endogamy. Then came trade and industry, and as in agrarian economy, groups got formed here too, of people of same trades, to protect their financial and survival interests. All these became castes of people in the same or similar trades, of the rulers in trade and industry and agriculture, of the serfs in various grades of employment, of the menials and scavengers, all having faith in their magician-priests and totems and taboos. Food was all that they essentially worked for, and it was considered sacred and it had a special significance in the religious and social structure. In the totemic and primitive belief it was considered to possess the capability to readily convey injurious qualities to the foes.

Agriculture brought villages and settled, organized life, and a stability in the social system. But even then the caste system could not have been that rigid and some mobility upwards or sideways should have been possible. Education by itself does not appear to have played much of role in the evolution of this system. Hypergamy, on the basis of colour or profession, must have created new castes. The arrival of Palaeo-Mediterraneans would have disturbed the existing balance and given rise to further combinations, and the lighter skinned Orientals and migrs from southern Russia would have made the situation even more complex.

However, the rigidity of the system, its endogamy, and the emphasis on commensality, has a lot to do with the primitive beliefs in totems, leading to taboos, magic, *mana* and what Hutton calls the soul stuff, i.e., the life force, that which is the essence of whatever comprises the creation. The belief was that whereever there was life force in abundance, there was happiness, and to make person fail it would help if his community's *mana* was diminished: *Mana* is the power residing within each person, including his belongings, and collectively it had, it was believed, a decisive influence on the fortunes of the tribe. The eclipse of an opposing tribe was sometimes sought to be achieved by performing acts which were taboo for that tribe, thus decreasing their *mana*, like serving them proscribed foods, or foisting upon them forbidden trades, and such like acts. Even the inert tools of the worker were believed to possess *mana*. The artisans worship the tools of their trade, howsoever briefly, every time they take them out for work; at least once a year elaborately, on the *Vishwakarma day*, around the time of Diwali, the Hindu festival of lights.

The idea of sacrifice, human, animal or otherwise, and head hunting and cannibalism, are based on this belief. By decapitation *mana* of the victim was sought to be secured. Likewise, by eating the flesh of another human being, securing a share in his *mana* was achieved. Additionally the magician priest had devised other methods for securing the same aim, like preserving the placentas of the women of the community, or eating the flesh of the dead elders before their burial, or seeking fulfillment of wishes by offering prayers at the graves of people who possessed recognized wish fulfillment power when they lived, though graves of even common people are respected for the power of the 'soul stuff,' the idea is to prevent the loss of *mana* of the community for the benefit of the community, or for the benefit of the person performing the ritual and make use of the power of the 'soul stuff, for gains and to ward off any evil or hardship. Movement of a person to a different tribe was considered to be loss of *mana*, a kind of a betrayal which the tribe resented and resisted. This could also be the argument for endogamy amongst tribals.

Thus, the foundation of the system lies in the Proto-Australoid, or earlier belief in *mana*, magic and the soul stuff. This had already brought endogamy and commensality.

With the development of trade and industry, guilds of artisans and tradesmen got formed. some of Dravidian extraction, but a large number of the pre-Dravidian people. This gave a new dimension to the caste system, incorporating groups based on profession, which eventually coalesced into castes. Another superimposition came with the advent of *varnas*. The Brahmanical religion emphasized the purity of race and sacrifice ritual, and also pollution (pollution is caused by proximity to people who are physically not clean, or do not wear clean clothes, or perform unclean jobs, or, in some cases, do not belong to the *varnas* of the twice born. All this tightened the caste classification. The *Karma* concept of the later Vedic period gave it further rigidity. Although the *Vaishnavas, Buddhists and the Jains* tried to break this rigidity, they failed. With time the roots of the system became deep and firm.

Food had a decisive influence on the system of taboos. The tools of the tradesmen are considered to be in possession of the soul stuff, or *mana*, for their usefulness, like the usefulness of a house, a boat, a machine, is proof of the soul power of the respective item. Likewise food also has soul-power, and it is important that this power is not lost by pollution. When food is served by strangers, or by people with whom eating is tabooed, there shall be loss of power. Besides, foods from sources outside the possession of the tribe, are considered harmful. Generally, however, accepting food from the twice born castes could be in order, though normally this is not permitted for fear of loss of spiritual power, *mana*.

Broadly, the following factors may be considered relevant to the evolution of the caste system.

(a) Geographical isolation of the peninsula, and mutual isolation of its regions on account of difficult and varying terrain. The isolation of the subcontinent prevented extensive interaction with neighbourhood countries. The tribes with different cultural background tended to nurse their prejudices, and that along with difficult terrain and undeveloped communications, lent to isolation and led to the growth of sectarian societies.

(b) Development and perpetuation of primitive customs and concepts about totem, *mana*, soul stuff, magic and power of food and working tools and other items of utility, including home and hearth. Even the words of the magician priest were believed to have power, *mana*. His incantations became *mantras* which were believed to have power. Movement out of the tribe was loss from the collective *mana* of the community. Even abandoning the family, or improperly eating outside with people of other families, or disregarding own totem or ancestor worship, was believed to adversely affect the *mana*.

(c) With the onset of industry there was evolution of guilds of artisans. Trades and professions became hereditary as the families and tribes tended become insular on account of their belief in totem, magic, etc. which gave rise to endogamy and commensality. The inter-family and inter-tribal contact thus was restricted, and the need arose, backed by primitive beliefs, for the family to keep the knowledge of its trade, a secret, loss of trade was like loss of its inner strength. Consequently opportunity to pick up trades from people outside the tribe was minimum.

(d) The ideas of purity and pollution and ablutions in ritual sacrifice.

(e) The colour, race and civilisational antagonism. Incoming people overpowered those already living here. They considered themselves superior and made every effort to preserve their own purity of race by strictly keeping away from the local inhabitants, while local people tightened their insularity to maintain integrity and identity. Under this head the clash between the patrilineal (like the Aryans) and the matrilineal (a large number of pre. Aryan tribes were matrilineal) societies is also covered.

These factors also contributed to the splitting of the people into small, mutually hostile groups, and exposed them to defeat in detail at the hands of the invaders, they just would not unify under one flag.

Shudras were classified as *sat* and *asat* shudras, asat being those who were placed higher in the caste hierarchy. The rest of them were placed in the category of "the rest". The Shudras were denied the privileges of the twice born and were not permitted Vedic rites for birth, death, marriage and other social ceremonies, nor could they use the sacred mixture made from cow's milk, curd, clarified butter and cow's urine and dung. But the *Sat* Shudras could take the help of the Puranas; this was called the *Namas* method, They were enjoined to perform all the daily sacrifices too on the basis of *Namas*, and execute welfare works and be charitable. Those who wanted to accumulate merit were advised to be virtuous. By the time of the later Vedic period, however, the *Sat* Shudras, which category included people like carpenters, masons or goldsmiths and similar tradesmen, or people who owned substantial land and other property or followed respectable vocations, or were pre-Aryan people of good means and education, though outside the Aryan fold, were treated well, and were allowed the services of a Brahman, though the ceremonies had to be based on the Puranas and not Vedas. In fact, during the post-Buddhist period the good Sudras with respectable means of income, were being equated with the Vaisyas, one amongst the many arguments for this equation being the origination of both Vaisya and the Shudra from the lower part of the body of Prajapati—the origination being from thighs (Vaisyas) and the feet (Shudras); Brahmans and Kshatriyas originated from the upper body, mouth and the arms respectively. Besides both *varnas*, i.e., Vaisyas and Shudras essentially provided services to the people in higher *varnas* and, therefore were placed on equal footing. According to Kautilya, the child born from a Vaisya on a Shudra wife is to be treated as Shudra. In fact, according to his *Arthashastra*, a work compiled during the post. Buddhist period, even an issue of a Brahman from a Kshatriyas wife is to be treated as a Shudra, which, of course is against the laws of Manu, which allow such an offspring to be treated as a Brahman. However, Brahman, after the introduction of this modification, could accept food offered higher Shudra, like he could from a Vaisya. The *Sat* Shudras could engage in trade and agriculture, like Vaisyas.

But Shudras never accepted the authority of the Brahmans, or the *Dharma Shastras*. There always was resistance, and few aggressive Shudras managed to claim higher *varnas*, e.g., Nandas ruling from Patliputra were Shudras, and imperial Guptas and Harsha Vardhana were Vaisyas. Many militant Sudra tribes ruled vast territories, and proclaimed their leaders as kings and their kinsmen as Kshatriya Rajputs, literally, son of kings. Any one daring to contest their pretensions, or any Brahman refusing to issue religious proclamations in their favour, was ruthlessly eliminated.

Vaishnavism is tolerant towards Shudras, and advocates non-discrimination, and emphasizes the importance of sincerity and purity of heart and goodness of deeds, irrespective of caste, in seeking the divine reality. It recognizes every individual's right to worship, and, consequently, his right to enter a temple. Both, Buddhism and Jainism do not recognise caste distinctions.

A number of original inhabitants continued as '*Asat Shudras*' generally as scavengers, village menials or those performing last rites for the dead people, or disposing of dead animals; they continued as underdogs right up to modern times. Often they were referred to as Ad-Dharmis, i.e., followers of the original religion, which implies people who follow Hindu faith but are not part of the Hindu Society. This has, in some cases, led them to adopt other faiths, like Islam, or Christianity, but after conversion the disadvantage of low birth has generally remained. In the Hindu society often humiliating restrictions have been imposed on them. In South India, where caste system was strong as compared to the North, the untouchables were forbidden wearing ornaments or gold, or their males wearing clothes below their knees, or wearing formal clothes like coats, slacks, shirts or ties, or using umbrellas against sun or rain, or getting a hair-cut, or their women covering the upper portions of their bodies, or using flowers for personal decoration. They could use only earthen ware, could never ride a horse for any reason whatsoever. Their children were forbidden education and were required to only tend cattle. The families were at the beck and call of the higher caste people and were required to work on miserable wages, and not own land, nor play music during their functions including marriages. In North India, however, the restrictions were not so severe, and higher castes valued the services provided by the Shudras, or the untouchables, or the *Chandalas*, and looked after them and provided them the wherewithal for survival, like land to build a house and foodgrains in return for work. Where such largesse was not forthcoming, because the village community could not utilize the full population on account of over population, they tended to turn into criminals. In eastern India, particularly in the hill areas of Assam and the adjoining states, the majority of the tribes are an admixture of Proto-Australoids and northern Mongoloids. They are treated as external castes. But being in majority, are compared to the higher Hindu castes and do not suffer the disadvantages to the same extent as the people of the external castes in the rest of the country.

It is, however, not to be assumed that untouchability is practiced only by the caste Hindus towards the exterior castes. Mahars, an exterior caste of Maharashtra do not like to be bracketed with *Chamars*, also an exterior caste mostly engaged in disposal of dead animals. *Chamars* in turn have distanced themselves from *Bhangis*, the scavengers, and so on. Taboos and endogamy are strict amongst these castes. Caste Hindus do not permit any of them to enter the temples, or accept food or water which might have been touched by them; even a shadow of these people falling on food or water is enough to pollute. Brahmans do not conduct their marriages or other ceremonies, nor are the barbers working for higher castes allowed to cut their hair. Because they are generally abysmally poor and illiterate and uneducated they do not have profitable vocations; their poverty compels them to borrow from the higher caste moneylenders, often to meet expenses of their essential ceremonies, and to clear their debts they are forced to work as farm hands or servants, as bonded labour often for their whole life.

In modern times, however, efforts have been made to improve their lot. Gandhi was strong champion of their cause. These depressed castes, classified as scheduled castes and tribes, constitute nearly 30 per cent of the total the Hindu population. They are either pure Proto-Australoids or a mix of Proto-Australoids and Palaeo-Mediterranean Dravidians. Essentially they are pacifists, dislike violence, and have borne the humiliations and hardships of their low social status, timidly. Some anthropologists have even advanced a viewpoint that they possibly have evolved from a sub-human species within South Asia itself. Their pacifism has made them extremely tolerant, giving up in adversity. They have a fanatical faith in fate, later in the retribution caused by Karmas, and strongly believe in magic to ward off the doings of a hostile fate rather than adopt a discerning attitude to enquire into the causes of failures. This has resulted in the almost total lack of development of science and technology amongst these people. Being at the receiving end, for most of them life has been a painful journey through pain and sorrow, and their religious thoughts were mostly dominated by this thought process.

The systems of endogamy and commensality that these people evolved, stayed till about the modern times; to a lesser extent it is there, amongst some tribes, even to this day. In the distant past some tribes had subsisted on food gathering when some people around them had become food producers. The gathering groups became dependent on the type of food that was available in their areas, which could be fruit, fish, birds, insects and so on, and this became their favoured food, totem, over a period of time, and its gathering accompanied celebrations and rituals, and sacrifice (even human). With time the clans exchanged food, on barter basis, and this brought contact and marriages within totem groups, improving diet and genes, and developed language, and increased the population of the clans that thus intermixed; others possibly became extinct through interbreeding. With the increased sanctity of the totem symbol, some relevant taboos were enforced, and that (and possibly for some other reasons as well) forbade sex within the totem clan. A tribe had several such clans and only inter-clan marriage was permitted (within the tribe and not outside it), but it was not permitted within the totem clan, outside the tribe. However, limited intermixing notwithstanding, the tribes were self-sufficient in most requirements and felt little need for extensive movement, or learning, or improving their living conditions by developing a scientific temper. For this reason culture of these people, including of the people who were more mobile and learnt the use of metals and evolved viable social systems, remained obsessed with religion and superstition. Whatever verve and scientific temper got generated, it was due to incursions from outside. Time stood still as far as these Proto-Australoids or Palaeo-Mediterraneans, or tribes born out of a combination of these two, were concerned. And they for ever lived in deprivation.

During the post-Buddhist period it was the ascendancy of Brahmanism, but the hold of the upper castes over the lower castes had relaxed to some extent, though in South India this relaxation was marginal, though whatever hold was there it was oppressive. There were reforms, and public movements against the system. The governments of states made laws to ameliorate the lot of low castes. During the rule of the Guptas (4th-6th century AD), who were Vaisyas, and ushered the golden age of Hinduism, a lot of time and resources were devoted to their welfare. Harsha Vardhana too, though a Vaishya and follower of Brahmanism, was well disposed towards other religions and castes. From time to time there appeared governments which were non-Brahman in substance, and under them the lot of the lower classes was even better.

During the early years of the fifteenth century, Brahmanism decided to follow the ritualism of the later Vedic period; this happened under the guidance of Sayana, an eminent Vedic scholar in the kingdom of Vijaynagar. This could have accentuated the caste divide, but for the efforts of the religious and social reformers of that time, who were striving for modifications of the rules of religion, and customs and practices. Although access to the religious literature was not allowed freely, their right to worship was accepted. Both Shaiva and the Vaishnava saints preached equality of all beings before God. A number of Shudra saints gained popularity in Maharashtra, for preaching *Bhagti* for every one, without class distinctions. Some of them composed religious poetry of high merit.

9

Brief History

Homo sapiens have lived on this subcontinent since the second interglacial period, i.e., for the last 200,000-400,000 years. The Ice Age was not as harsh or extensive over the subcontinent as in the countries to the north; in fact, southern and the eastern parts of the country escaped it entirely. The soil was fertile and there was abundant growth of vegetation, including growth of fruit and crops. People have survived basically on food gathering and cultivation. On the other hand hunter had to use his wit to ensnare his prey, be ingenious and tough in chasing it, and operate in teams to secure success. There is no such pressure on the food gatherer, although during natural calamities his situation is pretty hopeless. He has to wander in search of other sources. The food of the hunter is decidedly more nutritious, and he is physically tougher.

The period of Stone Age has varied in the different geographical locations. This was followed by the Copper Age. This metal all but replaced the stone tools. It could be produced from its ore in kilns no more technical than the pottery kilns; pottery is found along with the stone tools in the late Stone Age. Some parts of India, like western Deccan, almost completely missed the Copper Age, while some missed even the Bronze Age. Progressive stages of development, like moving from early Stone Age to the next stage, or moving from there to the Copper Age, were essentially brought about by the ingressing tribes.

There is no information about the human beings who lived on this subcontinent during the second interglacial or thereafter. They could have become extinet or been assimilated by the incoming tribes, like the Proto-Australoids, or these latter tribes may well be the evolved version of these inhabitants. The small statured and black Negritos, the first racial group to have been identified on this subcontinent, were possibly here 6,000 to 7,000 years back. Then appeared the near black Proto-Australoids. Some of their kind had fairly well settled in village communities five to six thousand years ago, tending to agriculture, but some amongst them were mere food gatherers. These people were followed by the Paleo-Mediterraneans, also dark, bordering on to black, people, who mixed extensively with the Proto-Australoids, resulting in a stock which have generally stayed at the lowermost rungs of the Indian social structure. They were followed by other groups like the dark Mediterraneans, the light skinned people emigrating from southern Russia, the Armenians, the Orientals and the like, and they caused the flowering of the Indus Valley Civilisation, one of the oldest to flower in the world. This culture was pretty widespread in the north-west of India, generally in areas which were well served by perennial water sources and were not in the midst of dense vegetation, for this was the time of the Bronze Age and cutting tools for clearing forests were not available; that had to await the onset of the iron tools, in the Iron Age. The Indus Civilisation had been well established by around 3500 BC and flourished unhindered for at least 1000 years. Its decline started by around 2250 BC with the incursions from the north-west, which included the ingress of the Aryans. The Aryans though not so numerous as the earlier groups, made lasting contribution to the culture of the people of the northern parts of the subcontinent. The historical details of these people up to the time of the later Vedic Age have been covered in the earlier chapters.

The Kingdoms

By about 600 BC Northern India had at least 16 well established big and small kingdoms, like Gandhara (Peshawar-Rawalpindi area), Kamboja (south-west Kashmir and parts of Kafiristan), Avanti (eastern Gujarat), Ashmaka (on river

Godavari), Shurasena (Mathura), Matsya (Jaipur), Panchala (Bareilly-Farrukhabad), Kuru (Thanesar-Delhi-Meerut), Vatsa (Allahabad), Chedi (territory between the Yamuna and the Narmada rivers), Malla (Gorakhpur district), Kosala (central Uttar Pradesh, around Lucknow), Kashi (Benares), Magadha (South Bihar), Vriji (North Bihar) and Anga (East Bihar). These states had their friendships and feuds, and the smaller states, particularly the republics, felt threatened by their more powerful neighbours. In course of time four out of these emerged as major power centres, being Avanti, Vatsa, Kosala and Magadha. The last named amongst these had a pre-eminent position.

Magadha, a non-Aryan kingdom was powerful. It has been mentioned even in the Mahabharata epic, as state ruled by a powerful king Jarasandh, an ally of the Kurus in the conflict. The state owed its strength to the rich and fertile soil, and its copper and iron ore mines, like in the Singhbhum district. These metals were used for the manufacture of agriculture implements and weapons of war. The sand of its river *Sona,* which joins the Ganges near Patliputra, modern Patna, carried gold. Its capital city, Girivraja, was surrounded by five hills which, with time, came to be strengthened by a stone wall. During the sixth and the fifth centuries BC it was ruled by Saisunaga kings. Bimbisara, whose father had abdicated in his favour when he was just fifteen years old, was about the most remarkable of this line. Immediately upon securing the throne in 545 BC, he got down to expanding his kingdom and entered into matrimonial alliances with Kosala and Vaishali, and founded the city of Rajgriha, modern Rajgir in the Patna district. He encouraged intellectual activity. Both Mahavira Jaina and Gautama Buddha preached in his kingdom. His rule brought name and strength to Magadha and served as a model for the kingdoms around, and even for the kingdoms that followed. This line had run its course in about a couple of centuries.

In his old age Bimbisara got killed by his son Ajatshatru and that provoked the joint hostility of Kosala and Vaishali, who had married off their daughters to him. But the new Magadhan king defeated them, even captured some of their territory. As part of his defence he fortified the village of Patligrama; within a few years this city became the famous city of Patliputra. He captured Vriji and took Kashi from Kosala; its king, Prasanajit, in order to appease him, had to marry off his daughter to him. In later years Prasanajit's successor and son is known to have massacred the tribe of the Sakyas, though the Magdhan king patronized both Buddhism and Jainism. But in the case of Buddhism he supported Devadatta, the schismatic cousin of the Buddha. Both Buddha and Mahavira died during the early period of his reign. The first Buddhist council was held during his time, to compile the scriptures and codify the discipline norms for the monks so as to ensure strict discipline in their conduct.

At least four kings of the Saisunaga line were parricide, being Udayain, Anrudha, Munda, and Kalashoka. The last named moved the capital of the State permanently from Girivraja to Patliputra, though he was also very fond of Vaishali; he kept it as his second capital. The second Buddhist council was held there during the tenth year of his reign, after 100 years of Buddha's Nirvana. This council too was called to rid the religion of heresy. In the year 376 BC the king got assassinated and the power came to ten young sons, who were all exploited by the powerful officials of the court, and that got the princes to get down to eliminate one another till by 345 BC in a matter of 32 years they were all gone and the throne was captured by Mahapadma Pati Nanda, who then founded the Nanda dynasty. He was a man of low origin and set about his task ruthlessly and exercised his rule over south Orissa and parts of West Bengal. He was succeeded by his eight sons, one after the other. This man is said to have been of low origin, though the Brahmanical *Varna* system was not in vogue amongst the Dravido-Austral people of that time.

Mahapadmapati Nanda was a man of ruthless ambition and expanded his empire as far west as the Punjab and exercised suzerainty over south Orissa and parts of West Bengal. He was succeeded by his eight sons, one after the other, the last of whom, Dhanananda had organized a powerful state with an army comprising 200,000 infantry, 20,000 cavalry, 2000 chariots and over 3000 elephants; some accounts put the strength of the army at a much higher level. To meet the expenses of the defence he had to impose heavy taxes, and that alienated his subjects and an adventure soldier, Chandragupta Maurya, advised and assisted by a Taxilian Brahman, Kautilya (also called Chanakya), took advantage of the prevalent disaffection and overthrew the king and captured the throne of Magadha for himself. Chandragupta, a non-Aryan, adopted the title of Maurya from the caste of his mother who, going by the caste system gradation, was of a low origin. By the Buddhist chronicles of Ceylon Nandas ruled from 345 to 323 BC. In this period the first king ruled for most of the time. But palace intrigues, treachery, murders were commonplace and took their toll and the aspirants eliminated one another without compunction to capture the throne and the power.

The north-west of the subcontinent at that stage was pretty unsettled. By about the middle of the sixth century BC Iranians had made inroads into the north-west India and Cyrus (522-486 BC), the most notable ruler of this line, had expanded his empire up to the present day Rajasthan. That brought him enormous annual tribute. However, the Iranian rule did not last for long after Darius, and the area got divided into a number of small free states; Pushkalavati (modern Peshawar) and Takshashila (modern Taxila) were important amongst them. Both states had flourishing trade and commerce; the latter was also known for being an important centre of learning, including the centre for the learning of the Vedas and the connected literature. *Mahabharata* is believed to have been first recited there.

Alexander the Great, 356-323 BC, was the ruler of Macedonia, the territory north of Greece, and has been one of the greatest conquerors who walked this earth. He was the son of the founder of the Macedonian empire, Philip II, and the pupil of Aristotle, and ascended the throne after the murder of his father in 336 BC (which he happened to witness). He forcibly united the warring Greek states and in 334 BC raised an army of 33,000 men and attacked the powerful Persian king, Darius III, at Issus and defeated him. By then he had already taken Asia Minor, Syria, and Egypt (where he founded Alexandria). He then invaded India, over the very difficult Hindukush Mountains, in 327-326 BC. The Indian king Ambi of Taxila, at the Indian border, surrendered to him without giving any fight, but further east the Indian king Porus decided to take him on in a battle in 327 BC. Porus lost, but the Indians gave a tough fight. Further east the Indian states defended even more resolutely, and made the conditions so difficult for the Greeks that they refused to advance any further. There was disaffection, for the soldiers had been out for too long and away from their homes, and that forced Alexander to call it a day and turn homewards. But he had to fight his way back through the Indian territory and during one of the battles he was severely wounded and had to be carried from the battle field. For the return journey he had divided his force into three columns: one column was to return over the hills in Afghanistan, the other by sea, while the third, which was under his personal command, was to take the difficult route over the Makran Coast. The journey was arduous and Alexander's condition deteriorated by the day and he died by the time his column reached Babylon. This was the year 323 BC.

Brahmans of north-west India were opposed to any foreign incursions into India and they played a central role in evicting the Achaemenian Iranians and were equally vehemently opposed to Alexander, for which they had to face latter's retribution. Alexander organized the conquered territories into Satrapies under local or Greek governors and placed some territories under vassal kings. Captured Indian territory was placed under the Satrapy of Seleucos Nikator who in 321 BC declared himself independent and in 306 BC, the king. A Taxilian Brahman, Chanakya, a recognized and respected teacher in a Taxilian university, well versed in state craft and common law, picked on Chandragupta to spearhead the movement against the Greeks. At this stage Chandragupta was operating as a brigand in the territory around the Vindhyas in Central India. He raised a force of mercenaries with the wealth he had looted, and, after Alexander was gone, he captured the territory east of the Indus; through guerrilla warfare waged at an ever increasing intensity, and made the Greek hold tenuous, and vulnerable to his assaults. Chanakya, possibly, also travelled to Magadha to persuade the Nanda king to join in the battle but, it is said, was rebuffed. This disappointed him, but he had sensed the disaffection of the Magadhans against their king, and advised

Chandragupta to attack and capture the throne, which the latter did in 323 BC after defeating the powerful Nanda Army which was commanded by their renowned Commander-in-Chief, Bhadrashala. It was a terribly bloody contest. Chandragupta had tried earlier as well to capture the Nanda empire, but had failed. The success came only after he had established himself in the northwest and had judiciously made use of the legions raised there; with the soldiers recruited in the north-west. Chanakya used all skills to secure success, including bribery, sex, extortion, competent intelligence: *Daam, Kaam, Dand, Bheda* !

Chandra gupta already possessed the territory north of the Vindhyas, including southern Rajasthan and the adjoining areas of the present day Gujarat when he took the throne of Magadha. By 313 BC he had annexed Avanti and Saurashtra, and in 305 BC he defeated Seleukos Nikator, the king of the Satrapy of Babylon and captured the trans-Indus provinces and most of the present day Afghanistan and Baluchistan. As part of the peace process Seleukos gave away to him his daughter in marriage. Jain records say that he was tilted towards Jainism during his last days and abdicated in favour of his son Bindusara, and spent his remaining days as a hermit. This information is not supported by any other account.

The Indo-Greek contact helped in the growth of trade. While Indians exported to Greece and the countries of the Levant, spices, jewels, muslin, turquoise, silk yarn, indigo, they imported pearls, copper, dates, gold, and slaves from Ethiopia, Arabia and the Mediterranean countries. Indians learnt from the Greeks their system of coinage, and astronomy. The most visible impact was on the Indian art, particularly, sculpture, the most notable example being the sculptures of Gandhara. The Greeks established settlements in the Punjab, but they did not survive for the people soon moved over to adjacent cities and towns. Some Maurya government agencies recruited Greeks as their officials to run the affairs of the state. But during the fading phase of the Mauryas these officials, along with others of their kind from the former Seleucid satrapies of Bactria and Parthia, carved out independent kingdoms for themselves.

The first Mauryan emperor developed an effective system of roads to the areas he annexed, the most notable being the (*Uttara Path*, or the northern highway, also called the Royal Highway (in modern times it has been named as the Grand Trunk Road), connecting Patliputra with north-west India.

According to Greek chronicles, a number of non-Aryan practices were prevalent during this time in the north-western India, and the focus of Aryan culture had moved eastwards. The independent republics were still functioning in some areas.

The Magadhans were dark skinned people, possibly an off-shoot of the Proto-Australoids. They preferred white clothes; one piece covering the lower portion of the body, waist downwards, while another covered the upper body, a kind of a wrap. Rich people wore ivory earrings and fancy white leather shoes of thick soles; this made them look taller. They used parasols for protection against the sun.

The greatest of the Mauryan kings was Ashoka. He secured the throne after an internecine struggle during which he eliminated his brothers (there was a large number of them) and other claimants. It took him almost four years of struggle to eventually clear all opposition, and hence his anointment as king was delayed by that much time.

Ashoka, like his forebears, was a great conqueror. He annexed the neighbouring state of Kalinga, in the twelfth year of his rule after a pitched and bloody battle, and with that he had the whole of the Indian subcontinent under his rule, including Afghanistan and Baluchistan, but excluding the Tamil country. He at this stage was the greatest monarch the earth had seen till then, and one of the greatest the world has seen even to this day. Whatever was left of the subcontinent was within his easy grasp, so also the tracts of Central Asia. His empire comprised settled village agriculture. He had put into operation an elaborate system of administration and tax collection, based essentially on Chanakya's *Arthashastra*, possibly the world's earliest treatise on statecraft. Chanakya was his chief minister during the early years of his reign.

After some years of his reign, after he had reached the pinnacles of glory and greatness, he came under the influence of the Buddhist teachers, and, may be, even the Jain saints; both kind of preachers were sweeping the country in his time. He developed aversion to violence. The bloody battle of Kalinga had infected him. He gradually turned his thoughts away from violence. He became tolerant towards all religious thoughts, and preached Buddhist Dharma and also respected Dharma as defined by Brahmans. He stressed the need to be good in thought and speech, clean in body and mind, and preserve life and not destroy it, be it animal or plant, and live in harmony with nature, in clean environments, and not cheat or tell lies, and cause pain and suffering to others through harsh speech or actions. He raised a special force whose job it was to teach this to the people at large; in fact, often he took it upon himself to teach Dharma, the importance of piety and morality. He communicated his messages to the people through engravings on pillars especially erected for this purpose, and also through engravings on rocks. He organised digging of wells, planting of trees for shade, cultivation of herbs for medicines, erection of hospitals, education of women and welfare of aborigines and subject races. He encouraged dynamic criticism of the Buddhist religious order so that it could be cleansed of corruption and superstitious accretions. For this purpose the third Buddhist council was held under his patronage. About him the famous historian H.G. Wells has said: "His reign of eight and twenty years was one of the brightest interludes in the troubled history of mankind."

Ashoka was a spiritual giant too after having been a great fighter, conqueror, ruler, administrator, and it was his great ability that turned Buddhism, an idea evolved by a small sect in the Gangetic planes, into a renowned world religion. He sent emissaries which included members from his immediate family, to the countries of South and South-East Asia to spread the message of the Buddha; his son Mahinda and daughter Sanghamitta embraced the order and crossed over to Sri Lanka and converted the whole island to the Buddhist faith. For his great achievements he is Ashoka the Great.

But the experiment of running an empire while following the Buddhist ideals, failed, and within a hundred years of his passing away, in 232 BC, his empire had been rendered non-existent. But Buddhism endured for many centuries, alongside Brahmanism, though it eventually lost to the latter and was almost wiped out, but not before it had been firmly entrenched in Sri Lanka and the countries of South-East Asia, and Korea, Mangolia, China and Japan, a development for which the great emperor had worked assiduously.

The empire was finally broken by the pressure of the Greek and the Kushan barbarians from the north-west. A number of their tribes managed to establish kingdoms and dynasties in western and central India. Constant war required heavy taxation and that alienated the subjects. By 187 BC the boundary of the Mauryan kingdom had shrunk to the outskirts of Patliputra. During one inspection of the troops by the king, Brihadharatha, his Brahman Commander-in-Chief, Pushyamitra Sunga, beheaded him in full view of everyone, and proclaimed himself the ruler, be bad the support of the army, and the officials of the civil administration who were dissatisfied with the heavy taxation and a string of defeats suffered at the hands of foreign intruders. The last few kings of this line were the followers of the Shaiva faith.

Pushymitra Sunga (187-151 BC) stabilized the north-western border of his empire along the line of Jalandhar—Sialkot in the Punjab. The rest of the north-west had been lost to the Greek invaders. He continued to rule from Patliputra while his son Agnimitra, stationed in north-western Madhya Pradesh, took care of the north-west. But he was soon threatened by Vidarbha whom he roundly defeated, but then came under pressure from Greeks from north-west, who had already secured, under their king Menander, Kabul, western Punjab and the lower Indus valley. Menander had also captured the present day Rajasthan and the upper Gangetic plain and was threatening Magadha itself till Vasumitra, son of Agnimitra, attacked the rear of the Greeks from the Sunga base in Malwa and forced a withdrawal on them to the line of Jalandhar-Sialkot.

With the rise of the Sungas the Vedic religion became the religion of the state and became the popular. But the Sungas could not last beyond 75 BC, and even the Kanvas who took the Magadhan throne from them, were all but extinct by 30 BC, after they had been wiped out by the Satavahanas; here and there some pockets of old ruling families continued for some more time.

Satvahanas ruled Andhra and parts of eastern Deccan. They captured Malwa from Kanvas. Their line was founded by Simuka, while the major expansion of the state was accomplished by Satkarni I after he had negotiated agreements with powerful Maratha chieftains of western Deccan. The empire had a setback on account of Scythian invasions, but the situation was restored by Gautamiputra Satkarni after he had driven out the Scythians, Greeks and Parthians from some of the territories that they had annexed. His empire included most of the present day Andhra, eastern Deccan and Malwa. Its king of renown was Sri Yajna Satkarni who took whatever territory Scythians had taken from his predecessors and brought about an era of great prosperity for his subjects. The Satvahanas declined after this period and by about the middle of the third century AD the line came to an end.

South of Magadha there were a number of states, including Kalinga, which had declared their independence, after having been periodically ruled by the Cholas, Pandyas and the Keralas. The most prominent ruler of Kalinga was Kharavela who had a, noteworthy strength and played a decisive role in the fortunes of the monarchies of southeast India. He was a constant threat to the Sungas of Magadha, but after him the power of the family declined and not before long the line became extinct. In the south the Cholas ruled the present Thanjavur-Tiruchirapalli tract, securing remarkable success in the fields of arts, crafts and military conquests, during the second century BC; they conquered even Sri Lanka. Pandyas ruled Madurai-Tirunelveli-Thiruvananthapuram and were great promoters of trade and learning. They had embassies in Rome and Athens. The Keralas ruled the area along the southern part of the west coast including Malabar, Kochi and Kottayam.

By about the first century AD the Greek rule had been all but eliminated and whoever of them stayed back embraced either the Vaishnav or the Buddhist faith. Their ruin had been caused by the Sakas, Pahalavas, Parthians, Kushans or the Yue-Chi tribes. Both Sakas and Yue-Chi were part of the same horde originally, but mutual disputes, most serious out of them being concerning the grazing areas, forced the Sakas out eastwards from the central Asian plains and they established themselves along the border of Central Afghanistan, *Sakasthana* or the present day Sistan, till in about the first century AD they found the Indian border weak and yielding. About this time the Parthians were also probing the Indian border, and with time Saka-Pahalvi kings won over large tracts from Afghanistan, going as far south as Malwa and upper Deccan, extending eastwards up to the upper Gangetic plain. It was only Gautamiputra Satkarni of the Satavahana line who held them and even made them to yield some ground Rudradaman (130-150 AD), the Pahalava king ruling from Ujjain, was one of the most powerful of this line. His rule extended from Sindh and Marwar in the north to Konkan in the south. He entered into a matrimonial alliance with the Satavahanas ruling the country to his immediate south. But when he was displeased with them he attacked and defeated them. His successors, however were not so powerful, and there were family feuds and loss of territory, till a line risen from the sons of the soil, the Guptas (no kin of the Mauryas) put an end to their State. But even before that the Yue-Chi nomads had assessed the weakness of the kingdom and moved closer to the Indian border, taking Kabul in 92 AD. Not before long the nomads were heading towards the Indian border, while parts of them had already hit China.

The great king of the Kushan line was Kanishka. In the Indian story he is a Saka potentate, since all the Scythians and Yue-Chi line have been grouped under one head. This king ruled for 23 years and founded the Saka era of AD 78. His Calendar was followed by his successors for many generations. He ruled from Peshawar (now in Pakistan) and his empire extended upto Benares in the east and in the west included most of the present day Afghanistan and Kashmir. He even threatened the Chinese in eastern Turkestan and secured a limited success. He followed some Iranian faith, but later changed over to Buddhism and became its ardent supporter, he got magnificent Buddhist monuments constructed throughout the length and breadth of his empire. The fourth Buddhist Council was held during his time at Jalandhar, or may be in Kashmir, in c. 100 AD. Since the followers of the Theravada school did not participate, the southern Buddhists did not recognise this council. The Council adopted the doctrine of Mahayana Buddhism (The great Vehicle) and recognized this as the main branch of this Faith and accepted the broader view of Buddha's teachings, permitting the local religious lores, ideas and deities into the Buddhist pantheon. This gave mythology to Buddhism. This Council also made Sanskrit the vehicle of Buddhist scriptures. Ashvaghosha, the philosopher, poet and dramatist, and the author of *Buddha Charita*, lived during his time and enjoyed his patronage.

Kanishka's successors held on to the boundaries of the kingdom. Huvishka even extended them. Such was their power that one of the descendants called himself the Caesar, in addition to the other titles he had adopted. By the third century AD, there were dissensions and the Yue-Chi formed four different kingdoms. These were broken by the Nagas and finally annihilated by the Guptas operating from Ayodhya.

The founder of the Gupta line, Srigupta was a king of a small state. His son Ghatotkacha ruled Patliputra and the areas around. But his grandson Chandragupta I (AD 320-335), was an ambitious, far sighted, brave and a shrewd person; he founded the Gupta line. He married princess Kumaradevi of the neighbouring state of the Licchavis, and this connection gave him status amongst the rulers of his time. He extended his rule over Magadha and Kosala, and appointed his son Samudragupta as the crown prince and associated him with the affairs of the state. Risen from the soil he was averse to the rule of foreigners, but he did not live long enough to secure any worth while success. But he left behind a tradition and a solid base for his successor to launch from.

Samudragupta (AD 335-380) was the greatest of his line. While working for his father he had concluded that lasting peace and prosperity for the Indian people could be possible only under a federation of states under one paramount authority. He had observed that many small states maintained luxurious courts and life style well beyond their means, and robbed their citizens through heavy taxation and other repressive measures. He had seen that the local officials committed predatory crimes against their subjects and that arrested all growth, financial, cultural or educational.

Their lavish life style made them easy prey to bribery and corruption and vulnerable to the inducements of the anti-state elements. He, therefore, set about to cleanse the state even when he was still the crown prince. He urbanized the forest tribes in Nepal, Assam, and Central India by clearing the land and placing the tribes in permanent settlements. This process had been started during the rule of the Mauryas, as laid down in Chanakya's *Arthashastra*, but was completed only by Samudragupta.

After ascending the throne and consolidating the state, he led his armies (330-336 AD) to subjugate the Gangetic plain and Central India. Then he returned to Patliputra and for the next eleven years just further consolidated his gains. By 347 AD he was ready to take on the South Indian Dravidian states, a difficult task by any account

South India had three noteworthy kingdoms, namely Pandya, Chola, and Kerala (also called Chera). Additionally there were fierce predatory tribes, which were mostly engaged in pillage and plunder and joined any one who they could profit from—the most prominent amongst them were the Pallavas; they had secured suzerainty over the three Tamil states by c. 226 AD. By the time of Samudragupta, the Pallavas, with Vishnugupta as their king, were ruling a formidable empire with the Capital at Kanchipuram, near Chennai, and had available to them, in addition to their own resources, the resources of the three feudatory states. Samudragupta, moving against them, first defeated king Mahendra of south Kosala in the Mahanadi Valley, then subjugated the tribes further south, in the forests of Orissa; he wanted no problems with his supply line. He then overpowered Kalinga and Vengi between rivers Mahanadi and Krishna and then attacked and defeated Pallavas. Vishnugupta was captured but was released after he had signed the treaty of submission, which was dictated by the emperor himself. Having completed his mission the emperor returned to Magadha by way western Deccan, enroute subjugating the states of Western Maharashtra and Khandesh, and by the year 350 AD when he got back to Patliputra, after covering a distance of over 2000 miles, he was the most powerful king on the subcontinent, ruling an empire comparable in size to what had been achieved by Ashoka, the Great. Some historians have likened him to Napoleon, but unlike Napoleon this emperor never lost an engagement.

The king now got down to consolidate his conquests. He deposed the incompetent small rulers of the Gangetic basin. Kings of Nepal and other Himalayan kingdoms were his vassals. To secure the north-western frontiers he entered into a treaty with the Kushan king who still ruled over parts of Afghanistan, including Kabul. To better administer his kingdom he moved the seat of his government from Patliputra to Ayodhya. The place not only facilitated better governance of the empire but also was connected with the legend of Rama, whose person was central to the mythology of the Hindus.

India during the days of Ashoka was mostly Buddhist, but during the Kushan rule it was partly Buddhist and partly following the religion of Shiva. Later Kushan kings were mostly Shaivas. Buddhism was one of the many religious cults flourishing in the Gangetic basin during the sixth century BC, and possibly not the most popular one either to secure the position of pre-eminence. But this was an ideology which was preached by a prince, and, besides, in course of time, it caught the fancy of two most powerful kings, namely Ashoka, and Kanishka. Although Hindu religion had been fairly on the upswing since the days of the Sungas, its hour of glory came after the later Vedic period, with the rise of the Guptas, many centuries after Ashoka and Kanishka. Till then it was in fierce competition with Buddhism. Guptas structured it on solid foundations.

Soon after arrival at Ayodhya the emperor performed the horse sacrifice with unprecedented magnificence, feeding hundreds of Brahmans, and doling out alms to the poor and the needy. The following year he concluded a treaty of alliance with Sri Meghavarana, the king of Sri Lanka; the latter sent his envoy to the imperial court with expensive presents, including jewels, and in return received permission to build a Sinhalese Buddhist monastery at Bodh Gaya. Ayodhya became an important centre of intellectual activity. The emperor was highly versed in scriptures, poetry and music and had around him the best talent of the country, an important scholar amongst them being the warrior poet Harisena. The religion and arts flourished under this king.

Both Ashoka and Samudragupta were great conquerors. The former chose the path of the Buddha and his empire was lost within 50 years of his death. The latter believed in intense military and intellectual activity. He believed that physical weakness and military inferiority brought misery and suffering to the rulers and the subjects alike, that only the intellectual activity propelled religion and sciences. His line flourished for almost two centuries after his death and made the most signal contribution to the stabilisation of Hindu religion and culture. Though the king supported Hinduism, he was equally well versed in the Buddhist philosophy, and often presided over friendly religious debates. He greatly respected intellectual activity in any field.

He was succeeded by his son Chandragupta II (c. 380-413) who in later years assumed the title of Vikramaditya, 'of the power of sun.' This king too was a great military leader, a legislator and a patron of arts and literature. He secured victories against the Saka king of Ujjain. He founded the *Samwat* era of 58 BC. His reign saw the peak of the Hindu renaissance, a process which introduced many changes and improvements in the religious, artistic and cultural concepts. Kalidas, the great poet and playwright worked during this time. The king had assembled in his court a galaxy of renowned men of arts and culture, religion and sciences, and the nine topmost litterateurs and others absolutely on top of their disciplines were in the prized band of "nine jewels". They made formidable contributions in their respective specialities. During this time the Hindu architecture began to break away from the Greeco-Roman influence, and great temples dedicated to Vishnu got erected in many towns of importance. Gupta emperors were devotees of Vishnu; the alter offerings were restricted to fruits and flowers, and like the Buddhists they protected animal life. Religion flourished. Although they followed the Brahmanical religion they patronized other faiths with equal zeal. Hindu religious literature was edited, and rewritten, including a number of Puranas, and even Upanishads.

The epics got their near present rendering during this period, the systems of Hindu philosophy were formalized, the *Bhagavad Geeta* got its final form, and also the *Vishnu Purana* and the *Bhagvata literature* and may be even the *Shiva Purana*. The heterogeneous ideas of Hindu religion were woven into a complete whole.

This was the period of effervescence in all branches of knowledge, like sciences, mathematics, astronomy, astrology, metallurgy and other basic and advanced sciences, industrial technology, military science and connected disciplines, trade, commerce, economics and arts, drama and poetry. Maximum attention was paid to education, including Buddhist education. A great Buddhist university, housing over 10,000 monks, flourished at Nalanda, near Gaya, financed by royal grants. By this time China had adopted Mahayana Buddhism and a number of Chinese travellers had become interested in India. Fa-hein, the Chinese traveller who visited during this period, has written that torture as an instrument of coercion, and the capital punishment were almost unknown, while those were extensively practised in China. The crime, he says, was the minimum; the people seldom had to lock their houses. There was general prosperity, and there was emphasis on education, and there was flourishing trade with the neighbouring kingdoms and, also with countries beyond the Indian shores. There was extensive trade with Rome involving export of gold, spices, scented resins and woods. There was trade with the countries of the Pacific rim, e.g., Cambodia, Thailand and Malaysia. This led to Indian settlements which developed into colonies; these colonies significantly influenced the ethos and culture of the region. To strengthen his position the Emperor went in for political marriages, like his predecessor had done. He gave away his daughter Prabhavati in marriage to Rudrasena II, the Vakataka king of the Deccan, an alliance that helped him to overpower Rudrasinha, the Saka satrap.

The successive Guptas enlarged their empire, defeating their enemies and defending against white Hun (Epthalites) invasions. Their soldiers fought with savage ferocity, and the Huns who had pulverized the Persian empire in 484 AD, reeled against the Indian counter offensive. Their Chief, Tormana, a Shaiva, was defeated in a fierce battle at Mandasor in Malwa in 528 AD, by Yashodharman, a powerful king of Central India, with the help of his allies. This broke the Huns and they were absorbed in the Hindu community as Rajputs. But this had weakened the Gupta empire and they soon went out of reckoning, but not without leaving a lasting imprint on religion and philosophy, arts and crafts, sciences, literature, and every other field, not only in India but even abroad, particularly Far East. Each of the Gupta emperors was a person of great ability, both in war and peace. Huns wrecked the powerful Sassanians in Persia (Iran), and quite a few powerful kingdoms in Europe. It is to the credit of the Guptas that they held them and finally broke them, although the process weakened them fatally. But they represent the spirit of India, a determination to stay free of foreign domination. They believed in being strong and just, for they believed that in this lay the secret to end human misery and suffering.

In the year 604 AD two young princes, Rajyavardhana and Harshvardhana, aged 19 and 15 respectively, both brothers and from the kingdom based in Thanesar, present day *Kurukshetra*, were fighting the Hun menace in the Punjab, when Grahavarman, the Maukhari potentate of south Magadha and husband of their sister Rajyasri, got defeated and killed at Kanauj by the king of Malwa. The elder brother immediately set out at the head of a force of 10,000 horsemen, to avenge the defeat, and rescue his sister who had been taken a prisoner. He defeated Malwa, but got assassinated, through a deceitful betrayal of trust by a Malwa ally, Sasanka, ruler of Central Bengal. Harsha took the throne in AD 612, and first task he attended to was the rescue of his sister, which he duly accomplished. He modernized his army, making it lighter, swifter and more mobile, and in a matter of five years or so, he had subjugated the whole of Northern India, and a greater part of Bengal and defeated and killed his enemy Sasanka. In the year 620 AD he was the dominant power and even the Pallavas of Kanjivaram in the south recognized his strength. He subjugated the important kingdom of Vengi located between rivers Godavari and Krishna, and then attacked the Chalukyas, his southern neighbours. The Chalukyas were strong. Their kingdom had been formed by a Rajput adventurer, Pulakesin Chalukya, and ruled during Harsha's time by his grand son Pulakesin II. He was a competent monarch who had brought the kingdom to the zenith of glory. He decided to resist Harsha's expansionist attempt. The two armies met on the bank of River Narmada, and in spite of several determined attacks, the Chalukyas remained intact. Finally the river became the boundary between the two states.

Harsha next turned his attention to Valabhi, comprising the whole of the present day Kutch peninsula and most of Gujarat, and by 665 AD had secured their submission. He later offered the hand of his daughter to Dhruvabhata, the ruler, to further strengthen the ties between the two kingdoms. It is possible that he did that in recognition of the claim of the Valabhis to their direct descent from Rama, the king of ancient Ayodhya.

Harsha ruled from Kannauj, which was already a flourishing city on the eastern bank of the Ganges, and had a large number of Hindu temples and Buddhist monasteries. The king, though following the Hindu religion, was soft on Buddhism, and this tendency did not please the Brahmans who believed Buddhism would weaken the state, as it supported unlimited tolerance. During his time Hiuen Tsang, a 43 years old Chinese traveller, came to India to study Buddhism at the Nalanda University. Because the Brahmans held their own religion in very high esteem, a situation of contention had arisen between the followers of the two faiths. During a joint Hindu-Buddhist festival in AD 643, organized by the king to honour the Chinese scholar, an attempt was made on his life; the conspirators were eliminated with rare ruthlessness. At the culmination of the festival the king gave generously to the poor and the needy and to the Brahmans and the Buddhist monks. The Kannauj festival was followed by another one of matching grandeur at the Prayaga, the confluence of the Ganges and the Yamuna. Both festivals witnessed lively inter-religious debates, but substantially emptied the royal treasury, which could have been resented by his subjects.

Rajyasri, the emperor's widowed sister, who exercised decisive influence over him, was already converted to Mahayana Buddhism. The king was a Shaiva by faith, but under the influence of his sister and the Chinese traveller Hiuen Tsang, he was very much under the spell of Buddhism, and this attitude permeated into every limb of the Government. Taking of meats was all but forbidden, and so was taking of life. But in spite of all this Buddhism was on the decline, for ultimate aim of the religion to achieve Nirvana was far too complex for the common man and difficult to comprehend, and did not enthuse him. An average being desires happiness in this world and in the hereafter. To most of them life was not an epitome of pain after all, filled with grief and sorrow and bereft of joy and happiness. To them it was a superb gift of God so long as it was not mired in problems. So they wanted to believe in a deity who could relieve them of their problems in this world as well as the next. Otherwise they loved life and enjoyed it. And Hinduism promised them a happy, healthy life in this world and a happier one in the hereafter, so long as a few simple rules were followed, and Dharma was respected, for Dharma ensured that not only the individual's personal life was fruitful and happy, but also of the whole community he lived and worked with. For the average Hindu the soul lived with the gods, in the *Swarga*; or heaven, reposed in ultimate bliss, or it attained *Moksha*, and got united with the source of creation, the fountain without limits of joy and bliss. In the Buddhist *Shunya* it is neither this nor that, neither happiness nor suffering. It is the state of absolute Zero, a vast, unlimited sea of tranquility. Mahayana Buddhism brought the concept of gods and compassionate incarnations of the Buddha, and developed, mythology to attract the common believer, but ultimately it was the *Nirvana*, a concept difficult for the common man to comprehend. It required a lot of monastic training and discipline. Besides, Hindu mythology was based on places a follower of the faith knew about and could relate to. It was not difficult for him to understand the essence of what was being put across; this mythology was a part of his culture.

Harsha honoured intellectuals. He himself authored three plays each of some merit: one about Buddhist religion, and two romantic dramas.

Kannauj, his imperial capital situated on the eastern bank of the Ganges, was strongly defended, and had well laid out gardens, water tanks and canals. People were prosperous and given to art and learning. His formidable army was primarily based on horse cavalry, and elephants, and he ruled over most of northern India: from the Himalayas in the north to the Narmada basin in the south, including Magadha, Orissa and Bengal. Kings of Assam, Sindh and Kashmir were his vassals. Bana, his Brahman friend and an eminent scholar, wrote Harshacharita (the deeds of Harsha), after Harsha's death to immortalize him.

According to Hiuen Tsang, Harsha's army had 60,000 war elephants, a 100,000 horse cavalry and infantry which could be as strong as 2 million. By contrast the Maurya army at its peak did not exceed 9000 fighting elephants, 30,000 horse cavalry and around 600,000 infantry, and yet the Mauryas held a vastly larger empire. Apparently Harsha's army was supplied by his vassals, and it was mobilized only during wars; it is quite possible that Hiuen Tsang's figures carry an element of exaggeration and may include some other non-specified elements. The policy of decentralization in every field was successfully adopted by the imperial Guptas. While the Mauryas emphasised a strong central control, Guptas left most of the state functions to their vassals and feudatories, including the provision of soldiers for war, all under their strict control. In return they provided protection and security, something like the 'Subsidiary system' which the British put into action in India while expanding their empire.

Harsha had no son and the line finished after his death in 646 AD, and the country got divided into numerous small kingdoms. Kashmir, which had all along been governed by one or the other major Indian empires, came to its own in the seventh century AD. In the ninth century Lalitaditya was ruling it. He caused the defeat and down fall of Yashovarman of Kannauj. His rule extended from Afghanistan in the west to Gauda or Western Bengal in the east. The famous historian Kalhana served in his court. The ruins of his great temple at Martand in the Kashmir Valley, can be seen even now. The line came to an end around 855 A.D.

By 836 AD Pratiharas were ruling from Kannauj and by the end of the century they controlled most of northern India. Their noble and notable king was Bhoja I. The stories of his concern for his subjects make part of the folklore even to this day. This king checked the eastward movement of Avantivarman, the king of Kashmir of the Utpala line, who ruled from about 855 AD. The westward expansion of the Utpalas was checked by the Indus kingdoms. In time this line was caught in internal strife and the state got divided into a number of fifefs, till in 1339 AD it finally succumbed to the Muslims.

Bhija's son Mahendrapala expanded the empire mostly eastwards, for in the southwest he had formidable foes in Rashtrakutas. Like his father, he too was a just king and assiduously worked for the spread of education. He recognized talent. He had the best of the scholars adorning his court. Till about AD 917 the Pratiharas were well entrenched in their kingdom, when Indra III, the Rashtrakuta potentate, defeated them and took Kannauj, though help from the Chandela king saved the throne eventually. In AD 1018, Kannauj was plundered by Mahmud of Ghazni and the state was severely weakened, and by about the middle of the eleventh century it had gone out of reckoning.

In the south the Vakatakas ruled in upper Deccan, i.e., Berar and the adjoining areas, or the present day northern Andhra Pradesh. Pallavas with capital at Kanchipuram near Chennai (Madras), ruled over territory comprising present day western Karnataka, southern Andhra and the whole of the Tamil country. Samudragupta, had given his daughter Prabhavati to Vakataka king Rudrasena II. Vakataka had matrimonial alliances with several royal houses, and that greatly helped to stabilize their rule. They ruled for many generations till they were overtaken by other rising dynasties.

The Pallavas, whose king Vishnugopa was captured by Samudragupta, around the middle of the fourth century, and then released, maintained a hold over this country till about the latter half of the sixth century AD, when they had a powerful king Simhavishnu, who captured the territories of the Cholas and defeated even the King of Sri Lanka. During the reign of his son

Mahendravarman I, a struggle erupted between the Pallavas and their northern enemies, the Chalukyas, which continued for several generations: Chalukya king Pulakesin II inflicted a crushing defeat upon the Pallavas, which was avenged by Narasimhavarman I of the Pallavas. In the first half of the eighth century Pallavas were routed by the Chalukyas and, thus weakened, they were finally eliminated towards the end of the ninth century by the Pandyas and the Cholas, their southern neighbours. Pallavas made a noteworthy contribution to the history of south India. They were the first to have had a great empire south of the rivers Penner and Tungabhadra. They supported the worship of Vishnu and Shiva. A number of saints of these sects flourished during the Pallava, rule. Kanchi, their capital, became a great centre of art and learning. They treated alike the learned men of Buddhist and Brahman faiths. The cave architecture and sculpture developed during their period, including temple design and temple architecture, was of high value. This set in new trends which were extensively followed in later years both in India and Far East.

Chalukyas were the rulers of Karnataka and had their capital at Vatapi, modern Badami in Bijapur. The line was started by a Rajput adventurer, Pulakesin I, an energetic brave man, who performed the horse sacrifice when he took the throne. The most renowned ruler of this line was Pulakesin II (AD 609-642), who captured the whole of the territory of northern Maharashtra, between the Narmada and the Kaveri rivers and held his own against Harshavardhana of Kannauj, forcing the latter to accept Narmada as the boundary between the two states. Mahendravarman of Kanchi feared the strength of this king and accepted his domination. Eventually the Pallava king, Narasimhavarman, the son of Mahendravarman, inflicted upon him a series of crushing defeats leading to the destruction of his capital Vatapi. His son Vikramaditya I, however, re-established the power of the crown, and three generations later Vikramaditya II did even better when he actually took the Pallava capital. Around 753 AD his son and successor was overthrown by one of his chiefs, Dantidurga, who started the line of Rashtrakutas. They formed a great empire which included Karnataka and Maharashtra.

During their hey day the Rashtrakutas ruled the most of the Indian peninsula, from south Gujarat and Malwa, going south to Tanjore. They had humbled the emperor of Kannauj, though the deltas of Godavari and Krishna were not under them. The Arab historians of this time have clubbed king Vallabharaja of this line with the emperor of China, the Caliph of Baghdad and the emperor at Constantinople, as the four greatest kings of that time, of the world.

The Rashtrakutas were patrons of arts and learning. The famous Kailasha temple at Ellora was made during their time. In later times their king, Dhruva, subjugated the Pratiharas and the Gauda kings. Under Govinda III, son and successor of Dhruva they were the most powerful, and received tributes from the Pallavas. Under Amoghavarsha (AD 815-877) they were engaged in a struggle with the Chalukyas of Vengi, while also engaged in checking the southwards advance of Bhoja I of Kannauj. Three generations later their Indra III defeated the Pratihara king Mahipala of Kannauj taking possession of his capital city. In 973 AD the dynasty was overthrown by Taila II, a feudatory who claimed descent from Chalukyas of Vatapi and founded the line of the Chalukyas of Kalyana or Kalyani. The successors of this line got embroiled with Cholas of Tanjore, descendents of King Aditya, who had inflicted a crushing defeat on Pallava king Aparajita.

Cholas rose to power under Rajaraja and his son Rajendra Chola. Around this time Bengal was ruled by the Palas who were overthrown by Vijayasena of Karnataka. He started the new line of the Senas. This line ruled western Bengal after defeating the Gauda king of the Pala line. They also ruled north Bihar, Assam and Orissa. Their king Lakshmanasena who ascended the throne around 1178 conquered as far as Varanasi and parts of Kalinga. He was a patron of learning; Jaidava, the author of *Geeta Govinda* was from his court. By this time the Chola armies had conquered as far north as the Gangetic plain, and their naval power had asserted in the overseas territories, including Sri Lanka and other islands. They also overpowered the Kalyani Chalukyas. Around the beginning of the twelfth century the Chola and the Kalyani Chalukyas families united through marriages, and the rule of the

Deccan was shared by these families. Vikramaditya VI, son of a Chalukya king from a Chola wife, was a great supporter of art and learning. Some important works of Hindu law were authored during his time. This king also established a new era in place of the Saka era.

After 1190 AD the Kalyani Chalukya empire split into three kingdoms, namely, Devagiri, Warangal and Dorasamudra, the last mentioned was ruled by Hoysalas. The Cholas, weakened with time, and its southern part was taken by Pandyas while Hoysalas and other neighbours, ripped apart the rest of the kingdom. Just around this time rose the new empire of Eastern Gangas of Kalinga and Orissa.

Yadavas of Devagiri promoted learning. They established a college of astronomy to study the works of Bhaskaracharya, the renowned astronomer. Works of Hemadri, Bopadeva and Gyaneshvara were compiled during their time. During the peak of their period Yadavas were ruling as far north as Maharashtra. But they, as also other small kingdoms, could not hold against the Muslim invasions of Alauddin Khilji's general Malik Kafur in 1306-07. By about 1317 AD, Yadava domination of Maharashtra had come to an end, and with that ended the Hindu rule there. Hindu rule revived only after the rise of the Marathas in the seventeenth century. Pandyas later became a part of the Vijayanagar empire. Orissa formed a strong kingdom and defeated Muslim invasions till it finally succumbed in 1568.

Upto the end of the first millennium AD the subcontinent, apart from short Buddhist and Jain interludes here and there, was ruled by Hindu kings. Hindus were then about the most accomplished people in the world. China was the only other country where people of matching capability lived. Otherwise civilizations did grow elsewhere but in terms of continuity, uniformity, homogeneity, the depth of religion and philosophy practised by the people, this one was unique. People here evolved sound and rational philosophical and religious concepts. Shankracharya and Ramanuja expounded the finer points of Vedanta, and the unity of the sub-continental culture, the Hindu culture, particularly the former. He established places of pilgrimage at the four corners of the sub-continent, viz; Badrinath in the Himalayas in the north, Puri in Orissa in the east, Rameshwaram in the gulf of Mannar in the south and Dwarka, on the Arabian sea in the west. A sound system of governance was evolved with the emphasis on simplicity in every walk of life. The sub-continent saw great kings, some amongst the greatest in the world, like Ashoka, and the Guptas, Harsha, Bhoja. These kings dedicated their lives to improving the lot of their subjects.

People generally followed the castes they were born in, though cases of switching the caste professions were not uncommon. Position of women in the upper castes was pretty strong, but subordinate to that of the men. Well to do Rajput, Rajanya, families practised Sati, but not on a large scale. Some classes of families forbade widow remarriage while some allowed *Niyoga*, the system under which a widow either automatically became wife of one of the brothers, or a man from of any of the close kin, or of a person of her choice if other options were not available; preference was for a man of the family or the extended family. Child marriage was not uncommon. Education for women was restricted, though this rule was not followed strictly amongst the well to do families. Importance of education was emphasized right from the village level, though its advantage was derived mainly by the Brahman community. Most kingdoms had universities for higher education. Present day Bihar is derived from Vihara, a collection of universities. Nalanda had 10,000 students during its peak time. Patliputra was a great centre of learning, so also Valabhi in western India, Bahur (devoted to Vedic studies) in the south, Devagiri (astronomy) in the Deccan; these were all great institutions of learning. With time the legal system became strict and punitive. The citizens, however, considered justice as their right.

The period also saw the countries of Central Asia being ruled from India. Afghanistan and the area immediately to the west of it was ruled from India right up to the time of attacks of Mahmud of Ghazni. Indian culture, religion and art found extensive acceptance in the countries of South East Asia. Between the second and the fifth centuries AD kingdoms of Malayan peninsula, Cambodia, Annam (present day Vietnam) and the islands of Java, Sumatra, Borneo and Bali were ruled by Shaiva Hindu kings, initially from the Indian sub-continent. Subsequently, for over one thousand years Hindu culture was dominant in this region. Cambodia and Champa (Annam) were Hindu, with Sanskrit as the court language, and the culture stayed at the peak till long after Hindus had suffered a decline in this country of their origin during the later part of the first millennium AD.

Buddhism was readily accepted in the east. It was also a fairly appreciated religion in the West till the advent of Christianity. But whatever of it remained after Christianity, that was gobbled up by Islam. Being essentially pacific it became an easy prey. There is similarity between Brahmanism and Judaism. The teachings of Buddha and those of Christ are essentially similar. Even the architecture of Christian structures bear resemblance to the Buddhist structures, like, for example, there is a strong resemblance between the Christian chapel and the Buddhist Chaitya (prayer) Hall.

Buddha was insistent that he was not deified after his death. He said the pleasure originating from colour and form caused desire, which caused attachment and consequent suffering. He emphasized Spartan simplicity and brotherhood of man; in fact a close bond between all life bearing entities.

The period also saw the growth of trade. Numerous port towns sprang up along the sea routes. Arts and sciences developed. Aryabhatta (fifth century AD) worked out that earth went round the sun, and also around its own axis, and on this basis eclipses were forecast accurately, and the Hindu Calendar of 12 months and 30 days was worked out. The division of time into smaller units was evolved. Some eras had their own calendars: Vikrami of 58 BC, Saka of AD 78, Harsha of AD 606. In mathematics Indians had nine digits and the Zero, and the decimal system, algebra, positive and the negative numbers and the like, and the quadric and the intermediate equations. Atom was the basic unit of matter. Metallurgy produced iron and coinage, and there were significant developments in surgery, general medicine and the study of the nervous system of the human body.

The Muslim Invasions

Towards the end of the millennium the subcontinent had been divided into numerous small, mutually hostile states, all conspiring against one anothers, possessing little fighting potential, extravagantly wasting their revenue to maintain a flashy, imperious court life. They had expended virtually little effort to update their fighting techniques, or done little study of the techniques employed by their potential enemies warfare. They held the Central Asian hordes in contempt, considering them plain barbaric, too inferior for any sustained fighting. But their enemies, though uncouth in manners and dealings, were a tough lot on the field of battle. Besides, people of the subcontinent were not unduly concerned about the demeanour, of the followers of Islam. They were prepared to treat them as people following a different ideology, and just that. They did not think they could be ruthless in the pursuit of their religion. They, in fact, were prepared to listen to their ideas on religion, and were pleased that their enemies were god fearing men In Kerala they even erected a mosque for their worship.

Arabs attacked Sindh ruled by Dahir, (he ruled a small part of the present day Sindh) in 711 AD under their young and energetic leader Mohammad-Bin-Kasim, and secured a signal victory with the help of the disaffected feudatories and office bearers in Dahir's court. Their advance eastwards or southwards was, however, checked by Chalukyas of Badami and the Gurjaras of Rajputana. The Arabs were generally mild and their rule brought good trade between Sindh and the Arabs. In 714 AD, Kasim got murdered, and after him within 30 years Sindh had been cleansed of all Arabs, thanks to the stronghold of the Brahmans in the Hindu ethos. After losing Sindh the Arabs made rapid progress in Iran where clergy was not that well organized.

The first major predatory ingress into India was by Mahmud of Ghazni, and he beat the hell out of the Indian states in the north-western and northern India. He looted the cities desecrated-

and plundered the holy shrines and temples, and during each of his seventeen odd destructive raids he carried enormous wealth, loaded on caravans of camels. India was rich compared to the countries of the Middle East and Central Asia. In spite of the philandering rulers of innumerable small states of that time, it had a competent trade machinery which had been in position for a long time, and generated wealth. Mahmud called the country the "Golden Sparrow", and pounced upon it like the proverbial hawk every time he needed money to finance his ventures in Central Asia. In the first attempt in 1001 AD he was resisted by Jaipala of the Brahman Shahiya line from Peshawar. But the latter suffered such a humiliating defeat and was so disappointed that he immolated himself. It has to be said to the credit of the kings of this line that they continued to offer determined resistance, sometimes rallying the neighbouring rulers, till in 1021-22 Trilochanpala, while leading an army of allies, suffered a crushing defeat on the banks of the Ramganga River, and was assassinated, and with the death of his son Bhima in 1026 the line of the Shahiyas, inspite of their sacrifices, came to an end. But their sacrifice had not been in vain, for Mahmud could not establish a firm enough empire along the sub-continents' northern borders and the country was left fairly to itself for a century and a half thereafter.

Next major incursion was by Shahabuddin or Mohammad of Ghaur in 1186. He captured Lahore which had been under Muslim rule from time to time after the fall of the Shahiyas. Chauhan Rajputs ruling from Delhi were unhappy about this development and a battle was fought between Prithviraj Chauhan, the king of Delhi, and Ghaun, in the year 1186, in whioh the latter was defeated. But the Rajputs instead of pursuing the defeated foes to complete their rout, let them go. Ghauri came again in 1193 and defeated Prithviraj; the latter died in fighting in battle. Ghauri left behind a governor, Qutbuddin Aibak, a slave of his whom he held in high esteem as a soldier and administrator, and stationed him at Ajmer; the latter conquered Delhi in course of time and declared himself the king (1206-10). He was succeeded by Illtutmish, Qutbuddin's slave and son-in-law (he was known for his sagacity and good looks). The line of the slave kings came to an end after Illtutmish's daughter had been dethroned around 1244 and the kingdom was seized by adventurers from the family and outsiders, with a lot of bloodshed. These kings had little authority outside Delhi and could not create a political state. They were no doubt recognized as some powers in the present day Agra, Oudh, some parts of Bihar, Sindh, Gwalior, Central India and Rajasthan, but the hold, at best, was tenuous and restricted only to receipt of Taxes whenever conditions were favourable.

The Khiljis ruled for 33 years, from 1288 to 1321. Alauddin (1295-1317) was their most notable Sultan. He was an uneducated tyrant and secured the throne by assassinating the ruling Sultan, his uncle and benefactor, Jalaluddin. He took Gujarat in 1297 and married the beautiful queen Kamla Devi, of the ruler, Karan Dev; she became his favourite queen. His trusted general Malik Kafur, a eunuch and former slave, annexed for him most of South India, including east coast and the Tamil land right up to Cape Comorin, where in 1310 he built a mosque to mark his victories. He looted an enormous amount of wealth during this expedition. In 1303 Alauddin had conquered Chittor and demanded that their chief queen, who was a beauty of fame of her time, be sent to his harem. The Rajputs of Chittor defied him and died to a man defending the honour of their women folk. The women folk alongside burnt themselves to death rather than be molested by their enemies. Custom of the men dying fighting defending their honour is termed as *Johar* and the women committing self immolation is called Sati. By 1312, the Sultan's health was fading on account of his excesses and the state was being ruled by Kafur, till in 1321 the Tughlaks captured the throne of Delhi.

The Tughlaks ruled from 1321 to 1414. Their noted Sultan was Mohammad-Bin-Tughlak, who took the throne of Delhi, as Allauddin had done, by ingeniously killing his father Ghiyasuddin. He ruled for 26 years (1325-1351), and committed some Himalayan follies during his rule. He embarked upon a plan to conquer China. His Army perished at the Himalayans, foothill itself. Then he decided to shift his Capital to the South of India, for he felt it was continuously threatened by the destabilizing menace of the Mongols from the north-west, and nearly lost his kingdom for he had badly exposed Delhi, his Capital, to the incursions of the Mongols. He then decided to move back to Delhi, causing enormous suffering and hardships to his subjects. His reign was marred by famines, sickness and mal-administration. There were revolts, and running between places putting out these fires he died at Tattah, Sindh, on 20 March 1351. His successor, Ferozeshah (1351-1388) though a mild king was a religious bigot, and in order to please his nobles, persecuted Hindus. Not that the Hindus were spared by earlier sultans either, but during his time the oppression reached new intensity. Even earlier the hated *Jizya* tax was imposed, a tax which underscored the fact that all non-Muslims were to be penalized by imposing taxes, because they were under the rule of the Muslims. The Muslim officials plundered the Hindu traders at will; during the rule of this Sultan the persecution levels reached a new intensity. This caused large scale dissatisfaction amongst the majority population, and that caused a downward slide of the rule. Amir Timur (Tamerlane) attacked during the reign of the last Tughlak, Mahmud, in December 1398 and struck such a deadly blow as to cause the demise of this line. After Mahmud the state was taken over by the governor left behind by Timur. Timur was a terrible killer, plunderer and destroyer. In Mongolian style he erected pyramids of the skulls of the people his soldiers killed in battle. He looted wealth and took along artisans to develop Samarkand, his capital city. The rule of the Sultan of Delhi had shrunk to the outskirts of Delhi after Timur's attack. The governors left behind by Timur found themselves in total anarchy and fled, leaving the field to the Lodis (1450-1526). The last of the Lodi line was defeated by Babar, attacking from Kabul in 1526 in the first battle of Panipat.

By the time of Babar's invasion the Hindus were like a people who might have turned on themselves. Their caste system had divided them into irreconcilable units working against each other, and their fundamental traditions had sapped their dynamism. They operated along a narrow groove, unwilling to change to keep pace with time. They had become a second rate agrarian society, fairly self-contained at the village level, lacking pathetically in dynamism, mobility, or developing a scientific temper. They submitted meekly to the humiliations piled upon them by their rulers, and were bereft of self-confidence and self-respect, or the courage to challenge the oppressor. Throughout the run of history they had been the rulers of Afghanistan. Afghanistan had been a part of or a province of the state of all Indian rulers. The degeneration they had brought upon themselves when they went under Afghan rule was baffling.

The successive Sultans had parceled out the land into *Jagirs*—farm holdings and awarded them, including the people living thereon, to their favoured nobles and officials, who plundered their subjects with impunity. Babar took Punjab in 1524. He had Allauddin Lodi, Ibrahim Lodi's brother, as one of his important allies. Delhi Sultanate at this stage had extended its hold eastwards, over the Gangetic basin, including a tenuous hold over Bihar, but excluding Bengal, which being farthest from Delhi, had declared itself independent. Sindh, Gujarat and Malwa were also under Muslim rule. Bahmani kingdom in the Deccan had split into five warring Sultanates of Ahmednagar, Bijapur, Bidar, Barar and Golconda. The founders of these states had been mere adventurers.

As for the Hindu states, these included Orissa and Gondwana, the confederacy of Rajput states of the present day Rajasthan, the powerful state of Vijaynagar south of the Bahmani states, covering the peninsula right up to Sri Lanka, Assam including Kamarupa and Nepal.

Babar defeated Ibrahim Lodi in the first battle of Panipat in 1526 and established the Mughal rule in India. His eldest son, Humayun, almost lost the conquered territory to Shershah Suri, who went after him tongs and hammer, and threw him out of Bengal, where during the retreat he nearly drowned while fleeing and attempting to cross the swollen Ganges; he got some respite only after he had reached Delhi, where also Suri did not allow him to rest and consolidate, chasing him all the way to the borders of Afghanistan, where his ruler brother refused to come to his assistance. Babar had more faith in the capability of his son, ruling Kabul, and for that reason was keen to establish him as the ruler in India. It is believed this idea provoked the hostility of Humayun and he poisoned him to ill health and one day while Babar was resting in his bed chamber, he smothered him to death with pillows. For outside consumption a story was coined that Humayun had fallen so sick that Babar prayed to God that his son's life be spared and instead his might be taken.

The kingdom came back to him because Shershah was dead, and Humayun had a reasonably free run. His son Jalaludin Akbar succeeded him. During his earlier conquests Akbar was ruthless and raised pyramids of the skulls of his enemies, but once he was firmly in control, he changed into a friendly ruler. He was an illiterate person, but he understood very well that in order to win over his subjects he had to keep them in good humour. His diplomacy had no place for the religious bigots. He had to take on Hemu Bakaal, who was a competent Hindu general of Shah Adil Sur, in the second battle of Panipat, and defeated him. Akbar's army was well organized on the most modern lines. It is significant that while the Mughal army was extensively using gunpowder fired weapons, the Hindu rulers were still dependent on bows and arrows. For that reason they just could not stand the intensity of attacks from invaders from Central Asia, or even Afghanistan. In order to cut the sanguine edge of Muslim fundamentalism he encouraged secularism, and promoted inter-community marriages. The princess Akbar had married from the ruling Rajput house of Jaipur, gave birth to Jehangir, his successor. The Rajputs, held positions of pre-eminence in his court, and he encouraged bonhomie between people of different classes and religions. He strove to give good administration to his people, and picked up the best brains specializing in different disciplines, to run his government, and improve trade, commerce and industry. All this brought prosperity. He was a just king and gave equal treatment to the people of all creeds and religions.

He opposed religious fundamentalism in any form, and held debates of intellectuals of different religions, and came to the conclusion that all extant religions contained seeds of fanatical thinking which could spell unhappiness to the different sections of the society. He often listened to the followers of different faiths and decided that for a happy contented society, the religions of the people had to be purged of fundamentalist thoughts. He in fact decided no religion brought people close to God, or to themselves. He therefore, designed a religious code of his own and called it *Din-I-Ilahi* God's religion. He did not get many followers for the faith he preached, but he used no coercion to secure followers. For all that he did to bring happiness to the people, he has been called Akbar-the-Great. He put a tradition in motion which for whatever time the Mughal rule lasted, remained the main stay of their governance.

However, his policies of cultivating friendly relations with the majority community got eroded during the reigns of the rulers who followed him. Under the influence of the Mullahs his son Jahangirs (1605-1627) twice revolted against him prompted by a conspiracy to seize the throne with the support of the Mullahs. But the royal family members interceded and dissuaded Jehangir. Besides, being from a Hindu mother the hold of the Mullahs was, at best, only tenuous. But when a conspiracy was hatched against him by his own son, after he (Jahangir) had been crowned, he acted tough and had the whole lot of the conspirators lanced and killed before his son's eyes. But in order to please the fundamentalist Muslims he did imprison his son Khusrau for his pro-Hindu leanings; the prince died in captivity in 1621. He made Islam as the religion of the state. By the time of Shahjahan (1627-1658) the hold of the Mullahs had become stronger and Muslims were predominant in all departments of the Government, including the army. Only non-government professions were open to the Hindus. Persecution of Hindus took alarming proportions during the reign of Aurangzeb Alamgir (1658-1707), and this led to large scale revolts, and ultimately, in a fifty odd years, resulted in the folding of the Empire to the gates of Delhi. At one time Aurangzeb had the whole of the sub-continent except the Tamil country and Kerala, in the south. During the latter part of his rule a number of centres of resistance had arisen, the notable ones being the Marathas, in the Deccan, the Rajputs in Rajasthan and the Sikhs in the Punjab. Besides, European trading nations who had been striving to secure the rich resources of the sub-continent, had also secured a significant presence, and they, together with other rebellious groups brought down the empire.

The Rise of the Marathas

In 1646 Shivaji started with the capture of the fortress of Torna near Pune and by 1678 when he died he was ruler of a formidable Maratha state. The same year Raja Jaswant Singh died while guarding the north-west frontier of the Mughal Empire and Aurangzeb offered to recognize his infant son as the successor only if he converted to Islam. Rajputs (Rathors) refused and joined the Marathas. Sambhaji, Shivaji's son, was a competent successor but lax in personal discipline. He was caught by the Muslims while he was hunting near Kolhapur, and was promptly sent to Aurangzeb who promptly had him beheaded. He was succeeded by Sahu, his infant son, under the regency of Raja Ram, who maintained pressure on the imperial forces through Guerrilla warfare. Aurangzeb died at Ahmedabad in 1707 at the age of 89. During his last days he was a harried person, running between places to stem the tide of the rebellions against him, with his treasury getting empty on account of the war expenses. Often he had to put his troops on frugal rations and spartan discipline to which his Muslim troops were not favourably inclined, since, being the masters, they were used only to comfortable living. He suspected his sons and never permitted any of them near his bed even when he was dying.

The Peshwa (the Prime Minister) of Raja Sahu did a good job of governance. But his successor usurped the power of Raja Sahu and put the royal family at Satara, virtually in retirement. By 1733, the Maratha army was controlled by three prominent families, being of Udaji Pawar of the area around Pune, Malhar Holkar of Indore and Ranaji Sindhia of Gwalior. Nadir Shah, the Iranian potentate, sacked Delhi in 1739-1740 and considerably weakened the Mughal rule. In 1748, Ahmad Khan Abdali or Durrani, an official of Nadir Shah who had established himself as an independent ruler of Afghanistan after Nadir Shah had been assassinated, attacked the north-western frontier, but was defeated by the Imperial troops. He came again in 1750 and took Punjab. In 1756 Abdali sacked Delhi; he called himself Ahmad Shah Abdali after the capture of Punjab. The Moghuls could regain their throne in Delhi only with Maratha help. During 1758, Raghoba, the Maratha leader, took Punjab from Abdali. The Marathas now visualized themselves as the rulers of Delhi, notwithstanding the fact that though they were the masters in irregular warfare they had little expertise for regular set-piece fighting.

In 1759, the Mughal king Alamgir II got murdered in a palace coup, and in 1760 Sadashiv Bhao, commander of the Peshwa's army in the north, took Delhi. This elicited immediate reaction from the Rohillas who wanted Delhi for themselves albeit under Abdali, for they considered Delhi to be a preserve of the Muslims. On 6 January the two armies faced each other for the third battle of Panipat.

During this battle the Marathas suffered the disadvantage of a long supply and command line. The control of the battle for the Marathas was from Pune, and this led to the development of a poor infrastructure for the battle. The administration had broken down even before the start of the battle; in fact it was this factor which forced Bhao to attack prematurely. The sickness rate was alarming, and the rations were frugal, and weapons inadequate, and practically no replacements of men and materials, including horses. Bhao's commanders told him they had long gone past the peak performance capability, and that with each passing day they were losing in their fighting potential. Besides, Marathas were not sufficiently trained in the technique of launching large scale combined infantry-cavalry attacks duly supported by guns, nor were they good enough in defence against them.

The Marathas fought hard and almost carried the day when, towards the evening, a tough attack by 13,000 fresh troops of Abdali turned the scales of the battle in his favour. The Marathas had no reserves at this stage. Both sides lost heavily in men and materials and the Marathas had to withdraw to the line of the Narmada river in the south, for reorganisation. Abdali, weakened, and his dream to rule from Delhi shattered, was hurried all along the communications lines, and was forced to withdraw to Afghanistan. In later years he made a few inconsequential forays in the north-west and was forgotten thereafter. Rohillas ceased to be a force of any consequence. Marathas failed to establish a Hindu kingdom at Delhi, and Peshwa Balaji Rao died of grief when he learnt of the debacle, and the Marathas split into a confederacy of four power centres, being Gaekwad at Gujarat, Bhonsley at Nagpur, Holkar at Indore and Sindhia at Gwalior, all operating under the Peshwa at Pune. In early nineteenth century they were the major force to challenge the expansion of the British, and could have been eminently effective, had they been united.

The British Ascendancy

A serious problem was in the meantime developing on the subcontinent's eastern horizon. In 1757, the British commander, Robert Clive, had defeated Siraj-ud-Daula, the Nawab of Bengal, by bribing his wazir Mir Jafar and was in effective control of Bengal, Orissa and Bihar. At this time the Portuguese, the French and the British were struggling hard to capture the trade routes and the trade with the east, and with this end in view had established sea fortresses along the seaways, including the Indian East and West coasts. In 1600 the British East India Company was formed and Sir Thomas Roe presented himself in the court of Jahangir in 1615 as ambassador of King James I. By 1639 the British had established the Madras outpost on the Bay of Bengal, and in 1662 they got the Island of Bombay from the Portuguese as dowry for King Charles II and in 1690 they acquired land in Hooghly, Bengal. By the end of the eighteenth century, they had defeated the French and the latter left with only a small enclave of Pondicherry. They had also overpowered the Portuguese and had confined them to their bases of Goa, Daman and Diu. By 1768 the British had taken the Northern Sarkars from the Nizam and in 1775 they seized Benares, and Ghazipur from Oudh. Tipu Sultan of Mysore was defeated in 1799; this gave them a consolidated block of territory from Malabar to Coromandal. The Mughals had ceased to be a power of any significance after the assassination of their king Alamgir II. Marathas were the only power who could prevent the British from taking the whole of India.

The European mastery of the sea was brought about by their galley type sea ship which originally started as fishing trawllers, but later got fitted with some arms to commit piracy and plunder on sea and land. Being big these ships carried men and materials to far off lands to engage in warfare. This was how the British came, through the sea routes, and established themselves. The guns on the ships attacked from a direction which had been the least prepared by their enemies for defence. The mastery of the sea routes gave them unhindered capability' to switch forces between the coast line around Madras, Bombay and Calcutta.

After its capture, Bengal was brutally plundered by the East India Company, and with this wealth arriving in Great Britain, started their Industrial Revolution of the seventies of the eighteenth century, setting forth an era of great prosperity for them. To ensure unhindered sale of their cloth in the mills in Manchester and steel in Birmingham, the Indian artisan and trader was maimed to a non-performing level; they went even to the level of amputating the workers. Bereft of the means of livelihood, people died by the thousands of hunger and disease. They did not possess even the means to procure the bare minimum farm inputs. The crops failed and there were famines to compound the already tragic situation.

The slide to grinding poverty had its roots in the fundamentalistic policies of the communally fanatic Muslim king Aurangzeb, and the pathetic passivity shown by the Hindus in taking the oppression unleashed against them by the British vested interests. In 1834, Lord Bentinck the British Governor General in India) wrote in his report (as quoted by Nehru): 'the misery hardly finds a parallel in the history of commerce. The bones of the cotton weavers are bleaching the plains of India'.

Paul Kennedy in his book *The Rise and Fall of Great Powers* has quoted Ashton's observation made as late as 1947, the year India secured its freedom:

> There are today on the plains of India and China men and women, plague-ridden and hungry, living lives little better, to outward appearance, than those of the cattle they toil with by the day and share their places of sleep by night. Such Asiatic standards and such unmechanised horrors are the lot of those who increase their numbers without passing through an Industrial Revolution.

That is what happened to the Hindus in India, for their passivity, for their failure to keep abreast of the political, economic, military or scientific developments elsewhere in the world, and stay vigilant and resist unitedly any external or internal threat.

Bengal saw a major famine in 1770, thirteen years after the take over by the Company, and it is believed that a third of the population of this fertile and densely populated region perished. The Indian traders class under the lungs and their henchmen had little political force. India had no middle class, the class of thinking elite who spear headed the industrial revolution in the west. Nevertheless, the Indian trader was a competent performer and had a sizeable share in the world transactions. According to Paul Kennedy, in 1150 the Indian share in the total world manufacturing output was 24.9 per cent as against 1.9 of the UK and 23.6 of the whole of Europe. At the beginning of the Industrial Revolution India was one of the leaders in trade, commerce and industry, but in a matter of merely 150 years it sank to the abysmal depths of total deprivation, because its industry never managed to make it to the level of an industrial revolution. The reason for it was the frozen, static out look, caused essentially by a lack of modern education, and an outmoded religious approach (religion played an important role in their day to day life). The surprising part is that the Indians sought the help of the British military strength from time to time, but never made an effort to develop superior weapons of warfare indigenously.

Peshwa Madhava Rao died in 1772 setting off a war for supremacy amongst the Maratha Chiefs, the two main contenders being Raghoba and Nana Pharnavis. The British stoked the fires of discord amongst and this ultimately led to the First Maratha War between the Marathas and the British which brought little gain to either side. There were some other engagements but they came to nothing. In late 1780 through an alliance the Maratha chiefs and Haidar Ali resolved to combine and throw the British out of India. But this hardly achieved anything.

Lord Wellesley took over in 1798 and with that started an era of extensive acquisitions. The declared policy of the Company now was to offer a ruler to become its subsidiary when he felt he was not in a position to hold on his own against his real or perceived enemies, internal or external, in exchange for a guarantee of protection of his rule. He was required to maintain a force of specified strength of Indian or British troops, under the command of British officers and to meet the expenses thereof, he had to cede territory, or pay from his revenues.

In 1799, Wellesley swiftly defeated Tipu and then embarked on the second Maratha War in 1803-05. The British forces were commanded by general Wellesley, the Governor General's younger brother and the later Duke of Wellington. The Marathas were defeated and had to sue for peace and cede Upper Doab, Rajputana, Broach, Ahmad Nagar and south-west Deccan. The subsidiary annexations brought Surat and most of southern Peninsula. In course of time under the subsidiary system the British suzerainty was recognized by nearly all the major Indian rulers. In 1803 even the Moghal emperor at Delhi accepted the British protection. This is the time when the British war machine was at the peak of its performance. The outbreak of war between Great Britain and France in 1744 had brought the war for the Caribbean trade and the war for Silesia together into a single global conflict which extended from North America to India. The struggle which intermittently lasted till 1815, eventually became a conflict between Great Britain and France, and all the kings and rulers in these lands, including Indian, fought as independent or subsidized allies of these powers. Though the British were not the outright winners, they came out better than France in this global conflict.

The British restored Gwalior to Sindhia under a new treaty in 1805 after the departure of Wellesley and that put an end to their conflict. During his term Wellesley introduced some educational reforms, like opening a college at Fort Williams for the training of new arrivals from England, and acquaint prominent Indian citizens with the British culture and civilization. There were some administrative reforms as well, particularly in the legal system.

Wellesley's annexations had created disaffection amongst the Indian rulers and prominent citizens and the Company decided it was time to observe restrain, since its main concern in India was with trade and commerce, and not with empire building. Marathas were not giving in easily. During 1812-17 they again organized to fight the British and had mustered the support of Pathans and freebooters, called the Pindaris. Early in 1817 the Governor General Hastings assembled a 120,000 army, the strongest in those times and set out to finally finish the Maratha presence. The Marathas had the will and the determination, but they were not sufficiently united, nor were they working under a joint command, for a common goal, nor did they possess the financial resources and the weaponry, or the organization, to wage a first grade war. The participants, or the constituents, were working to enhance their individual interests. In fact so poor was the Maratha showing in battle that a contingent of 27,000 men of the Peshwa were roundly defeated at Khirkee by a small British force of 2800 men. By the end of the year the Maratha power was finished, and their empire, founded by Shivaji in 1669 had ceased to exist. In the first few days of the year 1800 the Peshwa had been dethroned and the Raja of Satara recognized as the real monarch. He was of Shivaji's line; the power had been usurped by the Peshwas from Shivaji's grandson Raja Sahu in 1708.

The Sikhs also showed belligerence to the expansion of the British influence towards the Punjab. The first war was fought during 1845-46 which the Sikhs lost and the British entered Lahore on February 20, 1846. The second Sikh war was fought during 1848-49 which too was lost by the Sikhs, although they gave a brave fight at Chillianwala on the bank of River Jhelum. The Sikh weaponry, organization and skills were no match to that of the British. The Sikhs, in fact, were a fractured community, with any number of factions vying with each other to secure the position of pre-eminence with the aim of capturing the throne of Lahore. On March 12, 1848 Dalhousie annexed Punjab, disbanded the Khalsa Army, placed severe restrictions on the activities of the Sikh warlords and took away the priceless diamond the Koh-i-Nur which had been presented to Maharaja Ranjit Singh by Shah Shuja when the latter had sought shelter at Lahore after he had been driven out of Afghanistan. The diamond now adorns, broken into a couple of pieces, one of the crowns of the British monarch's family.

The Indian Independence

The great Indian Revolt was quashed, but not before a spirit of nationhood had taken roots. The Indian National Congress was formed in 1885 in Bombay with the blessings of the Government of India, and though it started as a tame annual gathering of affluent public men, it soon was spearheading a movement with the aim of eventually securing full freedom from the British Rule. In 1905, the British Government decided to Partition Bengal on communal lines. Already a movement had taken roots with the aim of securing the partition of Bengal on communal lines. The Indian National Congress opposed it, and it succeeded. But the division of Hindus and Muslims on communal lines became the corner stone of the British India policy and to achieve this they raised agents and stooges. After all, had the foundations of the British rule not been laid on bribery and corruption? Right from the time when Clive bribed Mir Jafar and taken effective control over Bengal, Orissa and Bihar and defeated his master Siraj-Ud-Daula, the Nawab of Bengal, to the time of the Great Soldier's Revolt of 1857, when the British managed to liquidate the core of the resistance to their governance, it had been one long story of treachery, engineered by the British. This was the time when Portugal, France and Great Britain were engaged in a struggle to capture the trade routes to the east, and had established sea fortresses along the sea ways, including sea ways along the Indian east and west coasts. In 1600 the British East India Company was formed and the British arrived in India with Sir Thomas Roe presenting himself in the court of Jahangir in 1615 as the Ambassador of King James I. Around 1639, the British had established the Madras outpost on the Bay of Bengal, and in 1662 they got the island of Bombay from the Portuguese as dowry to king Charles II and in 1690 they acquired land in Hoogly, Bengal. By the end of the eighteenth century they had defeated the French and the latter had been left only the small enclave of Pondicherry. They had also overpowered the Portuguese and had confined them to their bases in Goa, Daman and Diu. By 1768, the British had taken the Northern Sarkars from the Nizam and in 1775 they seized Benares and Ghazipur from Oudh. Tipu Sultan of Mysore was defeated in 1799; this gave them a continuous block of territory from Malabar to Coromandal. The Moghuls had ceased to be a power after the assassination of their king Alamgir II. Marathas were the only force who could prevent the British from taking the whole of India.

The European mastery of the seas was brought about by their galley type sea ships which were originally designed for fishing operations but were later fitted with arms for piracy and plunder on land and sea. Being big these ships carried men and materials for waging war. This was how the British came through the sea routes. The guns on the ships exercised flexibility and attacked from a direction least expected by their enemies. The mastery of the sea routes gave them unhindered capability to switch forces along the coast line around Madras, Bombay, and Calcutta.

After its capture Bengal was extensively looted and plundered by the East India Company, and with this loot arriving in Great Britain started their Industrial Revolution of the seventies of the eighteenth century, bringing to them an era of great prosperity. To promote unrestricted sale of their steel and cloth manufactured in the mills in Birmingham and Manchester, the, Indian artisans and traders were smothered out of existence. This was done ruthlessly, even by maiming the Indian crafts men. Denied the means of livelihood, people died of hunger and disease. They ceased to possess even the means to procure the bare minimum farm inputs. The crops failed and there were famines, compounding the already tragic situation.

The slide to the grinding poverty had its roots in the fundamentalistic policies of the rabidly fanatical Muslim king Aurangzeb, a Mughal king on the throne of Delhi. His rule was riddled with revolts and rebellions. Sikhs, Rajputs and Marathas rose against him. Although Mughal rule, in diminishing effectiveness continued for nearly a hundred odd years after his death, but it was a rule in anarchy, perpetuated by the pathetic passivity shown by the Hindus in taking it lying down. Lord Bentinck, the Governor General in India in his 1834 report wrote (as quoted by Nehru): The misery hardly finds a parallel in the history of commerce. The bones of the cotton weavers are bleaching the plains of India.

Paul Kennedy in his book *The Rise and Fall of Great Powers* has quoted Ashton's 1947 observation, in the year India secured its freedom: There are today on the plains of India and China men and women, plague-ridden and hungry, living lives little better to outward appearance, than those of the cattle that toil with them by day and share their places of sleep by night. Such Asiatic standards and such unmechanised horrors are the lot of those who increase their numbers without passing through an Industrial revolution.

That was how things went wrong in India, because the British, their masters, just did not bother to bring in any kind of Industrial Revolution. Or progress methodically in the process of advancement in any walk of life: educational, scientific, economic, military or whatever. Bengal went through a major famine in 1770, thirteen years after the take over by the Company, and it is believed that third of the population of this fertile and densely populates region perished. The Indian trader class had little political force. India, thus, had no middle class, the class of thinking elites, the likes of who were spearheading the Industrial Revolution in the west. Nevertheless the Indian trader was making his own contribution and had a respectable share in the world trade transactions. According to Paul Kennedy, in 1750 the Indian share in the world manufacturing output was 24.9 per cent as against 1.9 of U.K. and 23.6 of the whole of Europe. At the beginning of the Industrial Revolution, India was one of the leaders in trade, commerce and industry, but in the next 150 years it sank to the depths of near total deprivation, essentially because its industry never managed to make it to the level of an Industrial Revolution. One of the reasons for this, apart from acquisition of know-how and appropriate education and expertise in different fields of industry, was the attitude of stasis, 'a state of no change' which was brought about by backwardness and orthodoxy amongst people with whatever education. The scientific temper was poor and the Indians never managed to manufacture equipment and technology which could contribute to their fighting capability. Peshwa Madhava Rao died in 1772, setting off a war of succession amongst the Maratha chiefs. The two main contenders were Raghoba and Nana Pharnavis. The British stoked the fires of discord amongst the Marathas and this led to the Maratha war between the British and the Marathas. This brought little gain to either side. There were a few other engagements, but they came to nothing. In 1780 Haider Ali made alliance with Marathas and together they decided to throw the British out of India, but this also made little headway.

Lord Wellesley took over in 1798 and with that started the era of extensive acquisitions. The declared policy of the Company now was to offer a ruler to become its subsidiary when he felt he was not in a position to hold his own against his real or perceived enemy, internal or external, in exchange of a guarantee of protection of his rule. He was required to maintain a force of specified strength of Indian or British troops, under the command of British officers and to meet the expenses he had to cede territory, or pay from his revenues.

In 1799 Wellesley swiftly defeated Tipu and then embarked on the second Maratha War in 1803-05. The British Forces were commanded by General Wellesley, Governor General's younger brother and later Duke of Wellington. Marathas were defeated and they had to sue for peace and cede Upper Doab, Rajputana, Broach, Ahmednagar and south-west Deccan. The subsidiary annexations brought Surat and most of southern peninsula. In course of time the subsidiary system was recognized by nearly all major Indian rulers. In 1803 even the Mughal Emperor at Delhi accepted the British protection. This is the time when the British war machine was at the peak of its efficiency. The outbreak of war between Britain and France in 1744 had brought the war for the Caribbean trade and combined with the war for Silesia this became a global conflict that extended from North America to India. The struggle which intermittently lasted till 1815, eventually became a conflict for supremacy between Great Britain and France, and all the kings and rulers of those times, including Indian, fought as dependent and subsidized allies of these two powers. Though the British were not the absolute winners they came out better than France in the Global conflict.

The British restored Gwalior to Sindhia under a new treaty in 1805, after the departure of Wellesley and that put an end to their conflict. During his term Wellesley introduced some educational innovations, like opening a college at Fort Williams for the training of the new arrivals from England and to acquaint prominent Indians with the British culture and civilisation. There were some administrative reforms as well, particularly in the legal system.

Wellesley's annexations had created unrest amongst the Indians, and the Company decided it was time for restraint since its main concerns in India were with trade and commerce and Empire building. The Marathas, however, were not giving in easily. During 1812-17 they again organized to fight the British, and had mustered the support of Pathans and Freebooters called the Pindaris. Early in 1817 Governor General Hastings assembled a force of 120,000 soldiers, the strongest in those times, and set out to finish the Maratha presence. Though the Marathas had the will and determination, and they were incensed at the humiliations suffered by them at their earlier defeats, they were neither sufficiently united, nor were they working for a common goal, nor did they possess the financial resources, weaponry or the organization to wage a first rate war. Each chief was working to enhance his own interests. In fact so poor was the Maratha showing in battle that a contingent of 27000 men of the Peshwa were defeated at Khirki, near Pune by a small British garrison of 2800 men. By the end of the year the Maratha power was finished, and their empire, founded by Shivaji in 1669 had ceased to exist In the first few days of the year 1800 Peshwa had been dethroned and the Raja of Satara recognized as the true monarch. He was of Shivaji's line. The power had been usurped by the Peshwas from Shivaji's grand son, Raja Sahu, in 1708.

The Sikhs also showed belligerence to the expansion of British influence towards the Punjab. The First Sikh War was fought during 1845-46, and was lost by the Sikhs and the British troops entered Lahore on February 20, 1846. The second Sikh war was fought during 1848-49. This too was lost by the Sikhs, although they gave a determined fight at Chillianwala on the bank of River Jhelum. The Sikh weaponry, organization and skills were no match to that of the British. The Sikhs in fact were a fractured community with any number of factions trying to out do one another, with the aim of capturing the throne of Lahore. On March 12, 1848 Dalhousie annexed Punjab, disbanded the Khalśa Army, placed severe restrictions on the activities of the Sikh war lords, and took the priceless diamond Kohinoor, which had been given to Ranjit Singh by Shah Shuja when he had sought shelter at Lahore after he had been driven out of Afghanistan. The Diamond now adorns one of the crowns of the British monarchs family.

In 1848 the Raja of Satara died issueless and Dalhousie annexed the kingdom under the Doctrine of Lapse. Dalhousie also ordered a general war against dacoity, thuggee, infanticide, human sacrifice and such evil practices. In 1854 Jhansi was annexed under the Lapse Doctrine, but the Rani refused to give in and gave a tough fight during the 1857-58 rebellion. Oudh was annexed on 13 February 1856 because the ruler was incompetent. All these events taking place in quick succession created large scale disaffection amongst the common man and the rulers of that time. On 10 May 1857 the sepoys at Meerut mutinied. The immediate cause for this was the newly introduced ammunition which carried a preservative coating of a greasy substance which it was believed, comprised cow as well as pig fat. The word went round that this had been done deliberately to defile the Indian religions. The rebellion rapidly spread to other military centers, including Delhi, Lucknow, Kanpur (under Nana Pharnavis), Allababad and the adjoining areas. The Sikh and Gurkha troops saved the day for the British who had been taken by complete surprise at the uprising, and suffered heavy casualties in men women and children. In Delhi the rebels appointed the non-effective Mughal king Bahadur Shah as their leader, promising him the rule after the British had been thrown out of the country. The rebels believed that only a small force of the British was in control of the whole country with the help of a large section of Indian polity, that there was disunity amongst the Indians, with different factions out to secure personal gains, howsoever petty, that the British success was primarily due to their policy of divide and rule. By mid June 1858 the rebels had been defeated at all places. The Rani of Jhansi who took a stand to protect the interests of her adopted son and took the field at Gwalior, died fighting, but not before offering a stubborn resistance and there had been much blood shed. It is believed that the British had heavily bribed her soldiers who were responsible to man the fortifications including the gates of entry.

On 2 August 1858, by an act of the British Parliament, India ceased to be under the control of the Company and became a territory of the British Crown.

No account of the sepoy rebellion is complete without a mention of the role of Mangal Pandey, a soldier of the 34th Native Infantry whose attack on a superior officer came to be recognized as the event that sparked India's first War of Independence. The reader has to keep in mind that India at that stage was not a single united unit. It comprised several big and small states, each independent in their own right, exercising sovereignty over the areas ruled by them. The concept of one India did not exist then; it had not at any time earlier either. In earlier times, by and large the independent states acted in their own interests and entered into mutual alliances to further their own interests. Notwithstanding the geographical names like Bharata, or Hindostan, one-India came into being only after the territory-comprising it had been totally captured by the British, and then, after a gap of nearly two hundred years, the people had secured the country and their freedom in 1947 after a period of intense struggle. Whatever states in 1947 claimed right to exist as such under some treaties or understandings arrived at with the British at the time of take over by the latter, got wiped out and these territories became part of federal India.

That was how the British were seen and their authority came to be recognized. Their superior weapons, and ability to bribe key Indian officials in all engagements, civilian or military, got them to get the better of the kingdoms they set out to conquer. Barrackpore had been taken by the British, but a simmering resentment existed, not because of any all-India spirit, but other suspicions, amongst them defilement of the religious institutions, their customs and traditions. Men took the Company's employment because that gave them money to make their existence better, but they were averse to any thing that might put their social and religious institutions in a negative light.

On 29 March 1857, Pandey, the Purabiya-Sipahiya from amongst the east U.P. Bhaiyyas, strolled on to the Barrackpore parade ground and shot at two English officers, unsaddled one of them because his horse he had wounded, then called his comrades to take up arms against the British, shouting common sister related obscenity which still punctuates male conversation in north Indian towns and villages, and engaged them in a eight minutes sword fight, injuring both of them seriously. Some other sepoys hit the officers with rifle butts, but did not join Pandey openly. Nor were they identified by any one, not even by the injured officers. At this stage Major General Heassay his two sons in two, galloped towards Mangal Pandey. Rather than shooting at the officers charging at him, Pandey discharged his gun into himself. He was injured and captured and brought before a native general Court Martial presided over by Subedar Major Jowahir Lal Tiwari and 14 other UP sub-alterns. He was sentenced to death. At his trial Pandey offered no information about his motivation, aims or objectives. He neither cross-examined the witnesses, nor harangued the court. He admitted to taking *Bhang* and opium of late but maintained that he had acted on his own will. The record of the Regiment showed him to be of 'good character'.

He was born in the village of Nagwa, District Ballia, Uttar Pradesh. He was recruited in the 30 Native Infantry. On the day of the incident General Hearsay felt Pandey was in the throes of some sort of religious frenzy, and ordered the *Jamadaar* to arrest him, but the latter refused. The Rising had begun.

The court martial took place on 6 April 1857 and he was hanged at Barrackpore on 8 April 1857 though originally he was to be hanged on 18 April. As a collective punishment for his act the entire regiment was dismissed.

The Indian Independence

The great Indian revolt was quashed, but it gave birth to a spirit of *Nationhood*. Parochial interests gradually gave way to the feeling of *one India*. Indian National Congress was formed in 1885 in Bombay, even with the blessings of the Government of India, and though it started as a tame gathering of affluent public men, it soon started spearheading a movement whose aim was to eventually secure full freedom from the British rule; after all the new party had been formed against the backdrop of the *Ghaddar*, a revolt which though it had been defeated, nevertheless left a strong imprint on the political happenings of the country. In 1905, the Party launched an agitation against the Partition of Bengal on communal lines. It succeeded even though the British sowed the seeds of dissension in the Muslim and the Hindu communities. Although Mahatma Gandhi and the Congress did their very best to emphasise that they were for a secular India which would have nothing to do with communalism, the count was partitioned in 1947 to whet the aspirations of the Muslim community to satisfy their urge for a separate home land. There was no such thought initially, but as the freedom movement caught momentum the British vested interests raised a stooge in the form of Mr. M.A. Jinnah whom they made to insist that they would not settle for anything less than a split, giving a portion of the country to the Muslims; this product of the partition was to be called Pakistan. On 15 August 1947 the country was partitioned and two nations, India and Pakistan came into being. The British engineered this partition in furtherance of their policy of *Divide and Rule*. The expectation was that left to themselves though under the connivance of the British vested interests, the two communities would fight each other to exhaustion and eventually seek British intervention leading to British domination of the area. This, however, did not happen and that irked the British and they have been working against the Indian interests ever since. With Pakistan as a close ally and Indian interests not quite getting to benefit them, they have been opposing India on most fronts. They got Pakistan to start a movement to secure Kashmir, even though the latter had legitimately acceded to India after the Partition. For some reason India went to the UN Security Council, and there, under pressure from the western nations duly guided by the British, the Security Council has, time and again, ordered India to hand over Kashmir to the Pakistanis. If India has managed to hold on to their territory, it has been because of the Veto exercised in their favour by the Soviet Union. With time India has managed to convince the western world that any extensive tampering with the ground situation could result in serious consequences for the two countries and to the world as a whole. In gradual stages the world body, the United Nations, has come round to the view to let India and Pakistan mutually sort out their differences.

In retrospect it can be said that Hindu civilization, their religion and culture, is a synthesis of three distinct streams, viz., the Austric Australoid, Dravidian and the Aryan. In time there have been other admixtures with the people migrating into the sub-continent. Interaction between the Australoid and the Dravidian streams in the fourth millennium BC caused the flowering of the Indus culture which spread over whole of the northwestern sub-continent. If it did not travel further south or east, it was because it was the age of the bronze and copper tools and implements, and developing of farming land and large scale communications and means of travel were possible only up to a limited extent. It was essentially an agrarian culture but in its final stages it had turned urban, bringing an era of extensive trade and commerce, and prosperity. The philosophy of the culture was essentially pacifist. It believed in respect for all life and was totally opposed to destruction of any kind. Some of its sections possibly believed that even matter had life, and that it was indestructible, that atoms in different combinations brought about the manifest world. Both Jain and Buddhist religions were based on the essential thoughts of this culture.

The Sanskrit speaking Aryans arrived towards the end of the third millennium BC. They had a script. The hymns of the Rig Veda were already in composition. They arrived from far off lands, after wanderings of centuries. They explored the Indian subcontinent and visualized it as one country, which they felt ought to be under one rule. Although Iron-Age had not yet set in, these industrious people cleared the land in the Gangetic basin and in the area south of the Vindhyas, and expanded both eastwards and southwards. This had also been done by the pre-Aryans, partly in search of fresh areas for food gathering and cultivation, and partly to escape the insecurity brought about by the ingressing tribes from the north-west. By about the beginning of the second millennium BC the Aryans had gone as far south as the Vindhyas and the Satpuras. Their king Rama, it is stated, conquered Lanka (present Sri Lanka), an island south of the southern tip of the sub-continent. Even if some details of the Rama story may be mythical, the concept of one whole India had been kindled in the Aryan thinking. The philosophy of the Aryans was not pacifist. They prized conquests. Their god Indra wreaked thunderbolts from the heavens against their foes. Their religion was based on sacrifice which took its final form around 1000 BC. During the later Vedic period (1000-600 BC) the Aryan attitude towards the people already settled on the land, had mellowed, their extensive contact with the earlier people had brought about this change. During the Upanishadic period the mellowing had reached the final form. Animal sacrifice was replaced by floral and grain offerings.

The pacifist Austro-Dravidian stream, however, continued to be active. But it stayed dormant. Around seventh century BC it gave rise to Buddhism and Jainism. During the third century BC king Ashoka the Great, ruled over most of the subcontinent, Afghanistan and parts of Central Asia. But what harmed his empire was his acceptance of the pacifist doctrine of Buddhism, this in the midst of the problems posed by difficult communications. His was a vast empire, and he was in no position to run a government which did not enjoy a full support of his subjects. But the pacifist Buddhism could sustain his philosophy and the pattern of governance, for barely 59 odd years after him.

Next the subcontinent, or the most of it, came under one rule was during the fourth and fifth centuries AD, under the Guptas. Although these rulers were indulgent towards Buddhism (no ruler could ignore the wishes of a majority of his subjects), their rule lasted for over a century and a half. Brahmanism visualizes India as one country, and stresses the importance of safeguarding the rights of the people.

Mauryas were broken by the Kushans and the Scythians invading from the north-west. The Guptas were engaged, towards the tail end of their rule, in a struggle unto death with the Huns from Central Asia. They destroyed the Huns; it is another matter that in the process they got destroyed themselves. Under them the subcontinent saw its best days: peace, prosperity, general well-being of the people, flourishing arts and crafts, trade, commerce—the Golden Age of the subcontinent. Possibly such times never again visited the subcontinent.

The ruler of the last of the great Hindu empires was Harsha Vardhana. He was a great king, but he too leaned towards passivity and accepted Buddhism towards the concluding days of his rule. His empire did not last even for a day after his death.

The contest between passivity and aggressive dynamism has been a constant factor on the Hindu historical scene. The majority reposed faith in truth and non-violence, and have been at the receiving end for most of the time of the Indian history. The Arabs took a part of Sindh in 711 AD, but were thrown out within 30 years of their arrival. But Mahmud of Ghazni who first attacked in 1001, made the first dent in the Hindu defence system. Then he attacked during 1176-93. Had the Hindu rulers evolved some system to take on such raids unitedly, the history of the sub-continent would have been different. But the sub-continent was not a united whole. It stood fragmented in big and small states, each concerned only about their own interests, and waited as dispassionate onlookers while their neighbours were being stripped bare. Collectively they offered themselves to defeat in detail. After Ghauri the Hindus had virtually lost the control of their north-western border. The invaders came at will and the Hindus caved in before their ruthless ferocity, and their newly evolved techniques of warfare, and war machines; they showed little capability to organize an appropriate defence, and develop defence machines.

During the second millennium AD Alauddin sent his general and commander-in-chief, Malik Kafoor on the conquest of southern India, and thus ruled most of the sub-continent, even though the expedition was more in the nature of a series of raids for plunder than an endeavour to found an empire. Next ruler who ruled the whole subcontinent was Aurangzeb even though he faced severe opposition from his Hindu subjects and some of his Muslim feudatories, who strove to be independent. The British united the subcontinent under one rule after they had conquered the whole of it; they caused it to be one state, one nation. They, however, at the time of granting independence divided the subcontinent into three countries, viz.; India, Pakistan and Bangladesh.

With the arrival of the Europeans came their more lethal weapons, their superior battle field organization, and the naval warfare. Marathas had a formidable presence, but they could not do much to meet the new challenges. Size of the British-Indian Army was expensive. This impeded the development and welfare works and the country sank into poverty. Cities and towns languished for want of trade and commerce. In villages the common man had little else to do than get occupied with religion and tradition. Education was neglected. Customs like *sati*, infanticide, child marriages, *devadasis* came to be practised. The society was emasculated. People who had claimed to be the founders of one of the oldest civilizations, whose richness and prosperity had attracted migrants and invaders throughout the course of history, became the poorest in the world. The British under pressure to finance their industrial revolution and wars to expand their empire, sucked away everything that had any value, and left this land completely wasted. The intellectual inertia, the lack of scientific temper throughout the whole of the second millennium, caused all this. And then the British poured ridicule.

This is what Major General Sir George Younghusband had to say:

It is never wise to stand studied impertinence, or even the semblance of it, from any Oriental. Politeness and courtesy, by all means, and even camaraderie, as long as these are reciprocated, and all is fair and square, and above board. But the moment there is sign of revolt, mutiny or treachery, of which the symptoms not unusually are a swollen head, and a tendency to inactivity, it is wise to hit the oriental straight between the eyes, and keep on hitting him thus, till he appreciates exactly what he is, and who he is. Hindus have held on to their religion and culture tenaciously. The conversions into other faiths have been few; most of them were effected under state pressure. Even today some conversions take place on account of caste differentiations, and this will go on till the imbalance caused by such differentiations is not evened out. Hindus did not accept conversions into their faith but now they have somewhat modified the stance and some conversions have been reported. The process can gain momentum if the caste and the *Varna* distinctions are done away with. The Indians have been free for more than five decades now, and in this time their numbers have simply exploded. 85 per cent of the Indian population is Hindu, eleven Muslim, and the remaining are people from other faiths, including Sikhism and Christianity. Today Indians are at the threshold of the Industrial Revolution, 225 years behind Great Britain. It is the peculiarity of the onset of affluence that the population registers a rise. With the availability of the fruits of the scientific development, the first activity that attracts the attention of the common man is procreation; he is hardly capable of indulging in science and development; for he has yet to cover a lot of distance to acquire the know-how. But gradually he is past all this with the improvement in his educational levels and opens out into the open field of science, technology and development, gradually leading to higher standards of life.

Hindus have been and still are a very tolerant people. Ever since the gaining of Independence in 1947 from the British (who carved out Pakistan from the Indian land to serve their vested interests) on the basis of a vociferous demand from the Muslim community. Some sections of Muslims have carried a grudge against the Hindus for they believe the country is their field, that they had conquered it and it has to be in their occupation in perpetuity, not as a home land but a possession, under their rule. This attitude of the Muslim community was all too evident during the third battle of Panipat when Rohillas of India invited Ahmad Shah Abdali of Afghanistan and supported him to defeat Marathas so that Delhi might not fall under the rule of the non-Muslim Marathas, and remain under the Muslim rule of the Mughals. Mind set of the Muslims throughout the world today is to bring the whole world under Muslim rule. The Muslims throughout the world have been obsessed with this idea almost throughout their history. Nostredamus, the French astrologer and physician, has prophesied as far back as 1555 AD that the world shall witness a conflagration, a holocaust, when the Muslims of the world unitedly shall attempt to force their ideology on other people of the world. But, he goes on to say that this attempt would fail and peace and prosperity shall return to the human race. This is a real danger, but considering that Muslims are in a minority in India the chances are that this would be averted. But the danger shall remain.

In the meantime India has to work to take their industrial revolution to fruition, in order to bring prosperity to the people. For this, how ever, run away population growth has to be checked.

Index

N

O

P

Q

R